KU-078-241

Contents

Acknowledgements

The Bed-Sitting Room was co-written with John Antrobus. Q and *There's a Lot of It About* were co-written with Neil Shand. Many thanks also to the estates of Michael Bentine, Larry Stephens and Jack Mabbs. Paul Martin for his transcriptions on the website www.shutupeccles.com, and Janet Spearman, Dick Fiddy of the British Film Institute, Paul Hamilton, James Codd of the BBC Written Archive, Caversham, Mark Lewisohn for his indispensable *Radio Times Guide to TV Comedy* (BBC Worldwide Ltd, 1998) and the staff of the British Library. The publisher gratefully acknowledges Penguin Books for permission to reproduce extracts.

Special thanks to Norma Farnes, Spike's friend and manager for thirty-five years, for all her advice and support.

The Essential Spike Milligan

Spike Milligan was born in 1918 to a British military family enjoying the twilight of the Raj. After they transferred to South London, young Spike fought the Nazis in Europe before being invalided out. After the war, he took up the trumpet full-time and then wrote and performed in the series that made his name and occasionally broke his sanity throughout the 1950s, *The Goon Show*, with Peter Sellers and Harry Secombe.

In the 1960s he had success as a stage and film actor, but by the 1970s, despite some notable successes as an environmental campaigner, he felt overlooked by the BBC. Frail but still active into his eighties, his one-man shows were always sell-out events. In 1992 he was made a CBE, then in 2001, an honorary KBE, and in 2000 and 2001 he received two Lifetime Achievement Awards: for writing and for comedy. Spike Milligan died in 2002.

Alexander Games was comedy critic of the *Evening Standard* for six years and is the author of *Pete & Dud: An Illustrated Biography* and *Backing into the Limelight: The Biography of Alan Bennett.*

The Essential Spike Milligan

compiled by
ALEXANDER GAMES

HARPER PERENNIAL
London, New York, Toronto and Sydney

This paperback edition first published in 2003
First published in Great Britain in 2002 by
Fourth Estate
A Division of HarperCollins*Publishers*
77–85 Fulham Palace Road
London W6 8JB
www.4thestate.com

1

A catalogue record for this book is available from the British Library

ISBN 0-00-715511-5

Designed in Monotype Columbus by Geoff Green Book Design
Typeset by Rowland Phototypesetting Ltd,
Bury St Edmunds, Suffolk
Printed in Great Britain by
Clays Ltd, St Ives plc

Foreword

Spike Milligan: The Godfather of Alternative Comedy

He wrote *The Goon Show* in the 1950s. Those crazy scripts 'pushed the edge of the envelope' as astronauts like to say. From his unchained mind came forth ideas that just had no boundaries. And he influenced a new generation of comedians who came to be known as 'alternative'.

I first heard the Goons on Radio Dubai in 1974. (I told Spike this – he laughed and thought I was mad.) A suitably surreal medium to hear them on.

My dad said, 'I think you might like this.' We recorded the programme, on my brother's Sharp tape recorder – and I was hooked.

He was stationed in Bexhill-on-Sea during the war and I was stationed there during the 70s. He manned a gun – I sold ice creams. Both equally as dangerous (except mine wasn't). This was the connection that linked Spike to me and I needed that connection to believe I could make it out of Bexhill (I was digging a tunnel).

Spike was also in *The Three Musketeers* as Raquel Welch's husband who spies on her for Charlton Heston. A great piece of acting in a nightshirt. Spike went on to win the Nobel Prize for Scene Stealing with this role (well – he should have).

With his books and poetry and TV series and of course the Goons, his legacy will live on forever. His writings were timeless and so they age very well (try listening to the Goons now – it still kicks). In his later years I tried to do a gig in Rye (his home town) to see if he'd watch it and hopefully like what I did. I was looking for parental approval. I never did it in the end because I thought he might just tell me to 'fuck off' – as he would sometimes do on a summer's day (not just to me – to anyone).

But he was a giant of comedy and creation – who will not be forgotten.

Eddie Izzard

I

Tearing It Up

Crazy People: 1951

#1: Broadcast 28 May, 1951

All four Goons in their first ever radio show — reprinted here for the first time. For the first series, the BBC insisted on calling them *Crazy People*, but Michael Bentine left amicably when it was renamed *The Goon Show* in November 1952.

CAST
Harry Secombe
Peter Sellers
Michael Bentine
Spike Milligan

The Ray Ellington Quartet
The Stargazers
Max Geldray
Material compiled by Spike Milligan
The Dance Orchestra conducted by Stanley Black
Produced by Dennis Main Wilson

RECORDING: Sunday, 27 May 1951. 5.30–6.15 p.m.
TRANSMISSION: Monday, 28 May. 6.45–7.15 p.m. (HOME)

ANNOUNCER: (LIVE) This is the BBC Home Service.
DISC – FANFARE
ANNOUNCER: What is the zaniest comedy show on the air today?
SPIKE: Er – Today in Parliament?
ANNOUNCER: No, it's those 'Crazy People', the Goons.

(APPLAUSE)

ORCHESTRA: GOONS GALLOP (Up & under)
ANNOUNCER: At last here is a programme for listeners with
    three ears . . . . . one for Harry Secombe, Peter Sellers,
    Michael Bentine, and Spike Milligan. One for the Stargazers,

Max Geldray and the Ray Ellington Quartet, and one for
Stanley Black and his Zulu Bubble Dancers!! So pull your chair
up to the ceiling; fill up your glass with potassium cyanide and
let the Goons do the rest!

ORCHESTRA: <u>UP AND OUT</u>

(APPLAUSE)

PETER: Among the artistes appearing will be Arthur Cragworthy.

SPIKE: Hello.

PETER: Cloot Wilkington.

HARRY: Hello.

PETER: And Harold Vest.

MICHAEL: Hello.

PETER: And three parts will be played by . . . .

MICHAEL: Hello.

PETER: (SANDY FIELDS) Here, next to me, standing on the head
of the producer, is our author. We leave him to tell you his
story. Mr. Arnold Fringe.

HARRY: My name is Jones. I wrote this programme strictly for
the radio – but they said as a radio show, it was ahead of its
time.

PETER: When was that?

HARRY: 1852.

PETER: Continue.

HARRY: I shall . . .

HARRY: (laughs) I thought of many titles for the radio programme and finally I settled on . . .

SPIKE: 'Yuckabakaba'.

PETER: Why?

HARRY: Why not?

PETER: Touché.

HARRY: Mmmm! Bless you! Every day I phoned the BBC in
hopes of contacting some influential person – finally I managed to get one of the heads – this I mounted on a pike.

PETER: How jolly.

HARRY: Yes. At that time I was living in dire poverty – have you ever lived in dire poverty friend?

PETER: No, I have a little flat in Brockley.

HARRY: What a merry place to be sure – continuing my story – I was very, very poor . . . worry turned me grey . . . this gave me a peculiar appearance as I was completely bald at the time. As my last resource I opened up a little tobacconist's shop in Town. Unfortunately the little tobacconist caught me! He sent for the police, and so I . . . .

FADE OUT AND IN

F/X: <u>(GAVEL ON DESK)</u>

SPIKE: Order in court – first case.

MICHAEL: The prisoner, your honour, was found to be in illegal possession of two thousand half-smoked cigarettes.

PETER: (JUDGE) Two thousand cigarettes? Mmmm . . . what have you to say for yourself, Mr. Jones?

HARRY: (WHEEZY COUGH)

PETER: (OVER COUGHING) Fined forty shillings or seven days.

HARRY: I paid the fine with trembling fingers, but . . . they wanted money!

PETER: You were sent to prison?

HARRY: Yes! I was a fugitive from justice . . . Harried from pillar to post I had been finally spotted. A grim pursuit ensued. With a fast police car on my tail I sped like a mad thing through hamlet and village up the Great North Road – 60, 70, 80, 90 miles an hour. And they'd never have caught me, but for one thing.

PETER: What?

HARRY: My boots wore out!

<u>STARGAZERS & ORCHESTRA</u>: 'LET YOURSELF GO'

(APPLAUSE)

PETER: That was the Stargazers who appeared by kind permission of the Greenwich Observatory.

HARRY: Pip-pip (cough) pip – pip.

ORCHESTRA: FANFARE

ANNOUNCER: Motor Racing! The story of the B.R.M. The story of how it was born.

PETER: (GLENDENNING) The international car races will soon be in full swing. In past years the Italians have run away with all the prizes . . . in some cases before the race had even started. But this year they will have to contend with Britain and the B.R.M. Here to tell the story of this wonderful car is Captain Pureheart.

MICHAEL: Good evening.

PETER: Mmmmm. Yes well now, tell me what was the first race you ever won?

MICHAEL: The Old Crocks Race in 1892.

PETER: But that was before you were born!

MICHAEL: Do you imagine it was easy for me?

PETER: Ha ha ha!!! I think we'd better start your story.

MICHAEL: Yes. After the war an impoverished Britain put on an international car race at Silverstone – poor Britain, we had a very weak team – I shall never forget the dramatic finish of that first race.

F/X: (CROWDS CHEERING & ATMOSPHERE – MOTOR CARS RACING)

HARRY: (excited) And here come the Italian and German cars, neck and neck and it's the Italian pipping the German, as the chequered flag goes down on the finishing line! And here a long way behind coming into third place is Captain Pureheart the British driver.

SPOT F/X: (HORSE GALLOPING TO A STOP. NEIGH. WHINNY)

SPIKE: Woah boy woah! (FADE)

MICHAEL: Yes – British prestige sank pretty low – but I was determined. I decided to raise sufficient funds to

build a <u>new</u> car. So I hurriedly held a meeting with my
bankers.

ALL: (TALK VERY FAST)

HARRY: Hup!

MICHAEL: The answer was 'no'. I tried every possible way to
get money, finally I was successful, all I had to do was . . .

SPOT F/X: (SPLINTERING OF GLASS, POLICE WHISTLE)

MICHAEL: (Proudly) . . . . and six months. With this money I
gathered six car designers, we locked ourselves in a garage
and really went to town.

ALL: (SING) 'There's an old Mill by the Stream, Nelly Dean'
(FADE)

HARRY: They set to work with grim purpose. <u>This</u> was to be the
car that would recapture Britain's lost trophies. They rented a
factory at Berkhamstead and at dawn 3,000 pit workers
arrived at the works entrance. Soon the air rang with the
sound of their labours and by midnight the foreman reported
the result.

PETER: (COCKNEY) Well – now we got a 'ammer.

MICHAEL: Next I called on my technical adviser, Ernie
Splutmuscle.

PETER: Er, did you want me n'at Captain?

MICHAEL: Yes Splutmuscle, here's five thousand pounds, I want
you to go to Italy and bring back the finest motoring brains
that money can buy.

PETER: Righty-ho!

MICHAEL: Three weeks later he arrived back with a glass jar.
In it were the finest motoring brains that money could buy.

HARRY: In the meantime the engine had been completed and the
mechanics were fitting the body together.

F/X: (PHONE BELL)

MICHAEL: Hello.

HARRY: Hello Captain. The garage here.

MICHAEL: Good, how's she coming?

HARRY: Alright.

MICHAEL: Have you put the bonnet on?

HARRY: Yorst, and I don't 'arf look stupid in it. (laugh)

MICHAEL: Come the day when there she lay, the B.R.M. my
sleek new shiny monster was ready for her first trial run. I
checked her over with Splutmuscle.

F/X: (TAPPING)

MICHAEL: Splutmuscle.

PETER: Yais Captain?

MICHAEL: Have you checked the oil?

PETER: No yais, n'at.

MICHAEL: In <u>both</u> head lamps?

PETER: Yais.

MICHAEL: Splendid. Right, well help me into the cockpit, lad.

BOTH: (GRUNT GROAN)

PETER: Righty ho, all set n'at.

MICHAEL: Good. Now, when I say the word – turn her over!

PETER: Ever vigilant, n'at.

MICHAEL: Right! Turn her over!

F/X: (WHISTLE & CRASH)

PETER: Are you alright under there, Captain, n'at?

SPIKE: Yes, I see you must have had some rather trying
experiences.

MICHAEL: Indeed yes, I shall never forget the thrill of pulling
into the pits for the first trial run around the race circuit. As I
drove up ... (FADE)

F/X: (REVVING OF RACING CAR ENGINE)

PETER: Well, Captain, I timed you at 152 miles an hour.

MICHAEL: Oh splendid.

PETER: But how did she hold the record?

MICHAEL: Magnificently ... but I still think we should have
some wheels.

ORCHESTRA: LINK

MICHAEL: At last came the day when the car was completed

and Lady Quilter christened it. With due ceremony she broke a small bottle of champagne over the bonnet.

PETER: I name this car 'B.R.M.'

F/X: (GLASS BOTTLE BREAKING – PAUSE – SOUND OF CAR FALLING TO BITS)

MICHAEL: Rebuilding starts tomorrow.

PETER: A thoroughly disinteresting story, Captain, I assure you. One parting shot, why do you call your car the B.R.M.?

MICHAEL: Ha ha ha! The B.R.M.? Well that's the sound it makes, sort of brrrmmmmm! brrrmmmmm! (drives away into the distance)

PETER: (FADING) Goodbye! Goodbye!

ELLINGTON QUARTET: '<u>KEEP OFF THE GRASS</u>'

(APPLAUSE)

ANNOUNCER: You have just heard the Ray Ellington Quartet in 'Keep off the Grass'. Listeners will join us in wishing Mr. Ellington a speedy recovery from his laryngitis. And now to news of the moment. The call-up of Class Z Reservists may temporarily deprive many industries and professions of their key men. It may well affect radio too ... Let us therefore give you a more concrete example of what might happen if a shortage of radio artistes <u>did</u> necessitate existing performers taking on extra work. We present ....

SPIKE: Dick Barton! Special Agent!

GRAMS: '<u>DEVIL'S GALLOP</u>' (down for)

HARRY: In our last episode you will remember we left Dick, Jock and Snowey trapped in a gas-filled sewer (which you'll remember, was beneath a haddock-stretching factory in Park Lane). You will remember they were suspended by their feet. (You will remember they <u>had</u> feet.) Jock works himself free and cuts Dick and Snowey down.

PETER: Good work Jock.

HARRY: Ohhhhhh!

PETER: Good heavens! Snowey's fainted. Quick, Jock, you take his legs.

SPIKE: I can't, they're joined to his body.

PETER: Oh good! He's coming round. Are you alright Snowey?

HARRY: Yes, I'm alright, you alright, Mr. Barton?

PETER: Yes I'm alright Snowey, are you alright, Jock?

SPIKE: Yes I'm alright, are you alright, Mr. Barton?

PETER: Yes, I'm alright, you alright, Jock?

SPOT F/X: (TREMENDOUS PROLONGED NOISE OF DOOR BEING BROKEN IN)

PETER: Listen. (cautiously) I think there's someone trying to get in that door.

SPIKE: You're a genius Mr. Barton.

PETER: Yes, aren't I? But don't worry men, you can stand by me to rely on you.

SPIKE: Here Mr. Barton, you better have my gun.

PETER: No thanks Jock, I've got my two fists.

HARRY: Yes, pity they're both on the same arm.

F/X: (WHISTLE AND LARGE BUMP ON THE GROUND)

PETER: Look, they've thrown something through the door.

HARRY: Great Scott! It's an atom bomb!

SPIKE: What'll we do?

PETER: Quick men put your fingers in your ears.

F/X: (TREMENDOUS EXPLOSION)

PETER: (FAGAN) You threw an atom bomb in the cellar, didn't you, Sidney.

SIDNEY: Yes.

FAGAN: And you've blown Mr. Barton into little pieces, haven't you, Sidney?

SIDNEY: Yes. Yes.

ANNOUNCER: Listen again tomorrow to 'Dick Barton's Special Funeral'.

GRAMS: 'DEVIL'S GALLOP' (UP)

PETER: (SIDNEY) Yes! Yes!

HARRY: Well, Herschell, what did you think of that?

PETER: Shall we dance?

ORCHESTRA & MAX GELDRAY: (Echo on Harmonica) 'I CAN'T GIVE YOU ANYTHING BUT LOVE'

(APPLAUSE)

ANNOUNCER: That was Max Geldray playing 'I Can't Give You Anything but Love'. The next part of the programme follows as soon as it has been written. In the meantime it is our wish in this new programme to cater for all tastes. We have already presented items which we believe will not be to the taste of listeners to the Home and Light Programmes, and so it remains only for us to offer something which will not be to the taste of the Third Programme listeners. Therefore, we present . . .

ORCHESTRA: (DOING! – EASTERN MOOD MUSIC)

MICHAEL: (ON ECHO) 'The Quest for Tutankhamen!'

ORCHESTRA: LINK 1.

PETER: My name is Porridge, Sir Harold Porridge. For months my expedition had been digging for the lost tomb of the greatest of the Pharaohs, King Tutankhamen. Two thousand Khurdish coolies and their wives, 500 Bosarabian porters and their bags, and 600 dromedaries, all engaged in the task of excavating. For two years we dug every inch of ground – then, finally, we received a cable from the Egyptian Government. It said simply—

HARRY: 'Stop digging Hackney marshes – try Egypt!!'

PETER: Was this a trick? Was King Tutankhamen really buried in Egypt? The answer came in a mysterious way. One night my partner, Harold Vest, had a strange experience. (FADE)

SPIKE: (FADE IN) It was a hot night in June. Unable to sleep – I took out a sleeping pill. I then woke it up, and swallowed it. In the deep slumber that followed – I heard a sepulchral voice that said . . . . (FADE OUT AND OPEN FOR)

MICHAEL: (ON ECHO) Go to the Valley of Kings. There you will find the tomb of Tutankhamen!

SPIKE: But how do I get in?

MICHAEL: Tut-and-Kham-in!

SPIKE: But how – how will I know you?

MICHAEL: (ON ECHO) I will be wearing a re-incarnation! (FADE IN)

PETER: Vest recounted this unusual incident to me and we immediately organised a second expedition.

HARRY: But first we needed money.

PETER: Yes, so we approached the Governor of the Bank of England. To our request he replied . . . . .

HARRY: (HYSTERICAL LAUGH)

PETER: So we tried a money lender, and he said . . .

MICHAEL: Never . . . . never . . . . .

PETER: So we got it on the never-never. Day after day my staff interviewed potential members of the expedition. (FADE SLIGHTLY OUT)

PETER: (dramatic) Finally in April, the great expedition set off.

ORCHESTRA: VOODOO DRUM BEAT (Held Under)

PETER: Let me read you a few extracts from our diary, of the hazardous journey to Egypt.

HARRY: April 2nd, well on our way. Scouts going ahead on horseback with elephant guns.

MICHAEL: April 23rd, all men inoculated against the dreaded Black water fever. Lurgi pills issued. Morale very high.

SPIKE: May 13th, tension mounting to fever pitch as we approach our destination.

HARRY: May 15th, at last expedition arrives (DRUM STOPS ABRUPTLY) . . . . Victoria Station!

ORCHESTRA: SHORT LINK

ANNOUNCER: Finally on May 16th the expedition arrived at Dover. Sir Harold immediately sets about buying a ship.

F/X: (SEAGULLS WAVES ETC.)

PETER: Mmmmmm! She doesn't look very seaworthy.

MICHAEL: Ha ha ha, my dear sir this ship's only been used once before.

PETER: Really, who by?

MICHAEL: Hornblower.

ORCHESTRA: (LINKS)

PETER: And so the expedition sailed. The ship's log tells the story.

PETER: June 11th. In Bay of Biscay. Weather very cold.

EFFECTS: (HOWLING GALE – HOLD)

PETER: Captain awakened at midnight.

F/X: (KNOCKING ON CABIN DOOR)

HARRY: (Excited) Cap'n. Cap'n!

PETER: What is it, man?

HARRY: There's a fire in Number One Hold.

PETER: Oh! I'll come down right away. This cabin's freezing.

EFFECTS: (GALE OUT)

ANNOUNCER: Two months grim sailing and then from the crow's nest the news they had all waited for.

SPIKE: Der – land ahead!!

MICHAEL: (off mike) How far?

SPIKE: Oh! – ummmm – Der – lemme see now – orr – no prompting from the crew now – 4, 6, 5, 7, der – well I should say –

F/X: (SHIP HITTING LAND)

SPIKE: Der – mind if I go ashore?

ORCHESTRA: LINK 5

PETER: The ship foundered, but the crew managed to save the things we needed most – namely . . .

SPIKE: Women.

PETER: I won't bore you with the story of how we finally located the King's tomb – oh, I don't know, I might as well. One day a gigantic, burly native came in with the news.

MICHAEL: I've found the place.

PETER: Where?

MICHAEL: It's behind that sand dune!

ORCHESTRA: LINK 5

PETER: In less time than it takes to say . . .

SPIKE: Yakabakaba!

PETER: . . . we had found the sarcophagus of the Pharaohs! (dramatic) I was about to see the fulfilment of a lifetime's endeavour. Tense with excitement we all gathered around the Royal Tomb . . .

MICHAEL: I think everything is ready, sir. Shall we lift the lid?

PETER: Yes. Yes.

MICHAEL: Very well, Sir Harold. Ready chaps? Easy now . . . lift! . . . Again!

ORCHESTRA: TREMOLANDO STRINGS

ALL: (GRUNT)

EFFECT: (GRATINGS) HOLD UNDER FOLLOWING

HARRY: Look.

MICHAEL: I can see him!!

SPIKE: Look – King Tutankhamen!

PETER: Stop!!

MICHAEL: What is it?

PETER: We're too late!

MICHAEL: You mean . . . . . ?

PETER: (dramatically) Yes. He's dead!!

ORCHESTRA: LINK 6.

ORCHESTRA & STARGAZERS: 'HONEY I LOVE YOU BUT'

(APPLAUSE)

ORCHESTRA: FANFARE 4

ANNOUNCER: 1951. The Festival of Britain!

HARRY: In this memorable year that means so much to Britons everywhere, what more appropriate than a programme devoted to the old country herself. Shall we away?

SPIKE: (ECHO) Salute to Britain!

ORCHESTRA: 'LAND OF HOPE AND GLORY' (down under)

ANNOUNCER: (ECHO) The world salutes Britain!

MICHAEL: By radio from every corner of the globe come tributes and congratulations.

ORCHESTRA: FANFARE 'A'

ANNOUNCER: (ECHO) Australia salutes Britain!

F/X: (SLIGHT RADIO DISTORT)

PETER: Too right cobber, we are divided from you by 50,000 miles of land and sea. Let's keep it that way.

ANNOUNCER: America salutes Britain!

MICHAEL: (American) Yes indeed, without doubts, Britain can take it. Every dollar that we have sent Britain, Britain has taken.

ANNOUNCER: Food! Despite rationing a special effort is to be made in this Festival Year to make British Restaurants attractive to visitors.

MICHAEL: Stimulated by shortages, British culinary arts have risen to new heights of invention.

PETER: This is what a famous French Chef said after sampling one of our traditional meals.

HARRY: (AGONISED) OOOOOOOOH!!!!

F/X: (RAPPING ON DESK)

ANNOUNCER: Hygiene. In the department of sanitation Britain stands . . . alone. Despite the fuel shortage and the exhortations of Cabinet Ministers, the average Briton remains wedded to his weekly bath night.

F/X: (BATH WATER RUNNING AND SPLASHING)

HARRY: (SINGS)

MARIE: (Off) You in the barf, Fred?

HARRY: Yerst. Why?

MARIE: (Off) Well, I want to clean your boots.

HARRY: Oh blimey! Now I'll have to take 'em orf.

ORCHESTRA: 'LAND OF HOPE AND GLORY' (SOFTLY) (hold under)

MICHAEL: And so Britain has struggled valiantly on through the post-war years, fighting for a better standard of life for the pursuit of happiness for freedom . . . <u>Fighting</u> for her <u>very existence</u>! Until today the Motherland can still raise her proud face to the skies and say . . . .

HARRY: HEELLLLPPPPPP!!!

(APPLAUSE)

<u>ORCHESTRA</u>: <u>MARCH OF THE GOONS</u>
(<u>CLOSING</u> ANNOUNCEMENT FOR CRAZY PEOPLE) <u>6.45 p.m.</u>

(APPLAUSE)

CONTINUITY ANNOUNCER: (LIVE) Peter Sellers is now appearing in Variety at the London Palladium, and Michael Bentine in Variety at the Empire Theatre, Glasgow. We regret that Margaret Lindsay, who was billed in the *Radio Times*, was unable to appear.

The Goons: 1956

Ying Tong Song

The 'Ying Tong Song' — the B-side to 'Bloodnok's Rock 'n' Roll Call' — entered the charts on 14 September 1956 and stayed for ten weeks, reaching number 3. Both Goon hit singles from that year were produced by Marcel Stellman, and not — as legend has it — by Milligan's friend and future best man George Martin.

[Adapted from the transcription by Paul Martin on the website www.shutupeccles.com]

[Woodwind intro with string backing into harp accomp.]

Tenor: There's a song that I recall my mother sang to me. She sang it as she tucked me in, when I was ninety-three. [harp plays a rising chord . . .]

Bluebottle and Sprigs:

Ying tong ying tong Ying tong ying tong Ying tong iddle I po.

Ying tong ying tong Ying tong ying tong Ying tong iddle I po.

Ying tong ying tong Ying tong ying tong Ying tong iddle I po.

Ying tong ying tong Ying tong iddle I po, Iddle I po.

Ying tong ying tong Ying tong Ying tong Ying tong iddle I po.

Ying tong ying tong iddle

Bluebottle [spoken]: Ying tong iddle I po!

[short raspberry, Secombe]

Both:

Oh! Ying tong ying tong Ying tong ying tong Ying tong iddle I po.

Ying tong ying tong Ying tong iddle I po Iddle I po!

[brass solo]

Bluebottle:

Yeeng, Ying tongy tongy, Ying tong iddle I po.

Ying tong iddle I po. Ying ying ying tongy tongy.

Yeeng. Ying tong ying tong d'gy-n'o. Ying tong d'ga. D'g d'g d'ga.

Ying tong iddle I po.

Seagoon: Hear that crazy rhythm. Driving me insane. Strike your partner on the bonce. [thump]

Eccles: Nngh, I felt no pain.

[Bluebottle screeches]
Seagoon, Bluebottle and Eccles:
Ying tong ying tong Ying tong ying tong Ying . . .
[harp chord rises]
Soprano: Take me back to Vienna . . .
[Raspberry section, with band]
Bloodnok: Ohhhhh!
Eccles: Oh! [harp chord]
Soprano: Take me back to Vienna, where the . . . [crash!]
Seagoon, Spriggs and **Bluebottle** [far off]:
Ying tong ying tong Ying tong ying tong Ying tong iddle I po.
Ying tong ying tong Ying tong iddle I po –
[mad dash to foreground]
Ying tong ying tong Ying tong ying tong Ying tong iddle I po.
Ying tong ying tong Ying tong iddle I po –
Seagoon: LOOK OUT! [cry from Bluebottle]
[mad dash to distance] [hastily]
Ying tong ying tong Ying tong ying tong Ying tong iddle I po.
Ying tong ying tong Ying tong iddle I po [dash to foreground]
Seagoon: Ying tong –
[whine of bomb dropping: huge explosion]
[Double speed, but same tempo],
Ying tong ying tong Ying tong ying tong Ying tong iddle I po.
Ying tong ying tong Ying tong iddle I po Iddle I po . . .
Ying tong ying tong Ying tong ying tong Ying tong iddle I po.
Ying tong ying tong Ying tong iddle I po Iddle I po.
Bluebottle:
Ying! Tongy tongy tongy. Yiddy diddy diddy da daaa. Ying diddy.
Ying tong diddle. Yiddada boo.
[rhythmic thigh-slapping, raspberry]
All: Ying tong ying tong Ying tong iddle Ying tong iddle I po Ying
    tong ying tong Ying tong iddle I po Iddle I po.
Bluebottle: Whoooooh!

Silly Verse for Kids: 1959

On the Ning Nang Nong;
In the Land of the Bumbley Boo

Silly Verse for Kids contains many of Milligan's most popular poems for children.

On the Ning Nang Nong

On the Ning Nang Nong
Where the Cows go Bong!
And the Monkeys all say Boo!
There's a Nong Nang Ning
Where the trees go Ping!
And the tea pots Jibber Jabber Joo.
On the Nong Ning Nang
All the mice go Clang!
And you just can't catch 'em when they do!
So it's Ning Nang Nong!
Cows go Bong!
Nong Nang Ning!
Trees go Ping!
Nong Ning Nang!
The mice go Clang!
What a noisy place to belong,
Is the Ning Nang Ning Nang Nong!!

In the Land of the Bumbley Boo

In the Land of the Bumbley Boo
The people are red white and blue,
They never blow noses,
Or ever wear closes,
What a sensible thing to do!

In the Land of the Bumbley Boo
You can buy Lemon pie at the Zoo;
They give away Foxes
In little Pink Boxes
And Bottles of Dandylion Stew.

In the Land of the Bumbley Boo
You never see a Gnu,
But thousands of cats
Wearing trousers and hats
Made of Pumpkins and Pelican Glue!

Chorus
Oh, the Bumbley Boo! the Bumbley Boo!
That's the place for me and you!
So hurry! Let's run!
The train leaves at one!
For the Land of the Bumbley Boo!
The wonderful Bumbley Boo-Boo-Boo!
The Wonderful Bumbley BOO!!!

A Dustbin of Milligan: 1961

Letters to Harry Secombe

Milligan included five letters to Secombe in his first volume of poems, stories and drawings. This extract contains the first two.

S.S. Arcadia,
Near Aden.

Hello – Meagan Secombe! Sorry I haven't written before but I've been sea-sick. Gad, it's hot. Male passengers are going mad with the heat! With my own eyes I actually saw an Englishman *unbutton his dinner jacket at dinner*! He has since been certified. Gad, it's hot. The walls of the cabin pour with a screaming humid liquid vapour. Around us is the Red Sea, a festering green sheet of unskimmed molten brass. You can grab a handful of air and squeeze the sweat out of it.

Ah! but there's always the swimming pool. Lad! have you ever considered the spectacle of two thousand passengers, all jammed in a swimming pool made for twenty. They've been packed in there for three days now, and we can't get 'em out. We've managed to extricate one lady by pouring cokernut oil over her and prising her up with a crowbar, which gave her the effect of looking like an aged Venus rising from the sea.

Gad, it's hot. At two this morning one of the crew went berserk! Overcome with the heat he ran amok with his teeth out, shouting 'Eastbourne for ever, Eastbourne, pearl of the West!' and then proceeded to swallow pieces of cardboard with the word 'ice cube' written on it. To keep him quiet, I kept hitting him on the head with a piece of cardboard on which was written the word 'sledgehammer'. It was a night of real fun. Unfortunately the heat victim aroused several passengers by sliding the word 'noise' under their cabin doors. One annoyed passenger appeared in the corridor naked, save for a gladiator's helmet and a pair of corsets, and shouted 'Quiet please, we're not *all* mad you know' and threw himself over the side. As he floated aft, he shouted 'Help, drop me a line.' 'All right,' I said, 'What's your address?'[1] As he went down for the third time, he bellowed, 'I want my money back.' It was great fun next day auctioning off his effects. It's homely fun like this that makes us the great seafaring people we are.

This is really a first-class modern ship. The most interesting thing is the brass plate on the deck, saying 'Nelson fell here.' I'm not surprised. I fell over it myself.

Went to bed early, and, by sleeping at full speed, I managed to reach dawn ahead of the ship. The sun rose on the starboard side today. (The skipper turns the ship around each day so we all get a turn at it.) Looming in the morning mists are the great Volcanic Isles of Itfiflan, behind which lies Aden.

So that we could take photographs and oil paintings, the Captain ran the ship close inshore. He is a great sailor and navigator. Only a man with a great knowledge of the sea could take a ship so close inshore.

0800: All passengers in the sea helping push the ship off sandbank. Through a porthole the Captain, now purple with apoplexy, is shouting instructions and offering money prizes if we can re-float her before anyone spots us. All the crew stand at the rails shouting encouragement. What nice fellows they are. By mid-morning we had her afloat, and we sat down to a combined breakfast and lunch. Curried porridge and chips, fried fish with rice krispies. The Purser has a motto, 'Eat as much as you can, folks. You pay for it. The more you eat, the cheaper you travel.' I left a Scotsman trying to eat enough to enable him to travel free.

Slowly the great *S.S. Arcadia* steamed into Aden Harbour. Astern I saw a silver-white flash in the water, and the maw of a great shark as he gulped down some ship's waste. An old man saw it. 'Shoo, go away naughty fish,' he shouted. I learned later that he kept chickens in his cabin and was worried about them. As we neared the shore the water

[1] A joke.

became a mass of oil and it smelt something awful. The glare of the sun was immense. I said to the First Officer, 'Gad, that sun's hot,' to which he replied, 'Well, you shouldn't touch it.'

After lunch we descended the gangplank to the launch. At last I was to step on a part of the British Empire! Last time I was in Aden in 1933 it was just a dirty hot coaling station. Today it is just a dirty hot coaling station. Ashore the only thing that had changed was the ice-cream paper I had thrown in the gutter in 1933. It had grown older. A long thin Yemeni taxi driver beckoned us to his long thin taxi. 'We got Abadabar yaba dada doo, England very good man, how do you yardi boo.' 'Ying tong iddle i po,' I replied, and that settled it. Away we drove out towards the crater. There we hit the Arab caravan halting places. Everywhere there were miserable wretches moaning 'Buckshees.' Later I discovered they were all the tourist passengers off the ship. We saw one or two camels, and got their autographs on our shoes.

I got a lot of wonderful snaps of our ship as seen from the shore, the British soldiers on guard outside the British barracks, and the Union Jack over the port. What fun I'll have showing the people back home photos of the mysterious Occident. I shook hands with a friendly Arab . . . I still have my right hand to prove it. Nevertheless, everywhere are signs of organized British rule . . . all those happy fights in the café. We had a bomb explosion the day we were there. Of course, the café proprietor charged us extra for it. Those happy greetings that hang from every window 'Tommy go home.' In the harbour, with its guns trained on the shore, was the *H.M.S. Cambia* on a friendly visit. From the Yemen hills beyond came happy sounds of rifle fire. We were informed by the recruiting sergeant that we could partake in the fun if we signed 'this little bit of paper and put on this uniform'. As our launch headed back to the ship I couldn't help feeling we were getting out just in time. My suspicions were confirmed when, training my binoculars on the Governor's Palace, I could see him packing furiously, and his wife ironing a white flag.

Goodbye dear Neddy! My next report will be to describe the attacks of Arab Dhows as we sail from the shore.

Love to Myra,

Regards,

SPIKE

Hello, Ned – dear lad!

We left Aden on the evening of April 19th. The sun was setting, and Ned lad! the sunsets in this part of the world are almost miraculous. Shooting out from the perimeter of Old Sol are spears of light; pink, gold, red, yellow and crimson all fill the sky as the sun hurries to the horizon. The clouds look like the shields of a victorious army, then suddenly the sun is gone and lo! the curtain of night is down. The master tailor sews his bejewelled charges to the black canopy of the heavens. On high they cluster – the pendants of the constellation Castor, Pollux, Andromeda all glitter in the velvet darkness, like old oily chips on boiled haddock.

April 20th. What a day! The Captain mutinied and took over command of the ship. The crew turned really nasty and not one of them would dance with him that evening. The Captain finally won the crew around by promising them that they could all try on his hat.

April 21st. As the twilight encroached the ship a knowing looking Irish traveller said, 'Them's nice pigeons.' I corrected him, 'They're gulls.' 'Well,' he replied, 'boys or gulls, them's nice pigeons.' I was so enraged at his ignorance, I tied him to the mast and gave him sixty lashes with the cat. He's recovered, but the cat's right off its milk.

One day out from the Yemen Peninsula the heat started to play havoc with some passengers, i.e. at dinner a gentleman's shirt front exploded when he saw a lady in a low-cut evening gown. Mind you, her front looked as if it had exploded earlier with a wider area of devastation. The gentleman in question was Charlie Thud, a tea taster from Ceylon who had graduated from tasting soup in the Hebrides, and water at Tring. (Did you know that Tring was the inventor of the bicycle bell?) In the tourist lounge two Spanish girls and a Flamenco guitarist gave a very sultry concert of Flamenco dancing and singing. I watched spellbound the pounding insistent beat of Spanish rhythms, the red flashing lips of the Senoritas, the sensuous stamping of their heels. In the end, unable to contain myself, I tore off all my clothes, sprang to the middle of the floor and did the Palais Glide. Who said we British didn't have it in us? (I'm writing this from the ship's prison.)

April 22nd. Invited to cocktails with the Captain. He's a real son of the sea. He first became interested in ships when his mother approached him. 'John, your father wants you to build a boat at once,' she said. 'Where is father?' inquired John. 'In the middle of the lake, drowning,' was the reply. He told me he had the sea in the blood, and believe me you can see where it gets in.

April 23rd. Tonight was held the 'Ship's Gala Fancy Dress Ball'. I ate three tons of spaghetti, put on a turban and dark glasses, and went as King Farouk. How proud I was till I stepped into the ballroom. Have you ever seen five hundred King Farouks? The bewildered judges threw the prize in the air and we fought for it. Then it was time for some crazy rag (and bone) time rhythm dancing to the wild melodies of Arthur Lovelace and his Arcadian trio. The night grew hotter. Even the champagne was steaming. In the Paul Jones a stout lady grabbed me. 'You made a fool of me tonight, fighting for the prize with all those men,' and before I could protest she dragged me off to her cabin. 'Now take that silly turban and dark glasses off,' she said. I did so. She screamed, 'Help, there's a strange man in my cabin.' The night steward rushed in. 'The man is not my husband,' she whimpered. 'He's not mine either, mum,' said the old steward. Well, with five hundred identical King Farouks on board, I bet there was more than one strange moment during the evening. Anyway I was the only one down at breakfast the next morning.

Puckoon: 1963

Chapter One

Milligan's first novel, written over four years, was an Irish *Under Milk Wood*. In the first chapter we meet Dan Milligan, who takes his creator to task over the shape of his legs.

Several and a half metric miles North East of Sligo, split by a cascading stream, her body on earth, her feet in water, dwells the microcephalic community of Puckoon. This June of a Morning, the whole village awoke to an unexpected burst of hot weather. Saffron coloured in the bleach early sky, the sun blistered down, cracking walls and curling the brims of the old men's winter-damp hats; warm-bum biddies circulated air in their nethers, flapping their skirts and easing their drawers. Joyous voiced children fought for turns at the iron pump, their giggling white bodies splashing in the cool water from its maternal maw; bone-dreaming dogs steamed on the pavements and pussy cats lay, bellies upwards, drinking the gold effulgent warmth through their fur; leather-faced fishcatchers puzzled at the coarse Atlantic now flat and stunned by its own salt hot inertia. Shimmering black and still, it lay at the mercy of stone-throwing boys; the bowmen of the sands took respite from the endless cavalry charges of the sea. Nearby, Castle Hill groaned under the weight of its timeless ruins, while the distant mountains came and went in the mid-morning haze. Old Danny Conlon was already setting up the evening edition with ink-tinted fingers, 'Hottest Day in Living Memory', it took something like that to get the Pope off the front page; so lay Puckoon caught by summer in her winter thrall, as she lay thus dreaming 'twixt land and sea, all was light, and like a golden finger the morning was writ upon the scene.

Gleaming off-white at the foot of Castle Hill were the puzzled crumbling faces of the old peat cutters' cottages, their glass eyes now dimmed with cataracts of neglect and dirt. The peat had run out thirty years ago, and the peat cutters had run out not long after; some went to America, the rest stayed behind and hit each other with loaded sticks but it never really caught on and they dispersed. The cottages had been condemned as unfit to live in except during thunderstorms and depressions. The year after 'the troubles', the Irish Free State Government had bequeathed the cottages to those who had helped rid 'Houly Ireland' of the English, the Tans and for that matter, anybody. One such beneficiary was the Dan Milligan, son of a famous paternity order. With a roof over his head he had ceased work, living off his pension and his wits, both hopelessly inadequate. This sun-barbed morning the Milligan lay full length on the grass, head against the wall, his eyes lost in the shadow of his cap. His thoughts, few that they were, lay silent in the privacy of his head. Across the road, through a gap in the hedge, Milligan observed a nobbly brown dog snoozed down on the grass verge. Now it was one of those creatures that dozes with eyes half open, but, to Milligan, a Catholic, it would appear the animal was giving him a long sensual erotic stare: Milligan moved uneasily in his holy Catholic trousers. 'I wonder if he's trying to hypnotize me,' he thought, avoiding the creature's eyes. 'You can't be too careful these days wid all dem patent medicines about!'

In an attempt to break the white man's supremacy, Paul Robeson had once remarked 'All handsome men are slightly sunburned'. Milligan was no exception, he had also said it. He sat in the half upright. 'I tink,' he reflected, 'I tink I'll bronze me limbs.' He rolled his trousers kneewards revealing the like of two thin white hairy affairs of the leg variety. He eyed them with obvious dissatisfaction. After examining them he spoke out aloud. 'Holy God! Wot are dese den? Eh?' He looked around for an answer. 'Wot are dey?' he repeated angrily.

'Legs.'

'Legs? LEGS? Whose legs?'

'Yours.'

'Mine? And who are you?'

'The Author.'

'Author? Author? Did you write these legs?'

'Yes.'

'Well, I don't like dem. I don't like 'em at all at all. I could ha'
writted better legs meself. Did you write your legs?'

'No.'

'Ahhh. *Sooo*! You got some one else to write your legs, some one
who's a good leg writer and den you write dis pair of crappy old legs
fer me, well mister, it's not good enough.'

'I'll try and develop them with the plot.'

'It's a dia-bo-likal liberty lettin' an untrained leg writer loose on an
unsuspectin' human bean like me.'

It was a Dublin accent charged with theatrical innuendo; like all
Irish he could make Good Morning sound like a declaration of war –
which it usually was.

'Now, listen Milligan, I'll grant you a word wish. If you ever find
yourself in trouble just shout "Squrrox".'

'Squrrox?'

'Squrrox.'

'Alrite alrite, Squorrox, I'll remember dat. Squorrox,' he repeated,
'Right, Squorrox.'

He lay back, the sun grew on. 'I must admit you write nice weather,
mister.' He held one arm up to the sky and eyed the frayed cuffs of a
once-upon-a-time suit.

'It's goin' home at last, still a suit can't last for ever.' But on reflection
he remembered it had.

The shoulders were padded like angled flight decks, the trouser seat
hung a foot below the crutch and the twenty-eight-inch bottoms flapped
round his legs like curtains. He shook his head sadly.

'Ahh, they don't make suits like dis any more, I suppose the age of
Beau Brummel is dead.'

He recalled the day he'd bought it. The bride-to-be waiting at the
church while he, the groom, was still at home, standing naked in front
of a mirror, a top hat angled jauntily on his head. 'By Gor, she's getting
value for money,' he said.

'Hurry up, Dan lad,' his father was saying, 'you're late, and you
can't get married in that nude.'

'And why not?' said Milligan, admiring his honeymoon appendages, 'Adam and Eve done it and look at the fine honeymoon dey had.'

'Thank God,' said the old man, 'dere were no press photographers at dat weddin', or the Houly Bible would ha' been banned in Ireland for ever, perhaps longer.'

His two brothers had arrived with the suit just in time to get him to the wedding. He never forgave them, standing at the altar with two dirty great cut price tickets hangin' down his back. It was all so long ago. Suits were cheap in dem days, this one only cost a poun' ten shillin'. Prices must have gone up since then. 'Why, it must be nearly two thousand pounds for a suit dese days,' he reflected.

Kersploosh! A bucket of evil-smelling slops hit him square in his sleeping face.

'And there's more where that came from, you lazy bugger.'

The owner of the voice stepped from the cottage into the white sunlight.

'God forgive yez for dat,' spluttered the now reeking Milligan. 'Me hat! Look at me hat.'

With nostrils and legs akimbo, she towered over him like some human Yggdrasill, blotting out the sun.

'Owwwwwwwwwww!' shrieked the Milligan as she kicked the sole of his boot.

'If you don't get some work soon I'll –' she made the sign of slow manual strangulation. Milligan noticed that of a sudden there were no birds in the sky and the brown dog had fled.

'Owwww!' She kicked his other boot.

'Darling,' he whined – 'you know full well dere's no work round dese parts,' and he pointed as far as the fence.

'Poor Father Rudden is *still* looking for someone to cut the church grass, I'm going in for five minutes, if you're still here when I come out in half an hour –.'

'Owwww!' She kicked his boot again. Like an Amen the cottage door slammed after her. All the world went quiet.

'Holy God! Who in the blazes was *dat?*'

'That's your darling little wife.'

'Wife? Wife?' Agony swept across his face. 'Man alive, I thought it was a *man*. Good God, did you see dem arms? Jack Dempsey would be world champion again if he could get 'em. What kind of a writer are you? First me legs, and now this great hairy creature!'

'Don't worry, Milligan, I'll see you come out of this alive.'

'Alive?' He sat bolt upright. 'Holy Christ! Is dis a murder mystery? If so include me out, Mister. I'm a Catlick, a Holy Roman Catlick.' He listened towards the cottage. 'I better get after dat job.' He stood up, yawned, stretched, farted and lay down again. 'No need to rush at it,' he yawned. Kersploosh!! A bucket of evil-smelling slops hit him square in his face.

'I'm gettin' out of dis chapter, it's too bloody unlucky for me.'

Monty: His Part in My Victory: 1976

22 May

The third volume of Milligan's war memoirs covers the period from the fall of Tunis to the embarkation for the Salerno Landings. Milligan describes this period as 'playing at soldiers'. The book was nearly lost when he left the entire manuscript in a taxi, but fortunately the driver, a Mr. Moy, returned it to the publisher with no request for a reward.

CARTHAGE

22–23–24 May. Our long weekend leave was about to start. Friday till Monday! Where to spend it?

'Edgington,' I said, as I shaved with a thousand-year-old blade, my face a sea of cuts. 'All my born days I've wanted to see the ruins of Carthage.'

'I think you've only got a pint of blood left,' says Edgington.

'I must hurry.'

'What's a Carthage?' said Doug Kidgell.

'A great archaeological site.'

'Oh?' said Kidgell, 'why we goin', you got friends there?'

'It's to improve my education.'

'Can't we go to the pictures?' said Kidgell. 'There's Bing Crosby in "The Road to Bali" in Tunis.'

That evening, excited as schoolboys we drove off along the Tunis–Bizerta road, it was as though the war didn't exist, eventually we pull up on a sandy beach for the night.

There was no moon, but the sky was a pin cushion of stars. Great swathes of astral light blinked at us across space. We made a fire, glowing scarlet in cobalt black darkness, showers of popping sparks jettisoning into the night air. Tins of steak and kidney pud were in boiling water, with small bubbles rising to the surface.

'Ready soon,' said Doug, poking the fire, the only poke he would have for a long time.

Fildes and Edgington were making up their beds in the lorry.

Edgington singing while Fildes spoke to himself. It was interesting to hear; 'A cigarette that bears lipstick traces' – 'I think I'll put three blankets on top' – 'An air line ticket to romantic places!' – 'It's going to get chilly later' – 'A fairground's painted swings' – 'Better keep my socks on tonight' – 'These foolish things' – 'Where's that bloody pillow?' – 'Remind me of you.'

Kidgell in the driving cab is finishing off an 'I love you for ever' letter.

'You don't write many, Milligan.'

'I let 'em all worry.'

'What about your folks?'

'Well they worry about me *all* the time. Before the war they worried if I went to the toilet, even if I was in the garden they'd shout out "Are you alright son?" They'd wake me up in the middle of the night and say "Are you alright?" They're natural worriers. My father would wake up at 3 in the morning and worry about his job, and my mother would worry about him worrying about his job.'

'They sound a mite strange mate.'

'A mite? They're insane! Every night, when my father comes home from work, he gets his pistol from under the stairs then shouts "Hitler! if you're in this house, come out with your hands up." Let me tell you, Kidgell, *I'm* bloody worried about *them*.'

We sat around the fire, opening the tins with a Jack knife.

'Army cooks don't like tinned food,' says Kidgell.

'Why not?'

'They can't sod it up in tins. They like fresh stuff they can burn the Jesus out of. The motto of the Army Catering Corps is, Help wipe the smile off a soldier's face.'

'Got him!' said a triumphant Edgington, smashing a mosquito on his wrist, sending his marmalade pudding flying into the fire. 'Bugger,' he said, trying to retrieve it with a stick.

In a food frenzy he dashes to the lorry, returns at speed with rifle and bayonet. A heroic sight, as he lunged time and time again to retrieve the blackened duff. 'Don't forget – thrust – turn – withdraw,' said Kidgell.

'Gentlemen, a surprise!' I produced a small bottle of Schnapps. 'It fell off the back of a Major Chater Jack.'

'That is a spoil of war,' said Edgington, striking a dramatic finger-pointing pose.

'Well, it's not going to spoil mine,' I said, pouring out the white liquid.

Alf sipped and grasped his throat. 'Christ! If they drink this, they *are* the master race.'

It was fiery stuff.

'It'll kill us,' said Edgington.

He spat a mouthful on the fire, it exploded in a sheet of flame. 'See? When you go to the bog, for Christ's sake don't strike a match.' We mellowed. Harry got hiccups.

Edge: I wonder – hic – what's going to hickhappen to – us next –'

He didn't have long to wait for the answer – a spark shot out of the fire and burnt him.

We sat close to the fire. The smoke kept the mossies away – an occasional brave one would die under hand as it landed.

'Silly sods. I wouldn't risk my life to pass on malaria,' said Fildes. 'I think I'll turn in.'

Through the night a 3-ton lorry, with a mosquito net across the back, was home to four lads from London, who slept sounder and safer than those *in* bomb ridden London. It seemed all wrong, but it was alright by me.

A letter told of my eccentric father's career as a Captain. He had decided that the RAOC Depot at Reigate was wide open to paratroops. He took it upon himself to make a life-like raid on the Depot. He briefed a dozen NCOs. They chose mid-day. The officers are in the Mess, having a pre-lunch pissup – the men are queueing in the mess hall. Suddenly the cookhouse staff are surrounded by men with black faces and tommy guns. Their leader is speaking in a strange patois. ''Ands up, Schnell, git against that bleedin' wall, Englander please.' In the Officers' Mess from behind the bar arose 5 men with blackened faces, one wearing a German helmet, and holding a machine pistol,

'Last orders pliss undt hands up.' It was my father. The officers were then locked in an office where it was simple to phone the police. A constable arrived, and my father then explained the whole scheme. The Colonel said:

'You're a bloody fool,' and had him posted to RAOC, Elstree.

We were up at first light and away through Tunis on the Carthage road.

'Let's play some party games,' I said. 'I make up the first line and you have to rhyme the next, "There was a young gunner called Harry".'

KIDGELL: Told the MO he wanted to marry.
EDGE: The MO said Oh?
ALF: Is it Bexhill Flo?
ME: He said No, it's old Calcutta Carrie.

The blue Mediterranean flanked the road, we were as free as we would ever be in our lives. We pulled up at a lonely beach, plunged into the azure waters, with Edgington as base man we repeatedly tried balancing on each other. We got as far as 3, then collapsed with great artificial screams and dramatic plunges into the briny. One of us would submerge and sing a song and from the rising bubbles you had to guess what tune it was. Life was golden, and we were the assayers. Evening; we made camp by a sandy verge. We ate and talked. At 9.30 we bedded down. 'Good nights' were exchanged. At midnight we were still talking.

'This is marvellous, isn't it?' says Edgington. 'I don't like going to sleep 'cause I'll miss it.'

DOUG: Holidays in Africa, cor.
EDGE: You gone quiet Al!
AL: I was thinking of Lily.
ME: You dirty little devil, sleep with your hands on top of the blankets.
AL: You don't know what true love is, Milligan, there's too many birds in your life.

ME: I spread my investments! Keep as many on the boil as you can, I've got 7 going for me back in England, see there's –

EDGE: Look out! He's going to have a roll call!

ME: There's Beryl – Marie – Kay – Ivy – Madge – Betty – Dot – Doris.

DOUG: Companyyy! stand at easeeee!

AL: Don't they ever find out about each other?

ME: I keep the door locked.

EDGE: You're evil, Milligan, with all that shaggin' it's going to drop off one day.

DOUG: Believe me, it won't half make a noise when it hits the ground.

We awoke at first light, and played 'Who's-going-to-make-the-tea?' By ten past 9 no-one had given in, finally Edge arises, bent double, bladder bursting. 'I'll make it.' 'He'll only *just* make it,' I thought.

We heard him tinkering about outside, he broke into a little tune.

> Don't blame me,
> For falling in love with you.
> I'm under your spell
> But how can I help it don't blame – *BUGGER!*

'How's he going to rhyme that,' I thought. He'd burnt himself. With Edgington, striking a match could lead to anything. Edgington tying a boot-lace could end up with a broken arm. Edgington cutting his toenails could mean an amputated leg.

'Come and get it!'

We got it, fried eggs and sand. It was just after 10 a.m. when Doug put the lorry in gear and started following the signs.

'What happened at the Carthage?' said Doug, who was still puzzled.

'It was a great Naval Power! Had a war with Rome, I forget the score. The Romans razed the city, and ploughed the ground with salt.'

'How did you know all that?'

'Chambers Encyclopaedia,' I said, 'as a kid I loved reading. Given a chance I could have been a great scholar, even University.'

'You could have been a great University?'

'Everyone ought to get a university education,' said Al. 'I reckon if Harry had been through a university, he might be writing concertos instead of burning himself makin' the tea.'

'I think he'd burn himself writing a concerto.'

'Chambers Encyclopaedia?' said Harry. 'I thought that was the history of Piss Pots.'

Without warning, Kidgell burst into song. 'Loveeeeeee let me taste the wine from your lipssss,' and then went into hysterical laughter.

'He's goin' off his nut,' said Edgington, 'it happens to short arses like him.'

Doug frowned, smiled and grimaced as only a facial cripple could. 'Short arsed men are well known for their power. Take Nelson.'

'You're not,' said Fildes querulously, 'you're not lumping yourself in his class?'

A smile played across Kidgell's face.

'Answer, answer,' shouted Edgington, banging his fist on the dashboard and cutting his finger.

'Yes,' said Kidgell, 'I do, I have the same short arsed qualifications as 'im, it's just that I never had the same chances.'

Al turned and looked at Kidgell.

'What are you staring at?' he giggled.

'Christ,' chuckled Al, '*you* in charge of the H.M.S. Victory?'

'How do you know that inside me there isn't a brilliant naval tactician?'

'Say Ahhhh,' I said, 'and I'll look for him.'

'Personally you look more like a ½ Nelson,' said Edgington.

'Alright, alright, you think what you want, I still say short arses have a greater power over their fellow men by reason that they're nearer the ground and haven't got so far to fall.'

That baffled the lot of us and we gave up. Edington was bending his fingers over each other to make 'Crab Claws'. 'I learned this as a nipper,' he said. We set off again, sucking our ration of boiled sweets. We were doing 15 miles an hour, at that speed you could say

'Look at that', but, at modern speeds it's 'Did you see that?' Finally, CARTHAGE! We parked by a clump of trees, and walked to the ruins of the amphitheatre.

It was almost featureless now. What a sight it must have presented, clad in marble, as high as El Djem, the sun of Africa reflecting its white surface, the roar of crowds, the blood, the mangled remains, like Celtic vs Rangers.

'Is this it?' said Doug.

'Yes.'

'*This* is what I missed Bing Crosby on the Road to Bali for? It's terrible, it's like Catford.'

'One minute you're allying yourself with Nelson and when you see history you say it's Catford! You short arse, I only brought you here because the ruins were low enough for you to see over.'

'Well,' says Kidgell, 'I still say a Carthage is not as good as Bing Crosby in "The Road to Bali".'

We brewed our tea on the floor of the arena, it was hard to believe blood spilled here 2,000 years ago.

We upped anchors and drove on, finally Doug picked a spot adjacent to a heavily bombed French maritime repair docks.

'Ah!' says Kidgell. 'This looks more like a Carthage.'

He backed the truck under a large tree – a small group of Arabs with 3 donkeys and a camel are passing towards Tunis. They sell us oranges, eggs, dates and things that look and taste like Pistachio nuts, mainly because they were.

After a day of swimming, we are in bed smoking and talking.

'Got to be back by mid-day tomorrow – sod it,' said Doug regretfully.

'Good night lads,' yawned Edgington.

'Steady,' I said. 'You haven't had an accident for an hour.'

The 101 Best and Only Limericks of Spike Milligan: 1982

A Family Man

A family man from Siberia
As a father was very inferior,
But one operation
Revised the situation
And now he's a Mother Superior.

Goodbye Soldier: 1986

Graz

Maria Antoinetta Fontana, aka Toni, was Milligan's first serious girlfriend. The two met in Naples in June 1946 and the ensuing romance occupies most of *Goodbye Soldier*.

Next morning, I'm still discharging both ends. Wrapped in a blanket, doused with Aspros, I board the Charabong.

'How you feel, Terree,' says Toni.

'Terrible.'

I semi-doze all the way to Graz, showing no interest in food or drink. When we arrive in Graz, I hurriedly book in and make for my room. It's a lovely hotel with double glazing and double doors to the room, so it's very quiet except for the noise of me going both ends. I take a hot bath and take to my sick bed. I get visits from everyone. Do I need a doctor? I say, no, a mortician. Will I be doing the show tomorrow? Not bloody likely. Bornheim will have to take my place on the squeeze box; I am delirious. Toni visits me and tells me she loves me. That's no bloody good. I love her too, but I've still got the shits. Can she hurry and leave the room as something explosive is coming on. I fall into a deep sleep. I awake in the wee hours to do a wee. I'm dripping with sweat. What's the time? 3 a.m. I take a swig at my half-bottle of whisky. When I awake in the morning, I seem to have broken the back of it – it feels as if I've also broken its legs and arms. Twenty-four hours had passed away but I hadn't. In two days I'm back to my normal, healthy, skinny, self. How did the act go with Bornheim deputizing for me? It was great! Curses. So I rejoin the fold.

The show is at the Theatre Hapsburg, a wonderful, small, intimate theatre – one mass of gilded carvings of cherubim. This night the trio get rapturous applause from a mixed audience of Austrians and soldiers. Hall is stunned.

'Bloody hell,' he said. 'We weren't *that* good.'

'Rubbish,' says Mulgrew. '*They* weren't good enough!'

Dinner that night was a treat – first food for forty-eight hours. It's Austrian Irish stew. Bill Hall tells the waitress that his meat is very tough. She calls the chef, a large Kraut. He asks what's wrong.

'This meat is tough.'

'Oh,' says the Kraut. 'You are zer only von complaining.'

'That's 'cause I got all the 'ard bits, mate.'

'It's zer luck of the draw,' says the Kraut, who takes it away.

The waitress returns with a second portion.

'Yes, this is better,' says Hall. The excitement is unbearable.

I'm convalescing, so I have an early-to-bed. I'm reading Elizabeth Gaskell's *The Life of Charlotte Brontë*. First, I'm delighted to find that the father was Irish. The interesting figure in the story is Branwell Brontë, the piss artist. He's amazing. He writes reams of poetry, can paint and also write with both hands at once. How's that for starters. Yet, he is the *failure* of the family. My eyelids are getting heavy. I lay the book aside and sleep peacefully until the morning when there's a birdlike tapping at my door. It's morning-fresh Toni. She kisses my eyes. 'You very lazee, hurry up. Breakfast nearly finished!' She will see me after breakfast in the hall. 'We go for nice walk.' It's cold but sunny; we are quite high up.

I have a quick shit, shave and shampoo. I *just* make breakfast. I ask the waiter if I can have a boiled egg and toast. He looks at his watch. Is he going to time it? With an expression on his face as though his balls are being crushed in a vice, he says OK. Toni is waiting in the foyer. She is wearing a tweed coat with a fur collar and looks very pretty. We start our walk by strolling along the banks of the River Mur. Mur? How did it get a name like that? Our walk is lined with silver birch trees. We cross the Mur Bridge and I wonder how it got that name, Mur; through large iron gates into a park built on the side of a hill, called Der Mur Garten, and I wonder how it got that name, Mur. We walk up a slight gradient flanked by rose beds. It was then we did what must be timeless in the calendar of lovers: we carved our names on a tree, inside a heart.

> We carved our hearts
> On a tree in Graz
> And the hands of the clock stood still

Toni has found two heart-shaped leaves, stitched them together with a twig and scratched 'I love you Terry' on them. They still lie crumbling in the leaves of my diary. Ah, yesterday! Where did you go? I lean over and pick a rose only to get a shout, '*Oi, nicht gut!*' from a gardener. We climb higher to a lookout platform overlooking the Mur. How *did* it get that name? From here, we walk into the Feble Strasse, the Bond Street of Graz. As we cross the Mur Bridge, each of us tosses a coin into the river. 'That mean we come back,' said Toni. We never did. We never will.

We window-gazed. Why are women transfixed by jewellers, hand-bag and shoe shops? The moment Toni stops at a jeweller's, I feel that I should buy her a trinket.

'Isn't that beautiful?' she says, pointing to something like the Crown Jewels, priced thousands of schillings.

'Yes,' I said weakly, knowing that as I stood my entire worldly value, including ragged underwear, was ninety pounds.

The torture doesn't stop there. She points, 'Oh, look, Teree' – a fur coat valued at millions of schillings.

'Yes,' I say weakly, feeling like Scrooge.

'What lovely handbag,' she enthuses.

'Yes,' I say. Don't weaken, Milligan. As long as you can say yes, you're safe from bankruptcy. 'Look, Toni, isn't that beautiful?' I say, pointing to a small bar of chocolate for fifty groschen. Mur, how did it get that name? So, nibbling fifty-groschen chocolate, we walk back to the hotel.

During that night's show, Fulvio Pazzaglia and Tiola Silenzi have a row. Trained singers, their voices projecting can be heard on the stage. She empties a jug of red wine over Fulvio and his nice white jacket. Hurriedly, he borrows one that is miles too big. When he appears on stage, he looks like an amputee. On the way back in the Charabong, the row continues. She does all the shouting, he sits meekly in silence. It's something to do with money. She spends it and he objects when he can get a word in. We all sit in silence listening to the tirade. It is very entertaining and when she finally finishes, Bill Hall starts up a round of applause, shouting, 'Bravo! Encore!' She is beside herself with anger.

It was one unforgettable night in Graz that Toni and I consummated our love. When it was over, we lay quite still in the dark. Neither of us spoke. I could hear her breathing, then she started to cry.

'What's the matter, Toni?'

'I am different now. I am not girl any more.'

'Are you sorry?'

'No.'

With one act, everything was changed. We had made an invisible bond. Only time would test its strength. I lay watching her dress in the half-light – every move was etched in my mind. I can still see it quite clearly.

Next morning, when we met at breakfast, everything seemed different. Yet, it was only us. We seemed speechless, but our hearts beat faster. It was as though we were caught in an invisible net, each a prisoner of the other. Primitive emotions held us in their timeless grasp.

That afternoon, the Trio met in Hall's room for a practice of some new numbers.

'You're bloody quiet these days,' he says.

'I'm in love, Bill. That's why.'

'Love, me arse. All you want is a good shag and you'll be right as rain.'

'I'll bear that in mind.'

'Are you thinking of marryin' this bird?'

'It crossed my mind and body, yes.'

'You'll see, she'll be fat as a pig at forty.'

'Don't listen to him,' says Mulgrew. 'He should talk, with all those old boilers he goes out with.'

'They're not old boilers,' says Hall. 'They are mature, experienced women, who know all the tricks of love.'

'Tricks,' guffaws Mulgrew, 'like cracking walnuts in the cheeks of their arse.'

The session over, I rose to leave the room. 'You'll see,' says Hall, who is now playing the Trout Quintet. 'At forty, you'll be able to roll her home.'

I am writing home asking my folks for more razor blades and pile ointment – at the same time, telling them that I'm considering marrying Toni. My mother's reply is full of advice. I mustn't marry till I have a decent job and have 'settled down', whatever that means. Two *can't* live as cheaply as one. My ninety pounds' savings won't go far. I don't know, though; it's got as far as the Post Office in Lewisham. My mother should talk! In the days of the British Raj, her father was dead set against her marrying my father. He chased my father through the Poona Cantonments on a bicycle, my father escaping in a *tonga*.

Like all long-running shows, we are getting sloppy again. Lieutenant Priest assembles us all in the lounge. 'Look,' he says. 'It's getting to be like a private joke. It may be funny to us, but not the audience. We're going to have a full dress rehearsal tomorrow morning.' He is right, of course; we are all taking liberties. For instance, when Ricky Trowler is singing 'Let the Rest of the World Go By', he is barracked from the wings with raspberries and shouts of 'Drink up!' In the 'Close the Shutters, Willy's Dead' number, numerous ping-pong balls are bounced on the stage from each side. I think it's funny; Priest doesn't. Bill Hall plays disturbing obbligatos behind the curtain during the singers' spot, causing them to corpse.

It's a night with a hunter's moon. After dinner Toni and I go for a stroll down by the Mur. How *did* it get that name? We talked, the scenery drifted past unnoticed. We were now willing prisoners of each other. It had taken us by surprise; we were still in a state of amazement. Everything came through a rainbow-filtered haze. Toni was so childlike, I had a burning desire to look after her, to protect her. From what? God knows. Elephants? 'This is lak a storybook,' she said. 'We make it up as we go along.' Yes, one day the show would stop but we would go on for ever. This is how the story would go: the Bill Hall Trio would go back to the UK and become rich, then I would send for Toni! I would welcome her to England with a white Rolls-Royce, a glass of champagne and a complete explanation as to why the river was called the Mur!

We are finished in Graz and now to the dream city of Vienna sausage!

Call, call Vienna mine
Sing night and day with your song divine.

The Mirror Running: 1987

The Garden Fairy; My Boyhood Dog; Toni

The Garden Fairy
(*a true story*)

I saw a little girl
She was watching her father
He was taking rocks from the garden
And dumping them in the river
Her mother called,
'What was Daddy doing?'
'He's trying to make the garden lighter.'

My Boyhood Dog

Boxer, my Boxer,
where do you lie?
Somewhere under
a Poona sky.
Ah! my canine,
total joy
you were to me
when as a boy
we coursed the wind
and ran the while,
no end in sight,
mile after mile.
I was to you
and you to me
locked in a bond
eternally.
They never told me
when you died
to spare me pain
in case I cried.
So then to
those adult fears
denied you then,
my childhood tears.

1 April 1985

Toni

We carved our hearts
    on a tree in Graz
    and the hands of the clock stood still.
Down a timeless lane
    I can feel again
    that distant winter chill.
By the Wörther See
    when you came to me
    the wine of life was flowing,
But night and day
    time runs away
    and we know not where it's going.
As must we must
    time turns to dust
Like the long lost day together,
    on our wings of love,
    flew a dying dove
To leave us wondering whether
    that Capri day
    at our feet there lay
The time-drenched Faraglioni.
But the road we ascended
    had finally ended.
Addio amore, Toni.

Fleas, Knees and Hidden Elephants: 1995
_____

Knees

Knees (song)

You've got to have knees
You've got to have knees
They're the things that take stock when
    you sneeze
You've got to have knees
You've got to have knees
They only come in twos but never threes
You've got to have knees
You've got to have knees
In the winter fill them up with anti-freeze
You've got to have knees
You've got to have knees
Famous for having them are bees
You've got to have knees
You've got to have knees
If you want to see mine, say please
You've got to have knees
You've got to have knees
They help you run away from falling
    trees
Knees. Wonderful knees!

2

Cracking Up

The Goon Show: 1956

Series 7, programme 9: The Mystery of the Fake Neddie Seagoons.
Broadcast 29 November, 1956

This show comes from a series when the Goons were at the height of their popularity. It was co-scripted with Larry Stephens, and is reproduced here for the first time.

BILL: This is the BBC Home Service. Something follows almost immediately.

GRAMS: SERIES OF SOUNDS INDICATING A METAL MACHINE FALLING TO PIECES BIT BY BIT AT IRRITATING INTERVALS. SOUNDS MUST VARY WIDELY. ALL ENDS WITH DUCK CALL. (ALSO ON GRAMS)

HARRY: Ah – they don't make things like that any more.

BILL: What was it, Mr. Seagoon?

HARRY: Me.

BILL: You mean that at one time they were mass-producing Neddie Seagoons?

HARRY: Only a limited number for connoisseurs. You see – at that time there were only a limited number of connoisseurs.

BILL: Are you implying that there are other Ned Seagoons in existence?

HARRY: Yes – but there's only one signed original.

BILL: Who owns that?

HARRY: My wife.

GRAMS: FAST CHATTERING OF WOMAN'S VOICE AT HIGH SPEED

HARRY: Coming, dear! (WHISPERING) I'm the master, really.

BILL: (WHISPERING BACK, CYNICALLY) Yes – I'm sure you are, dear.

HARRY: Stop taking the mickey! I'm the funny man – I get the laughs in this show. Watch.

GRAMS: ROARS OF LAUGHTER – SEVERAL FEMALE HYSTERI-CAL SHRIEKS. (BELIEVE THE RECORDED LAUGHTER USED

BEFORE 'LAUGHTERMAKERS' PROGRAMME WOULD BE
IDEAL)

BILL: Mr. Seagoon – pull your trousers up at once. This is not
I.T.V. television! Now, if you'll just shave your head and put
on this bald ginger wig, you'll be ready for your part in –

HARRY: (QUIET 'WHAT-WHAT'-ING GOING ON BEHIND)

Bill: 'The Great Art Mystery – The Case of The Mystery of the
Fake Neddie Seagoon.'

ORCHESTRA: DRAMATIC MYSTERIOUS CHORDS

THYNNE: I'll never forget the day I met Neddie. The golden
morning sunlight was bathing the Devon hills as he made his
way through a reeking slum alley off Lisle Street.

HARRY: (HUMS TO HIMSELF) By the dustbins of Rome – I met
her . . . . . . by the dustbins . . . .

F/X DUSTBIN LID BEING LIFTED

SPIKE: (PUSSY CAT).

HARRY: (DRY) Ah – Percy Edwards' impression of a cat done by
Spike Milligan. Here – pussy – a fishbone for you . . . . . and
one for me . . . . . (GULPS)

GRAMS: SOUND OF FISHBONE DESCENDING GULLET. SUGGEST
KNIFE RUNNING DOWN SANDPAPER WITH VARIOUS
ADDITIONS

BILL: (OVER) Listeners – the sound you are hearing is the fishbone actually passing down Mr. Seagoon's gullet on its way
South. Only with the modern miracle of wireless is this possible. We now return you to the speaking end of Seagoon.

HARRY: (BURP) Ah – that's better. Now see what dainty moral
there is inferred.

F/X DUSTBIN LID OFF

HARRY: Pooh!

MORIARTY: Go away – this rubbish is reserved for members of
Rowton House.

HARRY: What are you doing in this dustbin?

THYNNE: We're waiting for the next delivery.

HARRY: I have the fishing rights for all these bins, I tell you. Out you get.

MORIARTY: Sapristi nobblers – take that!

F/X <u>LOUD WALLOP</u>

HARRY: (TOOTHLESS) Owww . . . . you devil of the dustbins.

THYNNE: Neddie – how dare you strike Moriarty in his Army Boot with the full force of your teeth!

ECCLES: What's going on here?

THYNNE: Nothing.

ECCLES: Oh – well, I'll clear off then.

BILL: The part of the mysterious stranger was played by Eccles. The rest of him was played by Rawicz and Landauer.

HARRY: (GOING OFF) All of you – clear off from these dustbins. Go on. Shoo!

THYNNE: (ON, QUIETLY) Moriarty – I've just recognised him. He's a Neddie Seagoon!

MORIARTY: Owwhh!

THYNNE: If he's an <u>original</u> Neddie Seagoon, he's worth a fortune. (ALOUD) Neddie?

HARRY: (APPROACHING, TOOTHLESS) What-what-what-what-what?

THYNNE: Neddie – we owe you an apology. Allow me to reset your teeth free of charge.

ORCHESTRA: <u>QUICK HOT BREAK ON XYLOPHONE – ENDING WITH GLISS (ANDO), UPWARDS</u>

HARRY: Ta.

MORIARTY: Neddie – let us escort you into your rightful dustbin.

F/X <u>SWANEE WHISTLE UP. LOUD CLANG OF DUSTBIN LID BANGED DOWN</u>

THYNNE: Got him!

HARRY: (MUFFLED) Let me out! Let me out!

THYNNE: Let's go and get the car from somebody's garage . . . . . . and take him to an art expert for cleaning and restoring.

MORIARTY: (GOING) Ooeeewww – money! The grisbee!

GRAMS: <u>TWO WHOOSHES OFF</u>

HARRY: (ON) Curse – trapped inside a dark, dank dustbin. But wait – (SLOWLY) – there's somebody in the dustbin with me! . . . . . . (WHISPER) He's coming over . . . . . . I'll pretend I haven't seen him.

GRAMS: <u>FOOTSTEPS – ON SLIGHT ECHO – APPROACH FROM DISTANCE AND STOP</u>

ECCLES: Hellooooo.

HARRY: It's the famous Eccles.

ECCLES: It's the famous Eccles.

HARRY: How did you get in this dustbin?

ECCLES: I got influence. I know the man on the door.

HARRY: Then you can help me get out of here.

ECCLES: Get out? Who wants to get out of a place like this? This is livin' – I never had it so good.

HARRY: SSShhhh! Listen!

ECCLES: What?

HARRY: Look – Dear listeners – through the bead curtains of the dustbin I saw a large dustcart draw up outside. To the sound of silent bugles, two dustmen slid to the ground and rowed themselves towards us.

ECCLES: Yer – that's the W.V.S. Dustbin Collection Society.

HARRY: Really – what's that for?

ECCLES: They make parcels of rubbish up for the poor people of Acton.

HARRY: What for?

ECCLES: What for! There's people in Acton who can't afford rubbish of their own.

HARRY: Even as Eccles spoke – our bin was hoisted aboard the ghostly dustcart and driven away to the sound of Max Geldray.

<u>MAX GELDRAY/ORCHESTRA</u>: 'BOO-DAH'

(APPLAUSE)

MAX: (OFF) (FADING YELL)

GRAMS: HEAVY SPLASH

BILL: That was Max Geldray playing an entrechat on an
    unloaded seagull. Next week 'Fifty Years of Song' arranged
    for wardrobe and Ernest Longstaffe. Book your teeth early.
    And now we return you to a certain type of entertainment.

ORCHESTRA: LAST EIGHT BARS 'LIMEHOUSE BLUES' PLAYED
    IN FAST 2/4 TIME

HENRY: Mm . . . . . . mmm . . . .

MINNIE: Where are you, buddy?

HEN: I'm trapped behind the rosewood piano, Min.

MIN: Oh – dear! Ah – which rosewood piano are you behind,
    Henry?

HEN: Which? How many rosewood pianos have we got?

MIN: I'll count them. Sixty-eight, Henery.

HEN: That's the one. I'm behind one of them.

MIN: Keep still! Heave! . . . . (AD LIB EFFORTS OVER)

F/X MOVING PIANO – JANGLING OF STRINGS – BOOMING VIBRA-
    TIONS – HEAVY BANGS, THUDS, ETC.

MIN: There you are. You can come out now, Hen . . . . Ououoh!

HEN: What's the matter, Min?

MIN: You're not behind this piano, Henry.

HEN: Oh dear – you'd better find me soon or I'll pass out.

F/X KNOCK ON DOOR

HEN: I'll get it, Bebe.

MIN: Okay, Ben. I wonder how many people will recognise that
    impression, Henry?

F/X DOOR OPENS

HENRY: What is it, gentlemen?

SPRIGGS: Pardon me, sir. I have a load of rubbish outside.

HEN: It's a music publisher, Min.

SPRIGGS: You don't understand, sir and Maurice Burman. What
    I mean is – we have a dustbin of selected rubbish specially for
    you – the poor people of Acton.

HEN: You mean it's free?

SPRIGGS: Not a penny piece to pay!

HEN: Ohh – <u>Min</u> – <u>Min</u>! . . . .

MIN: At least we can look our neighbours in the face. We've got our own rubbish!

HEN: Would you just leave it in the hall here, Mr. Man?

MIN: You must excuse the mess, sir, but we've got us in.

F/X DUSTBIN LIDS

SPRIGGS: (EFFORTS) There, madam – and there's plenty more where that came from. England's getting back on her feet, I tell you. Good-day.

F/X DOOR CLOSES

HEN: Ohh – look Min. Our own rubbish at last.

MIN: Where shall we put it, Henry?

HEN: On the mantelpiece, Min, where people can see it.

HARRY: (VERY MUFFLED GABBLE)

MIN: The rubbish spoke, Henry!

HEN: It's not dead yet, Min. (LOUD) It's still ponging. Come out from inside, you coward. Come out and fight Minnie Bannister!

F/X LID OF DUSTBIN OFF

HARRY: Please – please help me.

ECCLES: Please help him.

HARRY: I've been kidnapped!

ECCLES: He's been kid-

HARRY: Shut up, Eccles!

ECCLES: Shut up, Eccles!

HEN: Don't try and lie your way out of this. You're <u>our</u> rubbish!

F/X DOOR BURSTS OPEN

MORIARTY: Nobody move! We've got him, Grytpype.

THYNNE: Yes, Neddie. Don't try anything funny. We want the laughs here. Get inside that piano.

HARRY: But I'm not musical.

THYNNE: I know. I've bought your records.

HARRY: What-what-what-what-what?

MORIARTY: Sapristi! Stop the joking! Get inside that piano.

HARRY: No – it might be infectious.

THYNNE: Don't worry. I'll drive.

HARRY: I was forced at postul punt into the back of the piano
and driven away at break-neck speed . . . By a driver with a
broken neck.

GRAMS: CAR STARTING UP VERY FAST – WITH OVERLAY OF
PIANO-PLAYING AT HIGH SPEED. FADE UNDER:

MORIARTY: Faster, Grytpype. Can't this piano go any faster?

THYNNE: No, I'm out of practice. I haven't played for years.

GRAMS: DISTANT POLICE GONGING APPROACHING

HARRY: I'm saved. We're being gonged by a police piano.

GRAMS: PIANO/CAR PULLS UP SUDDENLY – GONGING STOPS

MUSIC SAXOPHONE – 'POLICEMAN'S HOLIDAY'

MORIARTY: Sapristi! Here comes a police saxophonist.

THYNNE: Yes. Keep Seagoon covered with this copy of Chopin's
Nocturnes.

HARRY: You devil, you know I don't know it.

BASS: (APPROACHING) 'Allo – what's goin' on 'ere? Do you
know you're breakin' the law?

THYNNE: What's the charge?

BASS: Playing the piano – on the wrong side of the street. Fined £5.

THYNNE: Well – naturally it's a French piano.

BASS: Then the fine will be five hundred francs.

F/X TILL

BASS: Merci – and here's an aerial photograph of a receipt.

ORCHESTRA: TAAA RAAA THIN CHORD CYMBAL

BILL: Part three – in which Neddie is taken to an art expert's to
discover whether or not he is an original Seagoon. Over then
to the expert.

ORCHESTRA: BLOODNOK THEME

Blood: Aeiough . . . Arggggggggg . . . . Blurnnnnn Orgeuegegeg
. . . . Aeolelelele. Never again. Now, Abdul?

ABDUL: Yes, major?

BLOOD: Here are those export masterpieces for the Americas. Just check this list. Original Portrait of Miss Marilyn Monroe by Michael Angelo.

ABDUL: Ha.

BLOOD: President Eisenhower by Gainsborough.

ABDUL: Gainsborough by President Eisenhower.

BLOOD: Good. Vincent van Gogh by Kirk Douglas, R.A. What's he doing in the Artillery?

ABDUL: Making a film.

BLOOD: Ohhhhhhhh –

GRAMS: WHISTLE – TRIANGLE – BASS DRUM – SPLASH – GONG – DUCK CALL. ALL DONE AT EVEN TEMPO

BLOOD: Answer the door, Abdul.

ABDUL: Ha.

GRAMS: A GREAT FURIOUS OPENING OF ABOUT TWENTY DOORS IN RAPID SUCCESSION

THYNNE: Thank you. Nervous of burglars?

MORIARTY: Bloodnok, we want you to see if this is an original Seagoon.

HARRY: What! You're going to examine me?

BLOOD: Only down wind. Now – as with all oil paintings like this . . . .

HARRY: What? I'm no oil painting.

BLOOD: I'll say you're not . . . . we must first remove the layers of centuries of dirt and grime.

HARRY: What-what-what-what!

BLOOD: Silung, painting.

HARRY: I tell you there's no need for this. I am the original Neddie Seagoon. I've got the signature on my bottom left-hand corner.

BLOOD: Whose?

HARRY: My father's.

BLOOD: Let me see.

F/X RIP OF CLOTH

HARRY: Oooops.

BLOOD: (READS) Fred Seagoon . . . yes – the signature's genuine. But wait! Your bottom left-hand-corner looks a forgery.

HARRY: It can't be. I use my bottom left-hand corner every day.

BLOOD: We'll soon see. Quick! Get him in this bath of turpentine.

GRAMS: <u>SPLASH</u>

HARRY: Ooooooeeeeeough! (BUBBLE)

BLOOD: Now – while he's soaking, let's listen to this oil painting of Ray Ellington.

<u>ELLINGTON QUARTET</u>: <u>'IT'S ALL RIGHT WITH ME'</u>

(APPLAUSE)

GRAMS: <u>HAMMER CHIPPING ON A STONE</u>

BILL: The sound you are hearing, folks, is Major Bloodnok chipping away the outer layer of the Neddie Seagoon in question.

HARRY: Ooops! Mind what you're doing down there, Bloodnok.

BLOOD: Silung – Gentlemen and Moriarty.

MORIARTY: Owww.

BLOOD: After extensive tests – I removed Seagoon's outer layer – and guess what I found underneath? A portrait of a man in his underwear. Gentlemen – this Neddie Seagoon – is a <u>forgery</u>!

HARRY: Me? A forgery! This is a trick – a plot – a plit – a trock – a plick – a trot – <u>I'm</u> Seddie Neagoon – I'll say that again – it's a kick – a plock – <u>I'm</u> Geggie Seadoon!

BILL: May I help?

HARRY: A trained talker. Proceed.

BILL: Thank you. (LOUD) It's a trick – a plot – <u>I'm</u> Neddie Seagoon.

<u>F/X</u> <u>CLANG OF DUSTBIN LID DOWN</u>

THYNNE: Got him.

MORIARTY: Well done, Grytpype. <u>So</u> – Wallace <u>Greenslade</u> is the original Neddie Seagoon – overpainted with a portrait of a BBC announcer.

BLOOD: Yes – it'll take years to remove all those layers of green slading.

HARRY: I tell you I am the original Neddie Seagoon.

BLOOD: Nonsense! You're only a head and shoulders.

HARRY: I'm a full-length portrait.

BLOOD: No man your size could be a full-length.

HARRY: Well, I was 6 ft 3 in as a child when I was young, but I was struck by a lift.

MORIARTY: Wait a minute! If you're an original, why are you such a funny shape?

HARRY: (DRY) I was done by Picasso.

THYNNE: Bloodnok, we're taking Greenslade to the <u>only man</u> who can tell us whether he's an original Greenslade – or a fake Seagoon.

HARRY: Who's that?

THYNNE: John Snagge.

<u>ORCHESTRA</u>: <u>THIN CHORD – CHOKED CYMBAL</u>

THYNNE: (BREATHLESS) We're back.

HARRY: Well?

MORIARTY: That Greenslade <u>was</u> a fake. After we removed the layers of green slade – look what we found underneath –

<u>F/X</u> <u>DUSTBIN LID UP</u>

BLUEBOTTLE: Hello, captain.

HARRY: Good heavens – a genuine Blue Bottle by El Greco.

B/B: Yes – Jim El Greco of Finchley. I'm going to be hung in the National Gallery.

HARRY: Splendid. I must get tickets. So – <u>you</u> were the person behind Greenslade!

B/B: I was the brains. I was just using his large-type front and posh-type talking to work my way to a position of importance in the BBC.

HARRY: Silly! There are no positions of importance in the BBC.

MORIARTY: Sapristi! The question is – where is the Original Neddie Seagoon?

B/B: My auntie's got an original Neddie Seagoon.

MORIARTY: Ow ow ow ow! Little friend of man – little nice cardboard mate – if I give you this quarter of Dolly mixtures would you show me this original?

B/B: (MAGIC) Coo! Dolly mixture – THINKS – with that quarter of Dolly mixture I can show him the original thing. Follow me.

ORCHESTRA: TA RAAAA THIN CHORD. CYMBAL CRASH

B/B: Part two –

F/X KNOCK ON DOOR. DOOR OPENS

THYNNE: Good evening, madame – er . . . we understand you have an original.

MIN: Oh come in, I'll . . .

B/B: Hello, Auntie Min . . .

MIN: Young Bottle, why aren't you at school?

B/B: It's broken up for the winter. They're using it as firewood.

MIN: Oh! I love those old Etonian customs.

THYNNE: (RESTRAINED IMPATIENCE) Ah ha ha, yes, madame – could we inspect the . . . er . . . original . . .

MIN: I don't know where Henery put it . . .

B/B: Never mind. I know where it is – in this dustbin.

F/X DUSTBIN LID OFF

ECCLES: Hello!

THYNNE: This idiot isn't an original Seagoon.

ECCLES: This idiot is the famous Eccles.

BLOOD: Wait a minute. I recognise that thin veneer. Quick – get him behind this X-ray screen.

F/X ELECTRIC BUZZER – CONTINUOUS SOUND

BLOOD: Just as I thought. He's had a plate of porridge for breakfast.

HARRY: (ASIDE) Feed line. (ALOUD) How do you know?

BLOOD: I can see the plate. Quick! Chuck him in this bath of turpentine.

GRAMS: SPLASH

ECCLES: Help – Oh, here . . .

GRAMS: SPLASH

ECCLES: Oh – here-here – Help!

GRAMS: SPLASH. THEN PRE-RECORDING:

GRAMS: (HARRY) Ooooh . . . . . help . . . .

BLOOD: Look! Just as I thought – the Eccles has washed away,
    revealing an original Neddie Seagoon by Elder the Breughel.

HARRY: Rubbish – that man is not an original Seagoon!

GRAMS: (HARRY) 'I'll have you know I am!'

HARRY: What-what-what-what-what-what!

GRAMS: (HARRY) 'Please don't do that full-face.'

HARRY: I can prove I'm the original Seagoon. Listen – (SINGS
    BRIEF FAST SCALE)

GRAMS: (HARRY) (SINGS SAME THING MUCH HIGHER)

BOTH: HARRY/GRAMS: (START ARGUING AND SINGING
    WILDLY)

BLOOD: Stop! Stop! Now – stand side by side. Now listeners –
    take a good look – and decide which one you think is the genu-
    ine Neddie Seagoon. The end follows almost immediately. Good-
    night. (MUTTERING, GOING OFF) I don't know how we get
    away with it . . . . .

ORCHESTRA: 'LUCKY STRIKE'

DURING CLOSING ANNOUNCEMENTS, BLUEBOTTLE ECHOES BILL

BILL: (OVER MUSIC) That was the Goon Show, a BBC recorded
    programme featuring Peter Sellers, Harry Secombe and Spike
    Milligan with the Ray Ellington Quartet, Max Geldray and the
    orchestra conducted by Wally Stott. Script by Spike Milligan
    and Larry Stephens. Announcer: Wallace Greenslade. The pro-
    gramme was produced by Pat Dixon.

ORCHESTRA: SIG. TUNE UP TO END. (1.50)

(APPLAUSE)

MAX & QUARTET: 'STOMPIN' AT THE SAVOY' (1.10)

(APPLAUSE)

Silly Verse for Kids: 1963

The Bongaloo; Soldier Freddy

The Bongaloo

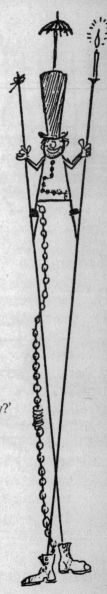

'What is a Bongaloo, Daddy?'
'A Bongaloo, Son,' said I,
'Is a tall bag of cheese
Plus a Chinaman's knees
And the leg of a nanny goat's eye.'

'How strange is a Bongaloo, Daddy?'
'As strange as strange,' I replied.
'When the sun's in the West
It appears in a vest
Sailing out with the noonday tide.'

'What shape is a Bongaloo, Daddy?'
'The shape, my Son, I'll explain:
It's tall round the nose
Which continually grows
In the general direction of Spain.'

'Are you *sure* there's a Bongaloo, Daddy?'
'Am I sure, my Son?' said I.
'Why, I've seen it, not quite
On a dark sunny night
Do you think that I'd tell you a lie?'

Soldier Freddy

Soldier Freddy was never ready
But Soldier Neddy,
    unlike Freddy
Was *always* ready and steady.

That's why,
When soldier Neddy
Is-outside-Buckingham-Palace-
on-guard-in-the-pouring-wind-
and-rain-being-steady-and-
ready,
Freddy – is home in beddy.

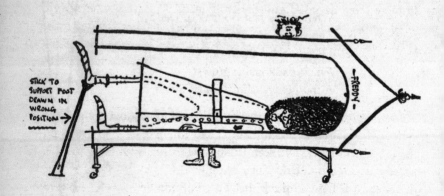

A Dustbin of Milligan: 1961

The Great Man

My Uncle Bertram Twitt was a great man. He told me so himself. One can't argue with facts like that. He was a tall, handsome, cross-eyed man with eczema. He walked with a pronounced limp, L-I-M-P, pronounced 'limp'. I was five at the time. Uncle Bertram was plagued with a bald head. It happened when he was twenty-one. 'I was wounded in the head whilst fighting Turko-Arab forces in Mesopotamia, and my hair fell out,' he told me. Latterly I discovered that he went bald naturally, but that was too ordinary for a great man. Hope came to him when the family were living in Poona. Uncle Bertram was approached by a Mr. Panchelli Lalkaka, a Hindu Holy man. For ten rupees, he guaranteed to cure my Uncle's bald head of baldness. The treatment involved my Uncle sitting naked in a darkened room, with a mixture of cow dung, saffron and treacle spread on his head. 'Stay in there three days sir,' said the Holy man.

It didn't work. My Uncle hit the Holy man with my brother's christening mug. I was now seven. My Uncle took to wearing a toupée. One day my Uncle said, 'Nephew, Nephew, there are many wicked landlords in this world, come, I must teach you to shoot.' He thrust a great Mauser Rifle at me. He put me in a bush overlooking a dried up Monsoon lake. He ran from boulder to boulder, and I fired blank cartridges at him and he returned the fire with an old Arab Pistol. Now the crows and hawks of India are much angered by rifle fire, which is usually directed at them. They took to diving on my Uncle. As he disappeared behind a rock a great hawk dived after him. It reappeared, clutching something in its talons. Uncle appeared a second later revealing a clawed bald head, and swearing above and beyond the call of normality. He threw rocks, sticks, clods, one of his shoes and discharged his pistol, but the hawk flew beyond the reach of the great man. That evening, wearing a handkerchief knotted around his heavily iodined head, he wrote a letter to England ordering a fresh wig and a powerful adhesive glue. For days after, he roamed the countryside with a pair of binoculars and a ladder. He searched every hawk's nest for fifty square miles around, but alas, never again did he find that wig, and never again did we play at shooting. Years later an Indian naturalist reported a strange find, a hawk's nest made from a wig; stranger still it wasn't my Uncle's. I was eleven at the time.

Puckoon: 1963

Chapter Five

Belfast is a big city. At one time it was quite small, even worse, there has been an occasion when there was no Belfast City at all. Thank heaven, those days are gone and there is now a plentiful supply of Belfast. Ugly and grey it spreads out, drab, dull, lacklustre streets, crammed with the same repetitive, faceless, uninspired, profit-taking, soul-breaking buildings. The only edifices worth seeing are those erected long before the coming of the local council and the builder. Beautiful buildings seemed to taunt them. 'Pull them down!' was the cry. 'The Highway must go through.' The world, beauty, tranquillity and fresh air were being sacrificed to a lump of compressed tin with a combustion engine. Stately trees were felled as a 'Danger to lightning', and when one questioned them the answer came from a faceless thing called 'Spokesman said'. Here, safe in its bureaucratic cocoon, we had the new vandalism of authority, power without conscience or taste; as it was with Belfast so was it with other cities, for now and ever after it seemed. In this metropolis lived many citizens. Most of them poor, with an additional burden, nowadays it costs more to be poor than it used to.

Inside sternly furnished wallpapered rooms at number 356 Queen Victoria Crescent, two young Customs officers were packing well-travelled suitcases.

Webster was short and handsomish, with ill-cut straight brown hair and grey eyes, all in all a bit of a ladies' man, one bit in particular. By comparison, Peter Barrington, his tall, blond, rather wavering room-mate, looked slightly effeminate. The two had nothing in common save the English language, and even then Barrington had a superior accent for it. As they packed, the tops of the red buses passed and repassed the windows with their never ending pageant of adverts. 'Beechams worth a guinea a box', 'Take Andrews Little Liver . . .' 'Gynon Salts for the regular. . . .' 'Exlax'.

The motive seemed to be 'Make people shit and get rich'. Strange, people won't believe in God, yet will swear by some blue pill that guarantees to rid them of baldness, bedwetting, distended kidneys, pox and varicose veins. Piles! A man with piles will believe any promise of a cure. Sitting on clusters of sore and distended veins, his mind goes awry and his judgement uncertain. Judge Jeffreys suffered from piles, and look at the havoc he wrought on the unfortunate followers of Monmouth. If it hadn't been for piles, Monmouth would have been alive today! Unaware of this historical truth, Barrington and Webster packed their cases.

'I cwan't sae I fwancy lwiving under cwanvas,' said Barrington, his accent almost obliterating the meaning of the words.

The upper class sound of it ruffled Webster. He didn't like Barrington, but two sharing a room was cheaper than one. Webster's background was Poplar, docks, dirt, pubs. He had been born in a cockney family when cockneys were perfectly content with their lot, made good workmen, great craftsmen, superb soldiers and were the first to put up flags for the King and Queen. In the twenty-five years since World War I that had all changed; gradually the adulation for the Crown grew less and less. Queen Victoria had gone to her grave with the streets choked with mourning citizens; it was a very thin funeral crowd that watched King George VI to his rest; it followed that the funeral of our present Queen was going to be downright embarrassing.

Behind the throne desperate efforts were made by those whose jobs hang by royal decree, to modify the Royal Family to meet the Social Revolution and make their little jobs more secure. The speech-writer royal was also under fire from the press; he had used the 'My husband and I' opening so frequently that it was always good for a laugh in comedy shows, and B.B.C. variety departments chiefs in search of O.B.E.s were quick to strike it from scripts, one of their rare positive gestures.

Barrington lit a cigarette. Unlike Webster, Barrington had been born into a class that denied him the joy of self-accomplishment; it had been all 'laid in' for him. His name was down for Eton three years before his birth, gilt-edged godparents, his baptism could be seen in

The Tatler, London Illustrated and, in *The Times*, a small notice to that effect. Despite all this he had been cashiered from the Guards for a certain incident with a young boy. It had been given three-inch head-lines in all Sunday papers, those Sunday papers that are always both 'shocked and distressed' at crime and degradation; so shocked and distressed are they, that every Sunday they re-shock themselves as a 'Public Duty'. THIS MUST BE STOPPED! says the front page.

Then the copy: Police Raid Den of Vice! Sixteen-year-old white girl found with black men! Working on information from one of our reporters, Scotland Yard Vice Squads this morning raided a Greek Club in Soho. Sgt. Henshaw C.I.D. reported seeing a hundred and twenty couples playing Bingo in the nude; when questioned the proprietor, Knessis Philominides, said that the players had felt 'hot'. Police removed certain appliances, an eight millimetre film projector, along with some films. Names and addresses were taken, among them eighteen-year-old the Hon. Maureen Campbell-Torrington of Bayswater. She was escorted by Pandit Nowarajee Gupta, Hindu seaman of no fixed abode. He told a Paddington magistrate, 'I had two whiskies and a small port wine and everything went black. When I regained my sensibilities I was in a Black Maria handcuffed to ten other men who were also naked.' Asked to explain 40 lbs of heroin in his pugaree he said, 'You are only doing this because you think I am Jewish!' He then showed them a photo of Gandhi and claimed diplomatic immunity.

In the same way, poor Barrington had been exposed to the nation.

His mother, Lady Norah, had been singularly unmoved by it all. As she told a reporter, 'I can't understand all the fuss, his father did this sort of thing all the time, and he got on *awfully* well,' but then she added, 'He worked in the Foreign Office.' An educated woman, she spoke eight languages and said nothing intelligent in any of them. She was one of those pale, powder-white, sedentary creatures who no matter when you called was always cutting flowers in the garden. As wars broke out she couldn't wait to start rolling bandages and knitting things for those 'poor men at the front'; in peacetime she ignored them completely. Lord Barrington himself was a devout Catholic and a practising homosexual; as he frequently said, 'practice makes perfect'. He was a fine military figure, and why shouldn't he be? From his ankles to his groins he wore Dr Murray's anti-varicose elastic stockings; from groins to mid-rib he wore severe male corsets, made secretly by Marie Lloyd's dresser; around his shoulders, laced under his armpits and knotted at the back were 'Clarke's elastic posture braces'; his glass eye gazed unseeing at the world, into its live companion was screwed a monocle. A stickler for fitness, he spent every morning lying on the floor clenching and unclenching his fists. In the '14–'18 affair, he served as one of Haig's military asses, saluting, pointing at maps, walking behind v.i.p.s, shaking hands, posing for photographs and forever reminding the General his fly buttons were in full view of enemy snipers, and so won Haig's undying gratitude. Now his young son Hon. Barrington had been seconded to the temporary obscurity of the Northern Irish Customs. Webster and he were both due to organize a Customs Post along the new border near Puckoon.

'Where the hell *is* Puckoon?' Webster was about to ask, when there was a combined knocking and opening of the door, the speciality of landladies in need of scandal, as was Mrs Cafferty: standing there, her bones almost escaping from her body, she smiled a great mouthful of rotten teeth, a salute to poverty and indifferent dentistry.

'I'm sorry yer goin' at such short notice,' she grinned, and handed the bill to Barrington.

'Two pounds?'

'That's one pound in lieu of a week's notice, sir.'

Barrington placed his cigarette on the window sill and took a five pound note from a registered envelope. From 'Mummy'.

'Oh,' said Mrs Cafferty, 'I'm sorry, we don't take cheques, sir.'

'Cheques? This is a five pound note.'

Confused and baffled by her ignorance of the higher currency denominations, she backed from the room, clutching the front of her flowered apron.

'I'll bring me husband up, he knows all about dem tings.'

Downstairs, his socks singeing in the heat of a near red stove, dozed the lord and master of the house. Robert Cafferty. Deep down in a fast disintegrating imitation leather armchair, he smouldered in mid-evening sleep. Around him his kingdom. On the stove, a blue chipped teapot was stewing the last life from its imprisoned leaves; on the mantelpiece a clockwork Virgin Mary, made in Japan.

'Wake up, darlin',' said Mrs Cafferty, striking him gently with her clenched fist.

'Ouch!' yelled Cafferty, leaping to his socks. 'Wassermarre, I'll kill the son of a –'

'Look at this,' she waved the five pound note.

'Oh,' he donned his glasses. 'It's a cheque . . . isn't it?'

'That's what I told dem, but dem says no.'

'I'll talk to dems.' He pulled up his braces and put his hat on as a sign of authority.

Webster and Barrington could hear them coming up the stairs in a flurry of whispers.

'Good morning to you both,' said Cafferty, appearing in the doorway, his face still drugged with sleep. 'Well, well –' he looked round the room in mock surprise, 'so you're leaving,' and without a break, 'Sorry we don't take cheques.'

Barrington snatched the note from Cafferty's hand, tearing it in half. 'For God's sake,' he said angrily, snatching the remaining half, leaving behind yet a smaller piece.

The Caffertys moved together for safety.

'Here!' Barrington hastily counted out four brown ten shilling notes. 'Brown, *dat's* the colour of money,' thought Cafferty.

'Sorry, we don't take dem cheques,' he said, leaving the room.

They could hear her hitting Cafferty as he stumbled down the stairs. One hour later Webster and Barrington sat side by side on hard black leather seats rocking sleepily on the train to Puckoon. Back in 356 Queen Victoria Road, Barrington's cigarette on the window sill was burning the house down.

'Hello, hello, Prudential?' said the smoke-enveloped Cafferty, 'Hello? I want to take out a fire policy . . .'

A most irreverent wind whistled through the seams of Major Stokes' military trousers. The rain whiplashed his violent overcast face. In the damp shadows behind stood members of his platoon, their identity lost in the timeless obscurity of a railway waiting room. There was no light, and the building was dank. The roof leaked, the gutters leaked, his hat leaked. He took a pull on his brandy flask.

'Puckoon! What a God-forsaken place.' He paced the weed-soaked platform breathing minced oaths. He stopped and beat a rapid military tattoo on his riding boot. 'Ouch!' he said. Stepping crisply into the street lamp's crepuscular glow, he took a nickel military watch from his pocket. The military time was nineteen hundred hours. The train was late. He rapped loudly on the ticket office partition; from behind came the sound of a rusty bolt being withdrawn; the partition slid half-way up, jammed, then slammed down again; a second time it rose, this time framed in the Gothic aperture was the unshaven, sandwich-chewing face of the Station Master, Donald Feeley. He peered into the dark at the Major's wet, white face.

'Where are you goin' to, sorr?'

'I'm not going anywhere.'

'Good, then you've arrived. Good night.'

'Wait,' the Major restrained him. 'I'm waiting for the train that was due here at sixteen hundred, the time is now nineteen hundred hours, you know what that means?'

'Nineteen hundred hours? No, sorr, my watch only goes up to twelve.'

'It's *three hours late* man! I'm supposed to pick up two Customs officers.'

'Oh?'

'Can't you 'phone, or something?'

'Dere's no 'phone here. We got a letter box.'

He stuffed another sandwich in his mouth.

'Is it usually this late?' shouted the Major, becoming openly vituperative.

'I meself have never timed it. Long as it goes backwards and forwards that's all we care.' He coughed, showering the Major with pointillisms of bread and sardines.

'You're a blasted idiot!' said the Major.

'True, sir, very true,' said Feeley, closing the partition.

Turning away in a fury, the Major fell heavily over a box. The darkness was filled with clucking chickens and swearing. 'What bloody idiot left that crate there?'

'I did,' said a voice.

He struck a match. It was a nun. This was all getting intolerable. He thought of London and Penelope, he thought of London and his wife, finally he thought of London and himself. A proud man.

A blow to Major Stokes' vanity had been going bald at the tender age of twenty-six while serving in Southern Command India. He had tried a remedy suggested by a doctor, Chanditje Lalkaka. Wagging his head, in a Welsh chee-chee accent, the Hindu physician had explained, 'It is made from a secret Punjabi formula, captured by Shivaji from the Rajputs during the Marhatta wars.' A bald man is a desperate man; but a bald *vain* man is a hairless Greek Tragedy.

The Major paid Lalkaka one hundred rupees. For five days and nights he sat in a darkened room, his head covered in a mixture of saffron cowdung and a curry-soaked handkerchief. Issuing forth on the sixth day, he discovered that what little hair he had had disappeared and so had Dr Lalkaka. For years after that he habitually and suddenly hit unsuspecting passing wogs and pointed to his head. Meanwhile, he took another pull at his flask and peered up the track into the sightless night.

Four miles up the line, showing no signs of life, was the six-thirty train for Puckoon. The carriage lights, strung like amber beads, hung lustreless in the squalling rain. A weak trickle of steam hissed from the outlet valve. On the foot-plate, O'Malley, the ginger-haired fireman, looked at the dead furnace.

'I can't understand it! Dat coal bunker was full on Thursday.'

'Well, it's *Friday* and *empty*,' said Driver Murtagh.

'Don't lose yer temper, Murtagh, all we need is somethin' to burn.'

'Oh! Wid a fine mind like that you're wasting yer time as fireman, and you're also wastin' *mine*!' Murtagh drummed his fingers in the throttle and spat into the dark.

'Now den! you listen to *me*! We passed a cottage a few yards back. Go and see if they've got a couple of buckets o' coal or peat.'

'O.K.,' said O'Malley, and he climbed down and crunched off into the darkness. From the carriages came enquiries.

'What we stopped for, mister?'

'Is this Dublin?'

'What happens if we can't. get started?'

'Well,' explained O'Malley, 'first class passengers will be taken on by private car.'

'What about us third class?'

'You get out and bloody well push.'

He continued on past the carriages, ignoring several cat-calls, two empty bottles and a passenger who couldn't hold it any longer. The cottage was dark save for a light in the back. There was no knocker. Hands in pockets, he tapped with his foot.

'Who's there?' said a female voice.

'Please, mam', it's the fireman from the Puckoon Flyer.'

'Did you fall off, then?'

'No, we've runned out of fuel.'

The door opened, a girl's face appeared, it appeared very pretty too.

'Come in.'

'Oh, tanks.'

The room was plain, a fire burned in a large inglenook recess. A crucifix and holy pictures hung on the far wall – a red light burned at a small altar. 'What is it you want?'

'Could we borrow a couple of buckets of coal or peat?'

'Coal I have. Would you like a cup of tea before you go? You look awful wet.'

He shuffled his feet.

'Aw, come on,' she said, pushing him back into a chair. 'That train's never been on time.'

She kept looking at him in a way. He sipped his cup of tea. She was looking at him in that way again . . . he finished his cup of tea . . .

Dear reader, it's a wonder how one bed can take so much punishment. The springs groaned under the combined assault of two activated bodies. It was an age-old story but neither of them seemed to have heard it before, and, they did it *all* on *one* cup of tea. Dear friends, a quarter of a pound of tea can be bought for as little as two shillings, and think of the fun you can have in the privacy of your own home.

From outside came an angry knocking on the door, from inside came an agonized coitus interruptus. 'Oh God,' gasped O'Malley, rolling off, 'who can it be?'

'How the hell do I know?' She was pulling on skirt, petticoat, stockings, but no drawers – after all this could be a false alarm. O'Malley wrestled frantically to tuck an unruly member into his trousers.

'Anybody in?' came the voice.

Relief showed on O'Malley's face. 'It's all right, it's me mate.'

The door opened on a wet engine driver. 'What the blazes has –' He saw the girl. 'Oh,' he said.

Carrying the buckets of coal back up the line O'Malley confided, 'Hey, you know why I was so long?'

'Sure,' grinned the driver, 'I was watching through the window, My, you've got a spotty bum.'

Saturday. Pay day! Ha, ha, Milligan rubbed his hands. Six days grass cutting at three shillings a day, six multiplied by three – 12 shillings! Ha! Ha! He looked at the church clock. 4.32. Time for lunch! He unwrapped brown bread, cheese, boiled potatoes and a bottle of stout. He took a long drink on the bottle and a long eat on the bread. By Gor, the old woman was starting to look after him dese days, perhaps work was the answer after all. The sun was warm again, he stretched out on a gently sloping gravestone. A breeze turned the trees into a rataplan of skirling leaves. He watched a cluster waving overhead. I wonder if they enjoy doing that? It looks as if they are. He finished his meal. 4.32! Just enough time for an hour's forty winks.

Milligan was awakened by the approach of an internal combustion engine. He could see the occupants. Polis! *And* the military! He dived instinctively into a pile of cut grass. There was a tread of military boots up the drive. They stopped.

'Anybody about?'

An English voice! What the hell were they doin' back here?

'Hello,' came the voice again. Through the lattice of grass, he could see a Corporal. He heard a soft gurgle as the soldier drained the last of his stout. 'I'll get him for that,' swore Milligan. A second man approached. It was Major Stokes. Milligan didn't know it was Major Stokes, but that doesn't alter the fact that that is who it was. They were joined by Sergeant. MacGillikudie.

'Any signs of life, Corporal?' A strange question in a graveyard.

'No sir. There must be somebody around, I just found this empty Guinness bottle.'

'Can I help you, gentlemen?' The voice of Father Rudden came on the scene.

'Ah, Vicar,' said Major Stokes. *Vicar?* The priest shuddered.

'My name's Stokes, o.c. 2/4 Ulster Rifles.' He extended his hand, had it crushed and returned.

'And what can we do for you, *Mister* Stokes?'

'We're here to build the new Customs Post and erect border fences.'

'Er – I don't see how I can help, I've got a bad back.'

The Major didn't seem to hear, he produced an Ordnance Survey map and pointed to a small red circle. 'This here is where it's to be, which lies approximately –' he pointed – 'over there.' The priest raised his eyebrows. 'A Customs shed. On CHURCH ground? I've heard nothing of this, it must be a mistake.'

'No, it's true, Father,' interrupted MacGillikudie, 'I had this official letter this morning.' Rudden glanced through it quickly. 'Well,' he concluded, 'I've received no notification. I shall have to write to Cardinal MacQueen in Dublin about it.'

'Can't wait for that, Vicar,' said Stokes. 'We have instructions to start right away.' Rudden rubbed his chin. 'Very well, if it's the law I can't stop it, but I think it's damnable to run a frontier through a churchyard.' He stormed back to the church ignoring the Major's attempts to explain. 'He'll be all right, sir,' said MacGillikudie with assurance. 'He's a fine man, he'll always give you a hand.'

'It'll be a long time before I give him mine again,' said the Major, feeling for broken bones.

Dan Milligan, in his grass prison, realized now there was no cause for alarm. He sprang to his feet like a herbal phantom. 'Good morning all,' he said happily.

'It's someone risen from the dead,' said the terrified MacGillikudie.

'Hands up,' said the startled Major.

'Don't shoot,' said the grassy spectre. 'It's *me*, Dan Milligan, aged 41.'

The Major had both hands on the pistol directed straight at Milligan's grass-covered head. 'Arrest this man, he appears to be in some disguise.'

'It's all right,' said MacGillikudie, realizing the truth, 'It's Dan Milligan, he's all right.'

'What the hell was he hiding for, then?'

'He says what the hell was you hiding for, Milligan?'

'I was havin' a sleep, Sarge.'

'He says he was having a sl —'

'I can understand what he's saying!' shouted the Major. 'Tell the idiot to be more careful in future.' The Major marched off, carelessly thrusting his pistol into the holster. There was a shot, a scream, and the Major took to clutching his foot and leaping. From nowhere the nobbly brown dog came snapping at his seat. What a noble sight. Man, beast and clutched foot, all leaping in perfect harmony. It was a great day for the Irish.

It was a greater one for the Jews. To Doctor Goldstein they took the wounded man. Laying on a stretcher, Stokes saw the nose of Goldstein hovering above.

'I say,' he said, momentarily forgetting his pain. 'You're a Jew. I don't want any damn Jew operating on me. Take me to a white man.'

'There's no other doctor for fifty miles and unless that bullet is removed you'll bleed to death!'

'Very well, then,' snapped the Major. 'Just this once then!'

Goldstein naturally knew of anti-Semitism. It was the most pleasant operation the doctor had ever performed. Without an anaesthetic.

The Bedside Milligan: 1968
————————————

The Singing Foot; The Sun Helmet

The Bedside Milligan contained drawings, stories, poems and letters written while he was writing *The Goon Show* and after.

The Singing Foot (A tale of a singing foot)

Woy Woy, Australia.
September 1967.

I have an Uncle. His name is Herbert Jam. He was 52. He worked in a laundry. One Christmas Eve he was homeward bound on a crowded bus when he heard what he thought was the sound of music coming from inside his boot; indeed, what was to make him famous had happened, his right foot had commenced to sing. Poor Mr. Jam tried to control the volume of sound by tightening his boot lace; it only succeeded in making the voice go from a deep baritone to a strangled tenor. At the next stop Mr. Jam had to get off. He walked home to the sound of his right foot singing 'God rest you merry gentlemen'; fortunately, Mr. Jam knew the words and mimed them whenever people passed by. It was all very, very embarrassing. For three days he stayed off work. His favourite T.V. programmes were ruined by unexpected bursts of song from the foot, he did manage to deaden it by watching with his foot in a bucket of sand, but, alas, from this practice he contracted a rare foot rot normally only caught by Arabs and camels. Worste was to come. The foot started singing at night. At three in the morning he was awakened with selections from 'The Gondoliers', 'Drake is Going West' and 'A Whiter Shade of Pale'. He tried Mrs. Helen Furg, a lady who was known to have exorcised Poltergeists and Evil Spirits, she tied a sprig of witchhazel round his ankle, intoned druidic prayers and burnt all his socks in the bath, but it wasn't long before the strains of 'The Desert Song' came lilting up his trouser leg again. On the recommendation of his doctor he visited the great Harley Street right-foot specialist, Sir Ralph Fees.

'Come in, sit down,' said the great man. 'Now, what appears to be our trouble?'

'It's my right foot.'

'Of course it is' said cheery Sir Ralph. 'And,' he went on, 'what appears to be the trouble with our right foot?'

'It sings.'

Sir Ralph paused (but still went on charging). 'You say your foot sings?'

'Yes, it's a light baritone.' said wretched Jam.

Sir Ralph started to write. 'I want you to go and see this Psychiatrist,' he said – at which very moment Uncle Herbert's foot burst into song! 'Just a minute' said Sir Ralph 'I'll get my hat and come with you.' The medical world and Harley Street were baffled. For the time being he had to make do with a surgical sound-proof boot and a pair of wax ear-plugs. Occasionally, he would take off his boot to give the lads at the Pub a song, but, Mr. Jam was far from happy. Then came the beginning of the end, E.M.I. gave him a £500,000,000 contract for his foot to make records. A special group was formed, called 'The Grave', the billing was 'Mr. Jam with One Foot in the Grave'. He was the news sensation of the year! But, it became clear that it was the right foot that got the fame, not Mr. Jam. E.M.I. opened a bank account for the right foot. While his poor left foot wore an old boot, his right foot wore expensive purple alligator shoes from Carnaby Street which cost £50 a toe. At parties he was ceaselessly taking off his shoe to sign autographs! Mr. Jam was just an embarrassment to his right foot! One night in a fit of jealousy Mr. Jam shot his foot through the instep. It never sang again! Mr. Jam returned to the obscurity of his job in the laundry. He was 52, happy, only now he walked with a slight limp.

The Sun Helmet

A pleasant three degrees below zero wind was blowing. The early morning Londoners shivered through the bitingly cold rush hour. Among them was a bowler-hatted Mr. Oliver Thrigg. The first snow of summer was starting to fall as he joined his 'AA members only' bus cue. Glancing to a bus que opposite (it was a different que to his cue, as the spelling proves), what he saw shook him to his foundation garment. There, in the que opposite, was a man wearing a sun helmet, eccentricity yes, but this fellow didn't have a stamp of a genuine eccentric, no, fellow looked far too normal! Curiosity got the upper hand, crossing the road he killed a cat. Once across he joined the que and left his on the other side. The sun-helmeted man caught a 31A bus, Mr. Thrigg signalled a passing 49A. 'Follow that bus,' he told the driver. 'Anywhere but Cuba,' said the driver. At Victoria Station the sun-helmeted man booked to Southampton, as did Mr. Thrigg, who kept him under surveillance until they reached Southampton, where by now the snow was 3 foot deep, which explained the absence of dwarfs in the street. The man continued to wear his sun helmet. 'Why, why, why,' said Thrigg, whose curiosity had killed another nine cats, making a grand total of one. 'I must follow this man etc.' The man booked aboard the Onion Castle and was handed £10 and an oar (Assisted Passage they call it). The ship headed south, and so did Mr. Thrigg and his enigma, which he used for colonic irrigation. During the whole trip the man appeared at all times in a sun helmet. Several or eightal times he was almost tempted to ask the man his secret. But no, as Thrigg was travelling steerage and the man 1st Class, plus the fact it was a special Non-fraternising Apartheid Cruise, no contact was possible. On the 12th of Iptomber the ship docked at Cape Town. Even though Thrigg got through Customs and Bribes at speed, he just missed the Sun Helmet as he drove off in a taxi. Thrigg flagged down an old cripple Negro driver. 'Follow that Sun Helmet,' he said jumping on the nigger's back. (The change from Negro to Nigger denotes change from UK to SA soil.) Several times Thrigg let the nigger stand in his bucket of portable UK soil so he could be called Negro. To cut the story short, Mr. Thrigg used scissors and cornered the man in the middle of the Sahara. The heat was intolerable as Thrigg walked up and said, 'Why are you wearing that sun helmet?' 'Because,' said the man, pointing at a 113° thermometer in the shade, 'the sun man! This protects the head.' 'I see,' said Mr. Thrigg. 'Well I better be off, I'm late for work.' As he departed for the caravan que, the man in the sun helmet spotted him. 'Good God, a man wearing a bowler hat! A bowler hat! Here, in the Sahara? I must find out why,' he thought as he joined the caravan cue behind Mr. Thrigg.

The Bed-Sitting Room: 1969

Act One (extract)

The Bed-Sitting Room, written with John Antrobus, received its première at the Mermaid Theatre in London. A movie version directed by Richard Lester and starring Ralph Richardson, Rita Tushingham, Michael Hordern and Arthur Lowe alongside Milligan was released in 1969.

CAST

Kak	Graham Stark
Lord Fortnum	Valentine Dyall
Mate	Spike Milligan
Other parts	Bob Todd
	John Bluthal
	Johnny Vyvyan

KAK WALKS TO HEAD OF THE COUCH, GOES TO SIT ON AN EMPTY SPACE. AT THE LAST MOMENT A DICKENSIAN CLERK HOLDING A CHAIR UNDER HIMSELF SLIDES UNDERNEATH KAK, SO THAT KAK IS SEATED IN HIS LAP. THIS IS ALL DONE IN ONE SMOOTH MOVEMENT.

KAK: Now then, start at the beginning, tell me all.

FORTNUM: My paternal ancestor Lord Crapologies Fel de Minge.

KAK: (quietly, without stopping FORTNUM speaking) Did he?

FORTNUM: What? Came over with the William the Conqueror, first class of course . . . it was Hastings 1066 . . .

KAK: (writes down on pad) Hastings Ten Sixty Six. Right, I'll phone him later.

FORTNUM: Yes, he'll bear me out. . . . Well, he was a tall man with garnished ginger knees and several ways about him. On Sundays they say he took a spotted woman to church. . . . Now in the late autumn of 1066, during an attack of Coptic Gadfly on the Knack-eeeeee.

KAK: Yes yes, needn't go back that far. How do you spell Knack-ee?

FORTNUM: I don't. Could you – er –

KAK: Oh, I'm sorry. (He re-agitates the feather) Now tell me something more recent.

FORTNUM: Well, if you <u>must</u> know, everything was going swimmingly until they dropped this terrible . . .

SOUND OF MULE RASPBERRIES. GROANS.

EVERYBODY ON STAGE LEAPS UP AND STARTS SWIPING AT INVISIBLE FLYING THINGS. THE PIANIST, WHO UP TO NOW HAS BEEN READING A PAPER BEHIND DRAWN CURTAINS, PULLS BACK THE CURTAINS AND LAUNCHES INTO A FURIOUS VERSION OF 'WHEN THE LIGHTS GO ON AGAIN'. AT THE SAME TIME A SMALL MAN IN A LEOPARD SKIN, ARMY BOOTS, GREAT GINGER WIG (AND IT MUST BE *ENORMOUS*) AND GREAT RED BEARD, ENTERS WITH A GREAT CLUB WITH WHICH HE BATTERS THE STAGE IN A FRENZY. THE NOISE STOPS, THE LITTLE MAN EXITS IN TEARS. PIANIST PULLS THE CURTAINS ON HIS PLATFORM. ALL REVERTS TO NORMAL.

KAK: The H-bomb?

FORTNUM: Yes, that's the one. Ever since then, I've been strangely troubled.

KAK: Did the noise keep you awake?

FORTNUM: No, I slept like a log, I do tree impressions as well. When I came to I discovered a marked change. As was my wont I toddled along for lunch at the Constitutional Club, and it had gone – rubble, nothing but rubble, and such small portions. I saw Lord Hailsham standing outside stark naked waving a Union Jack and shouting 'Vive le Sport'. I could see his membership had lapsed, so I ignored him. I wrote a stiff letter to <u>The Times</u>, then, <u>they</u> broke the news to me. While I'd been asleep, they'd had World War III. (Walks forward, looks up) I didn't get a chance to join the regiment.

KAK: There, there – that part of it came as quite a shock to me too; fortunately I managed to get there in time for a disability pension.

FORTNUM: Well, since the bomb I haven't eaten a thing.

KAK: Why not?

FORTNUM: (annoyed) Can't afford it! Bread at sixty-four gns per fine ounce. See this? (Shows signet ring) I had this bit of bread mounted this morning.

KAK: Gad, beautifully cut.

FORTNUM REMOVES RING AND HOLDS IT OUT TO KAK.

FORTNUM: Look, Doctor, all this, if you'll give me a prescription to alleviate malnutrition.

KAK: Right! (Writes on pad) T grams Brown Windsor Soup. Eggs and Chips. Jam and Custard. There, I want you to take this three times a day before meals, any good restaurant will make it up.

FORTNUM: I'll try Boots Café . . .

KAK: Good, anything else?

FORTNUM: Yes, ever since they dropped this bomb, I've had the morbid fear I might turn into a Bed-sitting Room.

HERE THE ACTORS MUST INTRODUCE GREAT TENSION.

KAK: A Bed-sitting Room?

FORTNUM: Yes!

KAK: Will you be empty? I – er – I mean – how would you visualise yourself as this Bed-sitting Room?

FORTNUM: A brick wall with brick wallpaper over it. A plastic draining board, fluorescent lighting, red bakelite door knobs and an outside wooden karzi. Oh dear, what should I do?

KAK: Well, I think you ought to stick out for thirty shillings a week – at a push you might get two quid.

FORTNUM: Two quid??? Look, you're not getting the point, I don't want to be a Bed-Sitting Room. You can't have a Lord turning into that sort of thing. Woburn Abbey, Blenheim Palace, where the takings are reasonable, but a Bed-Sit at two quid?

KAK: You sound quite Ad-Amant about that.

FORTNUM: I am <u>Ad</u>-Amant. I am.

KAK: You sound quite Adamant about that <u>Ad</u>-Amant.

FORTNUM: <u>I</u> am. <u>I</u> am. (<u>Stresses</u>)

KAK: Look, let's be practical – have you seen a good estate agent?

FORTNUM: Yes. (<u>Full of meaning</u>) He was quite quite beautiful.

KAK: (<u>worried</u>) What?

FORTNUM: But he refused to handle me until I'd become this blasted Bed-Sit. Two quid. The fool didn't realise, I'll do <u>anything</u> to stave off the prospect of becoming a Bed-Sit. I'll pay anything . . . even . . . (<u>He produces a gold coin</u>) . . . even Money!

KAK: (<u>falls on his knees</u>) Money!

BLACK OUT, DIVINE SPOTLIGHT FROM DIRECTLY OVERHEAD ON KAK. SOUND OF HALLELUJAH CHORUS BY HANDEL (VOCAL CHORUS). FORTNUM GIVES HIM THE COIN, KAK BENDS HIS HEAD IN RELIEF. LIGHTS UP. MUSIC STOPS. KAK TO HIS FEET.

KAK: Well, well, Lord Fortnum, I think we can do business. Roll up your sleeve.

FORTNUM ROLLS UP SLEEVE.

FORTNUM: Gad! An arm.

KAK: Say Ah.

FORTNUM: Ahhhh.

KAK: Good, you can get dressed again.

FORTNUM TURNS MODESTLY AWAY TO PULL DOWN SLEEVE.

KAK: Now, I want you to start taking these Anti Bed Sit Pills; take six a day, one every half mile.

FORTNUM: But I only live a mile away.

KAK: You'll have to move further out, then.

FORTNUM: But I . . .

The Two Ronnies: 1974

The Phantom Raspberry Blower of Old London Town,
#1. Broadcast 4 September, 1976

What became one of the most popular strands in *The Two Ronnies'* fifth series began as a thirty-minute single drama written by Milligan for LWT's *Six Dates with Barker* in 1971. When the idea was developed into a regular slot, Milligan wrote the first episode only, which appears here.

CAST
Ronnie Corbett
Ronnie Barker
Barbara Dickson

with
Stephen Calcutt
Jo Kendall
Vicki Michelle
Claire Nielson
John Owens
Johnny Wade

Produced by
Terry Hughes

EPISODE ONE

(AFTER TITLES SEQUENCE – A STUDIO CAPTION – AN OLD MAP
OF LONDON.)

DRAMATIC VOICE OVER: London 1898. This story starts on
the night of Tuesday October 3rd.

(CROSSFADE TO CALENDAR SAYING FRIDAY, APRIL THE 10TH)

EXT. DOWNING STREET. NIGHT.

(SWIRLING MIST. IN CLOSE-UP, A MATCH IS STRUCK. IT LIGHTS UP
THE NAME-PLATE 'DOWNING STREET'. WE SEE THE PHANTOM, IN

TOP HAT AND OPERA CLOAK, ONLY FROM THE BACK. HE WALKS,
WE FOLLOW HIM. HIS FEET AS THEY PACE TOWARDS NO. 10.
ANOTHER MATCH IS STRUCK – THIS TIME LIGHTING UP 'NO. 10'.
HIS BLACK-GLOVED HAND RAISES THE KNOCKER, AND KNOCKS.
SHOOTING OVER HIS SHOULDER, WE SEE THE DOOR OPEN. IT IS THE
BUTLER)

BUTLER: Good evening sir – May I assist you?

PHANTOM: Yes. Is the Prime Minister in?

BUTLER: He is, sir, but he doesn't see <u>any</u>body without an
appointment. Except Miss <u>Maureen</u> Body.

PHANTOM: In that case, please to give him my card.

(HANDS HIS CARD)

BUTLER: (MYSTIFIED) But why is there no address on it sir?

PHANTOM: I'm never at home.

BUTLER: Is there any message I may give to the Prime Minister
sir?

PHANTOM: Yes. Tell him this! (A GREAT RASPBERRY IS
BLOWN)

(THE BUTLER'S FACE DISTORTS WITH FEAR AND DISGUST, AS THE
FOOTSTEPS OF THE PHANTOM ARE HEARD RUNNING AWAY. THE
BUTLER CLUTCHES HIS HEART, STAGGERS IN THE DOORWAY)

BUTLER: Help – I – I've never been so – ooh!

(HE COLLAPSES. POLICE WHISTLES, RUNNING FEET, DRUM ROLL –
AND A CLOSE-UP OF THE VISITING CARD. A SMALL RASPBERRY IS
PRINTED NEATLY IN THE MIDDLE. THE MUSIC CRASHES IN WITH
THE 'PHANTOM THEME')

EXT. LONDON STREET. DAY.

(NEWSVENDOR [PLAYED BY A GIRL WITH A MOUSTACHE] IS
SELLING PAPERS)

NEWSVENDOR: Read all about it. Strange fiendish attack on
Prime Minister's butler. Police at bedside – Cor struth, strike a

light, Gard bless you Guv, read all about it. Police at bedside . . . .

(MIX THROUGH TO CAPTION STILL OF 'ST. GEORGE'S' HOSPITAL, WITH LIGHTED WINDOWS)

INT. ST. GEORGE'S HOSPITAL. NIGHT.

(OUTSIDE THE WARD – NOTICE ON DOOR SAYING 'SEBASTOPOL WARD')

(INSPECTOR CORNER, OF SCOTLAND YARD, AND HIS ASSISTANT, SERGEANT BOWLES, ARE TALKING TO A NURSING SISTER, YOUNG, PRIM, AND PROPER. SOMEWHERE BEHIND THEM, A SIGN ON THE WALL – 'MATERNITY WARD – DELIVERIES DAILY')

INSPECTOR CORNER: Good evening. I'm Corner of the Yard.

NURSE: You're the what?

BOWLES: He is Inspector Corner, of Scotland Yard. And I am Sergeant Bowles.

CORNER: How do you do.

BOWLES: How do you do, sir.

CORNER: I have to interview Mr. Butler, the Butler.

NURSE: Of course. You can come in now, Inspector, but you must be quiet.

CORNER: Pardon?

NURSE: (SHOUTING) You must be QUIET!

(A PATIENT IN A WHEELCHAIR FLIES PAST. WE HEAR A CRASH)

NURSE: How long will you be?

(THEY WALK THROUGH THE DOUBLE DOORS INTO THE SMALL WARD. AS THEY DO SO, SERGEANT BOWLES'S APPEARANCE CHANGES COMPLETELY – IN FACT, IT IS ANOTHER ACTOR. BUT HE STILL WEARS THE BIG RED BEARD WE ASSOCIATE WITH THE CHARACTER)

CORNER: Just a little while.

NURSE: Very well – but not a minute longer.

(THEY LEAVE THE SHOT – WE STAY ON A SIGN WHICH SAYS 'BRAIN SURGERY WHILE YOU WAIT')

(THEY WALK TO THE BED WHICH CONTAINS THE BUTLER)

BUTLER: Ooh! Oh! Ooh dear! (etc.)

CORNER: Good evening, sir. I'm Corner of Scotland.

BOWLES: Yard.

CORNER: Yes.

BOWLES: And I'm Sergeant Bowles.

CORNER: (MATTER-OF-FACT) I know that. We're hoping you might help us with our enquiries.

NURSE: That's all for tonight Inspector.

CORNER: Very well – we'll come back tomorrow.

(THEY ALL TURN AND WALK AWAY TOWARDS THE DOORS. A 'SUPERED' CAPTION APPEARS:– 'THE FOLLOWING NIGHT' WHERE-UPON THEY ALL TURN AND WALK BACK TO THE BED, IN THE SAME SHOT)

NURSE: Not too long, Inspector, he's still very weak.

INSPECTOR: I realise I am pressing you, Nurse; but it must be obvious to you that I have very little alternative.

(HE IS STANDING BEHIND HER)

NURSE: I didn't even notice. (SHE MOVES AWAY SLIGHTLY)

INSPECTOR: (TO BUTLER) Now. Did you see the man's face?

BUTLER: No – no – it was very dark.

INSPECTOR: A dark face, I see!

BUTLER: But it wasn't his <u>face</u>.

INSPECTOR: Well whose face was it?

BUTLER: It was the noise – oh. (HE SOBS)

INSPECTOR: Noise? Could you give us a rough idea of this noise?

BUTLER: Oh – I'm not – oh, the disgrace – it was so – oh!

INSPECTOR: You must try. It may be the breakthrough we've been looking for.

BUTLER: Oh, very well – Nurse – the screens.

(THE NURSE PUTS SCREENS AROUND THE BED. STAY ON THE NURSE AS SHE LISTENS TO THE CONVERSATION. WE CAN ONLY SEE THE OUTSIDE OF THE SCREENS, WITH THE NURSE IN FOREGROUND)

INSPECTOR: (OOV) Now sir – think hard – what was this noise?

BUTLER: It – it – sounded like – he went . . .

INSPECTOR: Yes? Yes? He went what?

BUTLER: He went (A PATHETIC ATTEMPT AT A RASPBERRY)
Ooh! Oh my wife, the disgrace . . .

(CUT TO INSIDE THE SCREENS)

BOWLES: (TAKING NOTES) I didn't quite get that sir.

INSPECTOR: He said the man went (RASPBERRY)

BOWLES: How do you spell it, sir?

INSPECTOR: Never mind the spelling, just put (RASPBERRY)

BOWLES: Very good sir. (HE BLOWS A SLOW RASPBERRY AS
HE WRITES IN THE BOOK)

NURSE: Oh – (SHE HAS BEEN GROWING MORE UNCOMFORTABLE AT
EACH RASPBERRY, AND FINALLY IN TERROR, SHE RUNS TO THE
WINDOW AND THROWS IT OPEN. A FLASH OF LIGHTNING ACROSS HER
FACE, A CLAP OF THUNDER, AND OVER THIS A GREAT RASPBERRY,
AND THE SOUND OF MANIACAL LAUGHTER. CRASH IN MUSIC)

INT. HANSOM CAB. NIGHT.

(THE INSPECTOR AND BOWLES, SITTING IN THE CAB. THROUGH THE
WINDOW AT THE BACK, OVERLAY OF OLD BLACK AND WHITE
LONDON STREET SCENES – CHANGING LATER TO SHOTS OF AERO-
PLANES, OR MONKEYS AT THE ZOO, ETC.)

BOWLES: But what is the point of such an attack – apart from
the shock? It's pointless – he must be a madman.

INSPECTOR: I know this sort of criminal well. A lifetime of frus-
tration – then, one desperate act. After that, nothing.

(BOWLES CHANGES ACTORS AGAIN)

BOWLES: You think he's blown himself out?

INSPECTOR: Possibly. Somehow I don't think we'll hear any-
more from this attacker. (A PAUSE) We seem to be taking a
devil of a time to get to the Embankment. I didn't realise the
road was so long.

BOWLES: It has to be sir, otherwise it wouldn't reach.

INSPECTOR: Yes, I see your point. (CALLING UP TO CAB-DRIVER) I suppose we <u>are</u> on the right road, cabby?

CABBY'S MYSTERIOUS VOICE: (OOV) Don't worry, sir; just put yourself in my hands. I'll look after you.

INSPECTOR: Of course you will. The British cab-driver is the salt of the earth.

(CUT TO BACK VIEW OF CABBY – IT IS THE PHANTOM SILHOUETTED AGAINST A VIOLENT-LOOKING NIGHT SKY)

PHANTOM: Thhh-ank you, sir. (HE BLOWS A SMALL RASP-BERRY ON THE 'TH')

(THE THUNDER CRASHES – INSPECTOR AND BOWLES LOOK AT EACH OTHER, SLIGHTLY MYSTIFIED)

DRAMATIC VOICE OVER: Inside that dim hansom cab, the dim handsome face of Inspector Corner of the Yard looked dim and handsome in the dim light of the hansom cab dim light.

Was the wind of change about to blow through the land?

Had he trodden in more than he could chew? Little did he realise – the world was to hear more from The Phantom Rasp-berry-Blower of Old London Town!

(MUSIC UP TO FINISH)

(END OF EPISODE ONE)

William McGonagall: 1976

The Truth at Last: Chapter IV

The breakneck-paced *McGonagall* books were written in collaboration with Milligan's friend and publisher, Jack Hobbs.

That night, under a full moon, McGonagall sailed from South Africa, in the hold as a slave. 'I want to see my solicitor,' he shouted through the barred hatch. 'Keep rowing or you'll have us all on the rocks,' shouted a friendly voice.

> It was the captain of the lugger
> Known as Captain Dan MacGrugger
> He wasn't fit
>
> . . .

And that was why McGonagall was rowing. 'What's the name of this ship?' said McGonagall. 'The Marie Celeste,' came the reply.

'I've got a nasty feeling,' said McGonagall.

'Well, keep it to yourself,' said the Captain, 'and I'll tell you what we'll do, we'll split the insurance.'

They spent the rest of the day pushing the crew overboard and setting the table for breakfast.

'Just before we lower the lifeboat,' said the Captain, 'put two sausages, bacon and eggs on every plate – That'll fool 'em.'

'It fooled me,' said McGonagall. But then everything did. As they rowed from the silent, fully rigged ship, the Captain gloated over the side. 'Oh wait till we collect the insurance on that,' he said, 'it'll come to a tidy sum.' 'How much is that?' said McGonagall. 'Five pounds each,' said the Captain. 'That's not much for the loss of a big ship like that,' said McGonagall. 'My God you're right,' said the Captain. 'Quick, after it.'

But row as he might McGonagall couldn't catch the fast disappearing *Marie Celeste*. 'She must be making all of twenty-three knots,' said the

Captain. 'Oh dear,' said McGonagall. 'I only know how to make two, and one of those is a granny.' Try as he may, they could not close the gap. With McGonagall at the oars the Captain rowed like mad, but steer as he may he had no effect.

LOG OF THE LIFEBOAT 321

DAY ONE: Enough food and water to last us for three months.

DAY TWO: All food and water gone.

DAY THREE: McGonagall lying delirious in the scuppers saying to himself 'Ooooooooooo Mrs Mountain's glorious Transport Cafe, where are ye in my hour of need?' to which she replied, 'I'm here in Lewisham cooking lunch for Scott Fitzgerald.'

DAY FIVE: Floating helplessly off the Azores.

DAY SIX: Floating helplessly off the Azores.

DAY SEVEN: Floating helplessly off the Azores.

FROM DAY SEVEN TO DAY TWENTY-THREE: Floating helplessly off the Azores.

DAY TWENTY-FOUR: Have decided to settle off the Azores.

DAY TWENTY-FIVE: Suddenly floating rapidly away from the Azores.

DAY TWENTY-SIX: Withdrawn application for permission to settle off the Azores.

DAY TWENTY-SEVEN: Captain acting strangely. 'This won't get us very far,' said McGonagall. 'What won't?' said the Captain. 'This won't,' said McGonagall, holding up a piece of knotted string. 'Give me that,' said the Captain. 'I will not,' said William McGonagall.

DAY TWENTY-EIGHT: The Captain said 'Give me that string.'

DAY TWENTY-NINE: McGonagall said 'No.'

DAY THIRTY: Fighting broke out around the lifeboat between McGonagall and the Captain. 'This is mutiny,' they both shouted. 'One of us must be wrong,' said the Captain. 'Land ahoy,' shouted the lifeboat – and there, three inches away on a hot summer's day, was the beach at Eastbourne, a pleasant resort, nestling on the South East coast, population 35,000 approx, and with the arrival of our heroes 35,000 plus two. There were regular trains to Victoria, and good connections by road to Brighton, Hailsham and Upper Dicker.

Good shopping centre and a wide choice of hotels, the Excelsior being the widest, recommended by the AA (Alcoholics Anonymous).

As they landed McGonagall cried,

'Ooo Beautiful Town of Eastbourne
A place where many people are born.
Because it's a nice place to stay
Not many people leave it to go away.
And I and my Captain are grateful it is here,
Because the moment we saw it we lost our fear,
And there are trains every hour from the
    station.
They go to Victoria and other parts of
    the nation.
And soon we'll be travelling along the
    iron line,
And I hope that during the journey I will
    feel quite fine.'

It was a new experience travelling in a dog crate in the guard's van but the Captain seemed to know what he was doing. How he got into that crate of pigeons McGonagall would never know. But it was cheap and safe provided you could keep up the barking and cooing. 'I'm going to woof, miss all this, woof, when we get to London,' said McGonagall.

At Victoria Station they broke open the pigeon crate and the Captain flew away, taking with him the vital insurance form for which

McGonagall had suffered so much and now had nothing. 'Ah well, easy come, easy go,' he said. He threw himself under a train, and missed. It wasn't his lucky day.

'Do you do this often?' said the wheel tapper. 'Not if you're successful,' said McGonagall, 'you should only need to do it once – does that answer your question?' and in one bound rejoined his wife and children in Edinburgh.

'Oh daddy's home, mummy,' said little Willie and little Sarah.

'Oh Willie dear you're back, your front, your legs and arms have all come home with you,' said Jeannie his wife.

'What's for dinner?' he said.

'Breakfast,' said Jean. 'It's only six o'clock in the morning.'

'Ah, that's the sort of dinner I like' he said, throwing himself on the bed and missing it. 'Do you do this often?,' said the wheel tapper. 'I thought I'd answered your question,' said McGonagall.

'I'm sorry Willie, we sold the bed – Does that answer your question?' said Jean. 'Suddenly your £500 a week cheques were cut off.' 'But I never ever sent you any £500 a week cheques,' he said. 'I knew it was something like that,' she said. 'Does that answer your question?' he said. 'Willie, why are you in such a terrible ragged condition,' she said, 'with nae shoes and nae trews?' 'It's something to do with shortage of money. Does that answer your question?' he said. 'But dinnae worry, I'm going to start my career as an actor,' he said, 'first thing tomorrow morning as soon as I've had a good dinner.' 'That's no good to me,' said the wheel tapper. 'I'm to report to Wilton's Music Hall,' said McGonagall, 'the manager wishes to see me.' So a perfect evening came to a close in the McGonagall household. With a roaring candle in the grate McGonagall gathered his children and the wheel tapper around him and told them a traditional Scottish fairy story.

'Once upon a time there were three overdrafts . . .'

'I think I'll be off now,' said the wheel tapper. 'There's no work here.'

EXTRACT FROM MCGONAGALL'S DIARY:

'Then next day Jeannie laundered my suit, boots, stick, hat and cape. As I sat naked by the fire I was concentrating deeply on my coming career, when suddenly everything went black and we didn't need to have the chimney swept for many a day.

It was a fearful task removing 80 lbs of soot from my body into a small hip bath, but once I'd got the hang of it it was quite enjoyable.

Starting with my feet I soon reached my neck when I beheld my black face suddenly in the mirror.

"Oh," I cried.

"Oh what?" said Jean.

"Othello," said I.

"Oh sod," said the wheel tapper, "there's no work here. Where's my penny Shakespeare Plays?"'

McGonagall composed a little tune called 'The Rattling Boy from Dublin Town' and played it to a musically-crippled friend who could play the violin in the kneeling load position. He also occupied the chair of music at the University, which they had specially made to fit him.

'It's a nice tune,' said the cripple.

'What do you think I should do with it?' said McGonagall.

'Take it to a garage,' said the cripple.

'Why?' said McGonagall.

'They'll drive it away for you,' said the cripple, 'and nobody need ever know.'

'But I don't want anyone else to drive it,' said McGonagall. 'It's only had one owner.'

'You mean it's still under guarantee?' said the surprised cripple.

'No it's under a tarpaulin in the garden.'

'What's it doing there?'

'It's waiting to be sung,' said McGonagall, then drawing on his last reserves of strength he said, 'Goodbye, I must go.' One hour later he was on the stage at Wilton's Music Hall singing the theme song from

Shakespeare's Macbeth. This had been a last minute change from his Othello act when a sudden squall had moved an entire week's soot from his face revealing an imposter.

'What are you going to do for us?' said the manager.

'Othello,' said McGonagall.

'But you're white,' said the manager.

'Can ye no turn the lights out?' said McGonagall.

The manager complied and McGonagall started his great act. From the crepuscular darkness came the sound 'Ooooooooo' followed by a pause, an agonized crash, and another 'Oooooooooo.' He had fallen into the orchestra pit. 'Thank God, the concrete floor has broken my fall,' he said.

It had also broken his neck. But with one bound he was back on the stage and although in great pain he gave the following soliloquy. 'Ooooooh God, Aaaaaah Christ, the pain in ma' neek (trans. my neck). I cannae go to work like this.' So, for an hour screaming in agony, he stumbled round the darkened stage until a voice from the gallery shouted 'What about Othello?' – 'Never mind about him,' said McGonagall. 'What about me?' and fell unconscious on the stage. As his body crashed to the floor he was given an ovation for the first time in his life. 'Encore,' they cried stamping their feet on the ground, but William McGonagall was resting. Unconscious, he was lifted to his feet by a kindly stage manager who hurled him back into the orchestra pit again. An enraged pianist hurled him back. An hour later the score was LOVE-40 in the manager's favour. McGonagall was only saved from another set by a Zeppelin raid on London during which he received a direct hit. It was a long time before McGonagall could play tennis again, but this did not stop his massive outpourings of poetry. Will anyone ever forget his immortal 'Ode to a Zeppelin raid over London'? – 'YES.'

Goblins: 1978

Fred Fernackerpan – A Mystery Goblin

I am a mystery fellow,
I'm Fred Fernackerpan,
I wear one sock that's yellow
The other dipped in jam.
I walk about the countryside
I walk about the town,
Sometimes with my trousers up
And sometimes with them down:
And when they were up they were up
And when they were down they were down
And when they were only half way up
He was arrested.

Unspun Socks from a Chicken's Laundry: 1981

The Boxer

I am a merry boxer,
I get into the ring.
Wallop! Wallop *Thud*! I go
Until the bell goes ding!

When the bell goes ding! again
I go back to my stool
And stare at my opponent,
The ugly little fool!

Ding! there goes the bell again,
I rush back to the bout.
Wallop! Wallop Blat-Thud-*OWW*!
Nine – ten – OUT!

101 Limericks: 1982

A Combustible Woman

A combustible woman from Thang
Exploded one day with a Bang!
The maid then rushed in
And said with a grin,
'Pardon me, madam – you rang?'

There's a Lot of It About: 1983

Jehova Boxer Sketch

The brilliant but unpredictable *Q* series took Milligan from *Q5* in 1969 to *Q9* in 1980. At this point, faced with calling the next series *Q10*, the BBC inexplicably backed away, and what would in fact become the final series was renamed *There's a Lot of It About*.

Jehova Boxer Sketch

SPIKE Now let's look at a group of people who are taking the violence out of boxing . . . run telecine.

SPIKE, AS HERBERT SCRACKLE, IS WEARING A PROTECTIVE SPARRING KIT, BLACK TIGHTS, BOXING BOOTS. HE IS JOGGING IN A PARK WITH SOME MINDERS AND KEEPS ON HITTING HIMSELF. A SPORTS INTERVIEWER STEPS INTO HIS PATH.

CAPTION: <u>A PAKISTANI DAVID COLEMAN</u>

INTERVIEWER Herbert Kid Scrackle, I noticed your peculiar training methods . . . could you explain?

SCRACKLE Yes, I have peculiar training methods because I am the current reigning Jehovah's Witness boxing champion.

INTERVIEWER How do you differ from ordinary boxers?

SCRACKLE We refrain from violence in the ring.

INTERVIEWER How does that work?

SCRACKLE I get a thrashing and he don't.

INTERVIEWER And what's the point of that?

SCRACKLE He goes away ashamed of himself.

INTERVIEWER And you?

SCRACKLE I go away on a stretcher.

INTERVIEWER What were you in before this?

SCRACKLE The lumber business.

INTERVIEWER Lumber?

SCRACKLE Yes, I was lumbered with a wife and four kids.

INTERVIEWER As a Jehovah's Witness boxer, who are your
 four favourite boxers?

SCRACKLE Gandhi.

INTERVIEWER Well, there you have it. We wish him every luck
 in his forthcoming fight with Alan Minter.

SCRACKLE AND MINDERS RUN OUT OF SHOT WITH MINDERS
BELTING SPIKE. CUT TO SPORTSVIEW SET. SPIKE AS HARRY
CARPENTER.

SPIKE Let's go over now to the ringside at the Alcock & Brown
 Memorial Sporting Tower, Brixton, where patrons are being
 paid up to 80p each to eat the dinner and another 40p to
 watch the fight.

COMMENTATOR Well it's time for good evening and expenses
 again. Here at the ringside it's standing room only. Someone's
 nicked all the chairs. (Interviewer in ring turns to Alan
 Minter who is wearing a dinner jacket and black tie and boxing gloves.) Alan, why are you wearing a dinner jacket for
 this fight?

MINTER Well, it's not going to take that long Harry.

COMMENTATOR What's it like fighting a boxer who won't hit
 back?

MINTER Well, it'll make a change from Haggler.

COMMENTATOR You didn't get much change from Haggler.

MINTER PUNCHES CARPENTER OUT OF SIGHT. BOXER ENTERING
MADISON SQUARE FOR WORLD TITLE FIGHT COMPLETE WITH FAN-
FARE AND SCREAMING CROWDS. SPIKE IS HELPED THROUGH THE
ROPES INTO THE RING BY TWO PRIESTS.

VOICE OVER And here is the challenger now. And just listen to
 those Jehovah's Witness boxing fans.

CUT TO STOCK FILM OF CROWD SINGING HYMN AT BILLY GRAHAM
WEMBLEY RALLY. BOXERS ARE CALLED TO THE CENTRE OF THE
RING – WE SEE NOW THAT SPIKE IS BOUND BY ROPES FROM THE
SHOULDERS TO THE WAIST.

VOICE OVER As you can see Scrackle's trainers are doing everything to make sure that he doesn't hit back, using the special Holy restraining ropes which were stressed and spliced by the Pope this morning.

REFEREE I want a good clean fight.

BELL GOES. LONG SHOT OF A REAL FIGHT SHOWING BOXERS COMING FROM THEIR CORNERS TO THE CENTRE OF THE RING. WE CUT TO OUR FIGHT SHOWING ALAN MINTER BELTING SPIKE.

COMMENTATOR And what a splendid lack of defence Scrackle is putting up here. That's fourteen tremendous blows to the head which he's brilliantly taken to the chin. Only a natural athlete could soak up this punishment. And look at the way he swung his chin into the path of that uppercut . . . Minter must be going out of his mind wondering what he has to do to miss him. Now he's on the floor again but is just fainting or has he just fainted. He's up again and he's down again. But you can't keep a good man down because he's up again and obviously you can't keep a good man up because he's down again. He's been saved by the bell and some say he's been saved by Jehovah's Witnesses as well.

(Spike's responses every time we see a blow land)

SPIKE . . . I forgive him for he knows not what he does (wallop) . . . Verily I turn the other cheek (wallop) . . . Hate not thine enemy (wallop) . . .It is better to receive than to give (wallop) . . . (when on the ground being counted out) . . . Thou shalt not kill (wallop) . . . Though I walk through the valley of death nought can harm me . . . Let him who is without sin cast the first uppercut . . . (Spike is on the ground) . . . And on the seventh day he rested . . . Only believe and no harm shall come to thee.

AT THE END OF THE ROUND WE CUT TO SPIKE'S CORNER. SPIKE HAS A BLACK EYE, STRAWBERRY NOSE, SEVERAL TEETH MISSING, SWELLING ON HIS CHEEK. ATTENDING TO SPIKE ARE TWO BRUISERS,

VERY MUSCULAR AND BROKEN-NOSED. THEY WEAR JEHOVAH'S
WITNESS BOXER T-SHIRTS WITH DOG COLLARS AND BLACK BIBS.

PRIEST 1 You're doing great, Kid. So far you haven't laid a
glove on him.

SCRACKLE Yes, I really had Alan worried in that round.

PRIEST 1 He thought he'd killed you.

BELL GOES

COMMENTATOR There goes the bell but wait, he's not coming
out. The doctor says he's not fit. He thinks he's dead.

STRAIGHT TO SPIKE'S CORNER WHERE THEY ARE ALL JUMPING UP
AND DOWN WITH EXCITEMENT.

PRIEST He's done it, he's done it.

SCENES OF EXCITEMENT AND MIX THROUGH TO THE DRESSING
ROOM WHERE SPIKE IS LYING IN A COFFIN.

INT 1 Well champ, how does it feel?

SCRACKLE Well, I was feeling it just before you came in and it
felt very nice.

INT 2 And what about the result?

SCRACKLE Well, it was a foregone conclusion. Alan Minter
didn't know what didn't hit him.

INT 1 What do you get for this fight?

SCRACKLE Injuries.

INT 1 I meant money.

SCRACKLE I meant injuries.

INT 2 But I thought you got a good screw for the fight.

SCRACKLE Oh yes. But I'd rather have money.

INT 2 Well, that's it – another triumph for Kid Scrackle, the
Jehovah's Witness boxer. This is Harry Carpenter looking for
expenses, Wembley.

SPORTSVIEW MUSIC. WE SEE THEM NAILING DOWN THE LID OF A
COFFIN AND CARRYING IT OUT.

THE END.

Startling Verse for All the Family: 1987

I Met A Greek; Have a nice day!

I Met A Greek

I met a Greek
   Who wouldn't speak.
I met a Turk
   Who wouldn't work.
I met a Dane
   Who was insane.
I met a Scot
   Who just talked rot.
I met an Arab
   Who gave me a scarab.
I met a Swede
   Who couldn't read.
I met a German
   Who gave me ein sermon.
I met an Italian
   Who sold me a stallion.
I met an Eskimo
   With only one toe.
I met a Moroccan
   With only one sock on.
I met a Mongolian
   Who knew Napoleon.
I met a Croat
   Who had a sore throat.
I met a Sioux
   Who was six foot tioux.
I met a Spaniard
   Who sold me a lanyard.

I met a Slav
  Who made me lauv.
I met a Cambodian
  Who was a custodian.
I met a Majorcan
  Who wouldn't stop torcan.
I met a Fijian
  Who'd just done his knee in.
I met an Iraqi
  Who had a bad baqui.
Now with a Swiss
  I'm ending thiss.

Have a nice day!

'Help, help,' said a man, 'I'm drowning.'
'Hang on,' said a man from the shore.
'Help, help,' said the man, 'I'm not clowning.'
'Yes, I know, and I heard you before.
Be patient, dear man who is drowning,
You see, I've got a disease.
I'm waiting for a Doctor J. Browning,
So do be patient, please.'
'How long,' said the man who was drowning,
'Will it take for the Doc to arrive?'
'Not very long,' said the man with the disease.
'Till then try staying alive.'
'Very well,' said the man who was drowning,
'I'll try and stay afloat
By reciting the poems of Browning
And other things he wrote.'
'Help, help,' said the man who had a disease,
'I suddenly feel quite ill.'
'Keep calm,' said the man who was drowning,
'Breathe deeply and lay quite still.'
'Oh dear,' said the man with the awful disease,
'I think I'm going to die.'
'Farewell,' said the man who was drowning.
Said the man with disease, 'Goodbye.'
So the man who was drowning drownded
And the man with the disease passed away,
But apart from that and a fire in my hat
It's been a very nice day.

Fleas, Knees and Hidden Elephants: 1995

Child's Prayer

Can you hear me God?
Can you? Can you?
Do you have big ears God
Do you? Do you?
Do they help you listen in
Or is it because the walls are thin
What's it like being God
Does it make you ever feel odd
Up there can you get apple-pie
How can you eat it up so high
Please can I see you God
Only just a peep!
If you're not here by 8 o'clock
I'm going off to sleep

3

Breaking Down

The Bedside Milligan: 1968

Letter to Rag Mag Editor; Manic Depression; A Nose: A World War II Nose; Dear Reader!; I had a Dongee

Editor, Rag Mag, Gloucester College of Education

You say your mag is in aid of mental health! Dear Lad, there's no such thing, if there was anybody in a position of power with any semblance of mental health do you think the world would be in this bloody mess? Young minds at risk is different. Anybody with a young mind is taking a risk – young means fresh – unsullied, ready to be gobbled up in an adult world bringing the young into visionless world of adults, like all our leaders. Their world is dead – dead – dead, and my God, that's why it stinks! They look at youth in horror – and say 'They are having a revolution', but what do they want? I say they don't know what they want, but they know what they don't want, and that is, the repetition of the past mistakes, towards which the adult old order is still heading. War – armistice – building up to pre-war standards – capitalism – labour – crisis – war and so on. I digress.

Mental Health. I have had five nervous breakdowns – and all the medics gave me was medicine – tablets – but no love or any attempt at involvement, in this respect I might as well have been a fish in a bowl. The mentally ill need LOVE, UNDERSTANDING – TOLERANCE, as yet unobtainable on the N.H.S. or the private world of psychiatry, but tablets, yes, and a bill for £5 5. 0. a visit – if they know who you are it's £10 10. 0. a visit – the increased fee has an immediate depressing effect – so you come out worse than you went in.

As yet, I have not been cured, patched up via chemicals, yes. Letter unfinished, but I've run out of time – sorry!

Regards,
Spike

Manic Depression

St. Lukes Wing
Woodside Hospital
Psychiatric Wing 1953–4

The pain is too much
A thousand grim winters
    grow in my head.
In my ears
    the sound of the
        coming dead
All seasons, all same
    all living
    all pain
No opiate to lock still
    my senses.
Only left, the body locked tenser.

December 1960

A Nose:
A World War II Nose

My nose, my nose lived dangerously
Its courage was no stunt!
And during the war in Germany
It was always out in front!

Yet when the battle was o'er
And we'd defeated the Hun
Suddenly, for no reason at all
My nose started to run.

Dear Reader!

Dublin
Nov. 1967

Human beings will become so used to being crushed together that when they are on their own, they will suffer withdrawal symptoms. 'Doctor – I've got to get into a crowded train soon or I'll go mad.' So, special N.H.S. assimilated rush hour trains will be run every other Sunday for patients. At 9 o'clock on that morning, thousands of victims will crowd platforms throughout England, where great electrically powered Crowd Compressors will crush hundreds of writhing humans into trains, until their eyes stand out under the strain, then, even more wretches are forced in by smearing them with vaseline and sliding them in sideways between legs of standing passengers. The doors close – any bits of clothing, ears or fingers are snipped off. To add to the sufferers' relief great clouds of stale cigarette smoke are pumped into the carriages. The patients start to cough, laugh and talk. They're feeling better already. But more happiness is on its way. The train reaches 80 m.p.h., at the next station the driver slams the brakes on shooting all the victims up to one end of the carriages. Immediately the doors open, and great compressed air tubes loaded with up to 100 passengers are fired into the empty spaces, this goes on until the rubber roofs of the carriages give upwards, and the lumps you see are yet a second layer of grateful patients. Off goes the train, and one sees the relief on the travellers' faces. Who wants LSD when you can get this? Ah! you say, the train can't possibly take any more. Wrong! At the next stop the train is sprayed with a powerful adhesive glue, and fresh passengers stuck to the outside, and so, crushed to pulp, pop-eyed and coughing blood, the train carries out its work of mercy. Those who are worried about their children's future in the 20th century need not fear. We are prepared.

I had a Dongee

I had a Dongee
Who would not speak
He wouldn't hop
He wouldn't creep
He wouldn't walk
He wouldn't leap
He wouldn't wake
He wouldn't sleep
He wouldn't shout
He wouldn't squeak
He wouldn't look
He wouldn't peep
He wouldn't wag
    his Dongee tail.
I think this Dongee's
    going to fail.

A Book of Milliganimals: 1968

The Bald Twit Lion

This is a story for children came originally from A Book of Milliganimals, published in 1968.

Once, twice, thrice upon a time the world was full of jungles going, 'Jung-JUNG-JUNGLE!'

But when night came all the noises stopped, because all the animals put on zebra pyjamas and went to bed.

The Lord of the Jungle was – The Lion!!!! Ger-owl.

'Today is my 21st Birthday. I've got this key to the Jungle. I found it under the mat.' Lion – whose name was Mr Gronk – was so proud he swelled out his chest, his legs and his arms and roared – very loud. Roarrrr! ROAR! It was so loud all the Jungle fell down.

The animals ran away, but worst of all – on his last GROWL – ALL – HIS – HAIR – FELL – OUT – AND – DOWN. Plip-ploppity-plapplap. 'Oh dear!' said Lion. 'How *terribly* terrible!!! Me? Bald? At 21?!!!!' All the animals laughed. Poor Lion was too frightened to roar any more or something else might fall off him. It was just like a nightmare.

He must find a solution to his bald twitness. He tried every solution in the Jungle but none was the right solution – and you can't stick hair on with none. 'I know,' said Mr Gronk, 'I'll *strain* until new hairs grow.' So he strained and strained but all the strain went to the wrong end and he got a hairy tail. He tried again. Things became worse.

Then he had a brilliant idea. He advertised in *The Daily Gnus*. A hairy anteater answered the ad. and took up residence on Lion's head. It was perfect for Lion but, oh dear, every time Lion growled anteater fell off and hurt his knee. 'Goodbye!' said anteater.

Lion was heart-broken and worse. He threw himself on the ground and *cried*!!! Drip-drip-drip went the tears for forty days and forty nights and flooded the Jungle.

All the animals swam round to see the strange spectacle of the Lord of the Jungle crying. And they laughed and they laughed. Mr Gronk persuaded the other lions they must shave their heads or their legs would fall off. But their wives were *furious*, and made their husbands wigs. Mr Gronk hadn't got a wife and as he had caused all the baldness no one felt inclined to make him a wig. Then he was discovered and went on TV. But Mr Gronk got tired of that. It was the bitter end. 'Stop,' said a lovely high voice above him. It was a lady giraffe called Emily Figgs. 'Why don't you paint rabbits on your head? Then people will think they are hares!'

'Giraffe called Emily Figgs, I love you!' said the elated Lion; and he threw his arms round and round and round and round her neck. Indeed Mr Gronk and Emily got married.

They had a super wedding – there were 100 animal guests and a table 50 snakes long piled high with every fruit in the jungle including red cabbages and green carrots from Ireland for the donkeys.

They all sang and danced and dear Mr Gronk and Emily lived happily ever after. Hip – hip – hooray!!!!

It was the happiest day the Jungle had ever known.

Small Dreams of a Scorpion: 1972

Onos; Metropolis; The Incurable; Me; Unto Us . . .

Small Dreams of a Scorpion was Milligan's first collection of serious verse.

Onos

We have cracked the midnight glass
And loosed the racketing star-crazed
    night into the room.
The blind harp sings in late fire-light,
Your hand is decked with white promises.
What wine is this?
There are squirrels chasing in my glass,
Good God! I'm pissed!

Metropolis

I see barbaric sodium city lamps
   pretending they can see.
They make a new mad darkness.
Beyond their orange pools
   the black endlessness of time beckons,
What, in that unseen dark tomorrow
   is waiting. . . . .
That *iron* tomorrow, coming on
   unknown wheels
Who is the driver,
Will he see me in time?

Woy-Woy
NSW
Oct. 1971

The Incurable

I have taken maidens
like pots of Vic
and rubbed them into myself
but was never cured
and so, the ailment stays;
I see it carried in each sauntering wench
and forever I seek the cure.
No alchemist has its measure,
no chemist its mix.
Till there comes the medicine
I'll make my own fix.
It may not cure
but will not harm.
It will make magic
but not the balm
and when, in some minded hay loft we lay
I'll not only make a woman –
I will also, make hay.

March 6th 1972

Me

Born screaming small into this world –
Living I am
Occupational therapy twixt birth and death –
What was I before?
What will I be next?
What am I now?
Cruel answer carried in the jesting mind
    of a careless God.
I will not bend and grovel
When I die. If He says my sins are myriad
I will ask why He made me so imperfect
And he will say 'My chisels were blunt'.
I will say '*Then why did you make so
    many of me*'.

*Bethlehem Hospital
Highgate 1966*

Unto Us . . .

Somewhere at sometime
They committed themselves to me
And so, I was!
Small, but I *was*.
Tiny in shape
Lusting to live
I hung in my pulsing cave.
Soon they knew of me
My mother – my father.
I had no say in my being
I lived on trust
And love
Tho' I couldn't think
Each part of me was saying
A silent 'Wait for me,
I will bring you love!'
I was taken
Blind, naked, defenceless
By the hand of one
Whose good name
Was graven on a brass plate
in Wimpole Street,
and dropped on the sterile floor
of a foot operated plastic waste bucket.
There was no Queen's Counsel
To take my brief.
The cot I might have warmed
Stood in Harrod's shop window.
When my passing was told
My father smiled.
No grief filled my empty space.

My death was celebrated
With two tickets to see Danny la Rue
Who was pretending to be a woman
Like my mother was.

Tel Aviv, 8th Feb. 1972

Open Heart University: 1978

Catford 1933; Goodbye S.S.; Feelings

On their return from India in 1933, the Milligan family settled in Catford, south-east London.

Catford 1933

The light creaks
  and escalates to rusty dawn
The iron stove ignites the freezing room.
Last night's dinner cast off
  popples in the embers.
My mother lives in a steaming sink.
Boiled haddock condenses on my plate
  Its body cries for the sea.
My father is shouldering his braces like a rifle,
  and brushes the crumbling surface of his suit.
The *Daily Herald* lays jaundiced on the table.
'Jimmy Maxton speaks in Hyde Park',
My father places his unemployment cards
  in his wallet – there's plenty of room for them.
In greaseproof paper, my mother wraps my
   banana sandwiches.
It's 5.40. Ten minutes to catch that
   last workman train.
Who's the last workman? Is it me? I might be famous.
My father and I walk out and are eaten by
   yellow freezing fog.
Somewhere, the Prince of Wales
   and Mrs Simpson are having morning tea in bed.
God Save the King.
But God help the rest of us.

Goodbye S.S.

Go away girl, go away
    and let me pack my dreams
now where did I put those yesteryears
    made up with broken seams
Where shall I sweep the pieces
    my God they still look new
There's a taxi waiting at the door
    but there's only room for you

Feelings

There *must* be a wound!
No one can be this hurt
                    and not bleed.

How could she injure me so?
                    No marks
                    No bruise

Worse!
People say 'My, you're looking well'
...... God help me!
                    She's mummified me –
                              ALIVE!

Bayswater
December 1977

Goblins: 1978

Jack Migger – A Rock Goblin Raver

'I'm a rock-and-roll Goblin,
With dancin' feet
A Skooby-do Daddy
From Basin Street,
Ah lurv ma baby,
Ma baby lurvs me,
A bim bam boogie,
And I'm ninety-three.'

So he went a-dancing',
But alas and alack,
He dropped out of the charts,
With a heart attack.

Mussolini: His Part in My Downfall: 1978

January 20, 1944

Volume four of Milligan's war memoirs begins in Salerno in September 1943 and ends in Afrigola in March 1944. Most of it was high-spirited, even farcical. Towards the end, though, Milligan's luck ran out.

January 20, 1944

GOING TO DIMIANO OP

I got into the jeep next to Alf and we set off; he didn't say much until we got through Lauro and then on to the railway track, now denuded of rails and used as a communications road. It was a lovely day, sunny. Suddenly Alf said, 'This is beautiful! Sunshine – birds singing, I could do with more of this.'

He told me the OP and the Major's HQ were both in 'dodgy' positions. Hart had been up the OP, and it had finished him – Jerry was ramming everything on to them. It all sounded grim, and I wondered what my lot would be. The sounds of Artillery faded as small arms, automatic weapons and mortars increased. We were passing a steady stream of ambulances; one I noticed had shrapnel holes in the sides.

We turned off the railway embankment on to a country 'road', really a cart track; a one-mile sign read 'Castleforte 5 kilometer'.

'How's Jenkins been behaving?' I said.

Fildes smirked. 'He sends everyone up the OP except himself. I think he's shit scared, that or barmy.'

I didn't fancy being in any way mixed up with Jenkins, he was humourless. I didn't understand him at all, no one did; God help me, I was soon to find out what a lunatic he was. I was already tired having been awake for two nights, and the piles were giving me hell. We approached the ferry bridge over the Garigliano. Jerry was lobbing occasional shells into the smoke that was being used to obscure the crossing. From the smoke loomed the Pontoon Ferry bearing its load of wounded. Some looked pleased to be out of it. Others looked stunned, others with morphia were just staring up from their stretchers.

'Any more for the Woolwich Ferry?' says a cheerful cockney voice. We and several other vehicles move forward, among them a truck loaded with ammunition – a few more Jerry shells land in the river. By the sound they are close, can't see for smoke – we stop. Through the smoke, a figure with outstretched arms to stop us going off the end as apparently had happened earlier. A jeep driver, thinking it was a continuous bridge, roared off the end, surfaced swearing. 'Where's the rest of the bloody bridge?' More shells. We are moving.

We pull off the other side; to our left looms Mount Dimiano.

'That's what all the trouble's about,' says Fildes, 'our OP's on there somewhere.'

Off the road to our right is a cluster of farmhouses, some shelled, some intact.

'This is it,' says Fildes, as we turn right into them.

We pull up in front of the centremost one. A two-storeyed affair – all around are dead Jerries. MG bullets are whistling overhead as we duck and run inside.

It was a large room. On a makeshift table was a 22 Set. There was Jenkins. Laying down at the far end of the room, 'Flash' Gordon, Birch, Fuller, Howard, Badgy Ballard, Dipper Dai – all looked as gloomy as hell.

'It isn't the war,' said Birch, 'it's Jenkins.'

'Milligan – you can get on the set right away,' says Jenkins.

I took over from Fuller; immediately, Jenkins sends RHQ a series of pointless messages. 'It's very stuffy in the room.' 'There are eight ORs, two NCOs and myself.' 'Thornton coming back.' 'The Germans are shelling us.' 'The Germans have stopped shelling us.'

I don't exactly know what his job was supposed to be. The people who were taking the stick were Lt. Budden and party, who were being 'stonked' unmercifully. In the room, save for a direct hit, we were comparatively safe. From the time I arrived (about 4 pm) the bastard kept me on the set all night, a total of seventeen hours with the headphones on. It was my third night without sleep, just the noise of the interference was enough to drive you potty. To get a break I said, 'Do you think, sir, under the Articles of War, I could be relieved, so I can relieve myself?' Even then he said, 'Well, hurry up.' I felt like saying, 'I will piss as fast as I can, sir – would you like someone to time me in case I loiter?'

Outside a young Lieutenant was talking to a Sergeant. '. . . Then why didn't they stay inside. I mean those inside didn't get killed.' I presume he was referring to the unburied dead who lay without the walls. It was dark. A stream of MG bullets whined over the roof, God knows what he was aiming for – there was nothing behind us.

Overhead, stars shone. Back in Major Jenkins' Salon for the Morose, I went back on the set. At that moment a terrific explosion shook the farm; it was a Jerry 155mm shell, and he continued to carry out harassing fire throughout the night. I think it was the road to the ferrybridge he was after, but he moved around a bit. I continued to relay our lunatic's messages. 'The Germans have started shelling us', 'There's an interval of two minutes between each round', this his most unbelievable one. 'Every time we transmit a message – he shells us.'

The idiot was implying that Jerry had a device that made it possible to locate the position of a wireless set by its transmission. Of course, there was absolutely no truth in his statement – when we didn't transmit Jerry shelled us – so how did he become a Major? Men's lives were in his hands. Like all lunatics he had unending energy – as dawn came he got worse. I was almost numb with fatigue, and my piles had started to bleed. I should never have volunteered. One of the lads makes breakfast – while I'm eating it Jenkins tells me, 'Bombardier, I want you to take Gordon, Howard, Birch and Ballard to the OP with fresh batteries and a 22 set.' Great, all I have to do is carry a 50lb battery to the top of a mountain, anything else? Like how about a mile run before in medieval armour?

Ballard apparently knows the way. At 9.00 we put on Arctic Packs and strap on one battery each. We set off single file on the road towards Castleforte, which sits in the near distance on a hillside full of Germans.

We turn left off the road into a field; we pass a Sherman Tank, a neat hole punched in the turret; a tank man is removing kit from inside. Laying on a groundsheet is the mangled figure of one of the crew.

'What a mess,' says the Tankman in the same tones as though there was mud on the carpet.

I grinned at him and passed on. Above us the battle was going on full belt; coming towards us is Thornton, dear old 35-year-old Thornton; he looks tired, he has no hat, and is smoking a pipe.

'Hello, what's on?'

He explains he's been sent back. 'I'm too old for that lark. I kept fallin' asleep.'

I asked him the best way up. He reaffirms, 'You go up a stone-lined gully; when it ends start climbing the hill, it's all stepped for olive trees. Of course,' he added, 'if you're in the gully and they start mortaring, you've had it.'

'Thanks,' I said, 'that's cheered us up no end.'

He bid us farewell and we went forward, we reached the gully. In a ravine to the left were Infantry all dug into the side; they were either 'resting' or in reserve. So far so good. We reach the end of the stone gully and start climbing the stepped mountain – each step is six foot high, so it's a stiff climb. CRUMP! CRUMP! CRUMP!, mortars. We hit the ground. CRUMP CRUMP CRUMP – they stop. Why? Can they see us? We get up and go on. CRUMP CRUMP CRUMP – he can see us! We hit the deck. A rain of them fall around us. I cling to the ground. The mortars rain down on us. I'll have a fag, that's what. I am holding a packet of Woodbines, then there is a noise like thunder. It's right on my head, there's a high-pitched whistle in my ears, at first I black out and then I see red, I am strangely dazed. I was on my front, now I'm on my back, the red was opening my eyes straight into the sun. I know if we stay here we'll all die . . . I start to scramble down the hill. There's shouting, I can't recall anything clearly. Next I was at the bottom of the mountain, next I'm speaking to Major Jenkins, I am crying, I don't know why, he's saying, 'Get that wound dressed.'

I said, 'What wound?'

I had been hit on the side of my right leg.

'Why did you come back?' He is shouting at me and threatening me, I can't remember what I am saying. He's saying, 'You could find your way back but you couldn't find your way to the OP', next I'm sitting in an ambulance and shaking, an orderly puts a blanket round my shoulders, I'm crying again, why why why? Next I'm in a forward dressing station, an orderly gives me a bowl of hot very sweet tea, 'Swallow these,' he says, two small white pills. I can't hold the bowl for shaking, he takes it from me and helps me drink it. All around are wounded, he has rolled up my trouser leg. He's putting a sticking plaster on the wound, he's telling me it's only a small one. I don't really care if it's big or small, why am I crying? Why can't I stop? I'm getting lots of sympathy, what I want is an explanation. I'm feeling drowsy, and I must have started to sway because next I'm on a stretcher. I feel lovely, what were in those tablets . . . that's the stuff for me, who wants food? I don't know how long I'm there, I wake up. I'm still on the stretcher, I'm not drowsy, but I start to shiver. I sit up. They put a label on me. They get me to my feet and help me to an ambulance. I can see really badly wounded men, their bandages soaked through with blood, plasma is being dripped into them.

When we get to one of the Red Cross trucks, an Italian woman, all in black, young, beautiful, is holding a dead baby and weeping; someone says the child has been killed by a shell splinter. The relatives are standing by looking out of place in their ragged peasants' clothing amid all the uniforms. An older woman gives her a plate of home-made biscuits, of no possible use, just a desperate gesture of love. She sits in front with the driver. I'm in the back. We all sit on seats facing each other, not one face can I remember. Suddenly we are passing through our artillery lines as the guns fire. I jump at each explosion, then, a gesture I will never forget, a young soldier next to me with his right arm in a bloody sling put his arm around my shoulder and tried to comfort me. 'There, there, you'll be alright mate.'

We arrived at a camp. I was put into a tent on a bunk bed. An orderly gave me four tablets and more hot tea; in a few seconds they put me out like a light. I had finished being a useful soldier. I've had it . . .

I wake up, it's very early, am I now stark raving mad? I can distinctly hear a brass band, right outside the tent, they are playing 'Roll Out the Barrel' at an incredible speed. I get up, look outside. There in a circle stand a collection of GIs, all playing this tune; they are in a strange collection of garments, some in overcoats with bare legs and boots, some in pyjamas, others in underpants, unlaced boots and sweaters, an extraordinary mixture.

I looked at my watch. It was 0645. This I discovered was the American Reveille; the tune finished, the men doubled back to their beds. But where was I? It was a large hospital tent, full of bunk beds with sleeping soldiers. I was the only one awake, and was still fully dressed save my battle-dress jacket. For the first time I felt my right leg aching. I sat on the side of my bed, took the plaster off my leg to look at the wound. It was a wound about two inches long and about a quarter of an inch deep, as though I had been slashed with a razor blade. Today you can only see the scar if I get sunburnt. It wasn't hindering me, so what was I here for? I lit up a cigarette. It was one of my five remaining Woodbines, now very crushed. Two RAMC Orderlies enter the tent, young lads, they go around the beds looking at the labels; they woke some of the men up, gave them tablets. They arrived at me. I asked them where I was. They told me it was 144 CCS, I was labelled 'Battle Fatigue'. I was to see a psychiatrist that evening. Meantime there was a mess tent where I could get breakfast. I told them I didn't have any small kit. 'Don't worry, lad, they've got knives and forks there.'

Lad? So I was Lad now. It was a wretched time. No small kit, no towel, no soap, no friends. It's amazing what small simple things really make up our life-support system, all I wanted was for some cold water on my face. I went across to the American Camp and from a GI (of all things smoking a cigar) I scrounged a towel. He was more than generous, he took me to his Quarter Master, who gave me two brand-new khaki-coloured towels, soap, and a razor. I'm afraid I was still in a terribly emotional state, and I started to cry 'Thanks' but apparently they were aware that the Camp next to them were Battle Fatigue cases.

I wandered through a mess of tents till I found the Ablutions. It was still only 7.30, but the place was full; there was the terrible silence of a mass of people who don't know each other. I washed in silence, and the cold water made me feel a little fresher. The seat of my trousers are all sticky. Oh God, what a mess, blood, the curse of the Milligans is still working. What I really want is a bath. I'm given two different-sized pills. I ask what they are, the orderly says, 'I don't know, chum.' (I'm Chum now.) He knows alright, but it was early days for tranquil-lisers. 'Take them after breakfast.' I have absolutely no recollection of eating breakfast, I think that I took the tablets right away; next thing it was evening time, I'm very dopey.

'You got to see the "Trick Cyclist",' says the young orderly. I had no idea what 'Trick Cyclist' meant. I asked. Psychiatrist? That was for lunatics. Was I one? I was to find out. In a small officer-type tent, behind an Army folding-table covered with a grey blanket sits a stern, or rather attempting to look stern, officer. He is a Captain. Middle aged, a small, almost pencil-thin, moustache. He asks me all those utterly boring questions, name, religion, etc. . . . He asks me what happened. I tell him as much as I can recall. He is telling me that it takes 100,000 shells before one soldier is killed, he ends with (and in a louder voice than before), 'You are going to get better. *Understand?*' Yes, I understand. I'm back in my tent, still a bit airy-fairy in the head. I've never had mind drugs before.

I get an evening meal. There's no lighting in the hospital tents, the orderlies come round with a Tilly Lamp, and I get more knock-out pills. Next morning, 'Roll Out The Barrel'; it's a great place for Battle Fatigue, a week here and it would be 'Roll out the Battle Fatigue'. I am to be sent back to the Regiment. I suppose they know what they are doing. Time was to prove that they didn't.

How I got back to the Battery I don't know, this was a time of my life that I was very demoralised. I was not really me any more.

The Mirror Running: 1987

To My Daughter Jane; Lo Speccio

To My Daughter Jane

I cannot tell you in words,
I cannot tell you in sounds,
I cannot tell you in music
How much I love you.
I can only tell you in trees,
In mountains,
Oceans,
Streams.
I might be heard to say it
In the bark of a seal on moon misty nights.
It can be heard on the hinges of dawn.
Tho' my muse is slain,
All else says I love you Jane.

Flora Bay
Cape Town

Lo Speccio

Someone left the mirror running
I pulled the plug out
   it emptied my face
   and drowned my reflection.
I tried mouth to mouth resuscitation
   the glass broke
   my reflection died
Now there's only one of me.

6 January 1981

It Ends With Magic: 1990

The Home

It Ends With Magic was a rather charming home-spun tale starring Milligan's family, renamed the Sparrows. This extract begins in Edwardian England after Florence, widowed and poverty-stricken mother to Laura, Séan and Silé, has had to be admitted to hospital, leaving her with no choice but to send the children to. a 'Home for Needy Children'.

The Home

On the Monday morning the child welfare officer, Mr Spencer Cringle, a grey man destroyed by years of filing and signing, put the children and their scant belongings on the nine-twenty train from Victoria. The carriages looked resplendent in their tan and yellow Southern Railway livery. Smoke and steam arose from the great black trains coming and going, porters' trollies rattled along the platforms. There was the shrill whistle from the guards. The children travelled in the guard's van, in the care of Mr Harrold Fagg. He was a tall, thin man, with a droopy moustache which hid his mouth. To eat his dinner he had to lift it up like a drawbridge. He was very kind and did his best to cheer them up.

'Don't worry, your Mum will be better soon,' he said. 'Look, I'll make a nice cup of tea for you, yes?'

'Does tea stop the cry?' said Silé.

'Of course it does,' said Mr Fagg starting his Primus stove. 'British soldiers drink lots of tea, that's why they never cry.'

'My Dad was a soldier,' said Séan. Mr Fagg nodded.

'Now you watch for that kettle to boil, while I start the train.'

As an afterthought Séan added, 'My Dad didn't cry.' Mr Fagg stepped on to the platform, observed his railway watch; at nine-twenty he waved a green flag, blew a shrill blast on his silver whistle; the great engine let out a hiss, steam shot out from everywhere, the great black train eased itself forward, shuddering, clanking and snorting like a wild untamed stallion. As they sipped tea from Mr Fagg's brown

enamel mug he told them the train could travel at 'forty miles an hour!'
'Cor,' said Séan. 'Forty!!!'

'Is that faster dan me?' said Silé.

'Yes, it is,' said Mr Fagg. 'It faster than anyone can run.'

Soon the train was pulling clear of the drab, black south London
buildings and into the countryside.

'Look,' said Silé. 'It's all goed gween!'

'If I was a train, I'd go puff-puff everywhere, even in the lounge,'
said Séan.

At the next station Mr Fagg let Silé wave the green flag and Séan
blow the whistle.

'Oh! I started the train, did you see?' said Séan proudly.

'I made some of it goed, too,' said Silé still waving the green flag
out of the window.

'No more, missy,' said Mr Fagg taking charge of the flag, 'or the
engine driver will think I'm drunk.'

Laura had her head out of the window. 'Look, I'm eating the wind,'
she said, opening her mouth.

'It makes a music in your mouth,' said Silé trying it for herself.

Séan was squatting near a basket of homing pigeons, on their way
to Bexhill. He put his fingers between the wickerwork to stroke the
soft feathers on the neck and observed the way the different feathers
interwove to make different hues. 'They're racing pigeons,' said Mr
Fagg, 'we carry quite a few in the summer.'

Silé, getting restless, lay on her back kicking her legs in the air,
saying, 'Ooley dooley, Ooley dooley.' When she got tired of that she
said, 'Fisssssh, fisssshhh. Arig-ger, Ariiif-ger. One, two, three, eleven,
six, ten.'

Laura sat on the guard's seat, her hands folded in her lap, a girl
with natural dignity. 'How much longer, Mr Fagg?' she said. Mr Fagg
looked at his big Southern Railway pocket watch on a chain. 'We
should be there in about, er, twenty-two minutes.'

Sure enough, twenty-two minutes later, the train slowed into Win-
chelsea, a small country station with a short platform, two gas lamps,

a rubbish bin, a small ticket office, a bench and potted geraniums. Gilbert Croucher was the porter. He was round and fat like a football with legs and a hat; he was also ticket collector, gardener, and station master, it all depended on what hat he was wearing. When the children alighted he wasn't wearing any. It was his day off. As the train stopped, however, he put on his ticket collector's hat. 'Ah, you must be the Sparrow children. Someone's waiting for you.'

A big man with a red face like a boiled ham and a brown Derby approached them. He smiled, showing huge brown teeth. 'Oi am Dan Butterworth and h'I 'ave cum ter pick-a you h'all up.'

'Hello,' said Laura timidly.

'Ah,' smiled Dan, 'let's gie you a help with yer parcels, missy.' With a large hand he collected the children's belongings and said, 'Vollo me.'

Outside he seated the children in a black gig pulled by an equally black horse. 'Can I sitted next to you?' said Silé.

'Ah, that you can, missy,' said the kindly Dan, lifting Silé and her parcel on to the driving seat where her legs dangled. Laura and Séan mounted the back, and away they trotted.

Coming from a smoky city, the children were seeing for the first time in their young lives England's rural greenery.

'It's h'only a miule down the road,' said Dan.

'You talk very funny,' said Séan, who had never heard a country accent before.

'Arrr, that's cors h'I speak w' a Sussex dialect.'

'What's die-lick?' said Silé, who was wiggling her fingers.

'Thart's me accent, they waoi oi torke,' said Dan laughing.

'Does your horse had a dielick?'

'Weel,' said Dan, grinning all over his face, 'I don't know. Oi ain't never 'eard 'er tork yet.'

'What's his name?' said Laura.

'He's not a he,' said Dan. 'E's a she, her name is Blossom.'

'That's a nice name for a horse, if I had a horse I'd call her Blossom,' said Laura, 'or, or Buttercup.'

Séan the artist watched the shapes and colours of the trees, grasses and wild flowers that he had never seen in such profusion before, only dead ones in the Kensington Natural History Museum. To children living in a smoky city this open countryside was like returning caged birds to the sky. They talked excitedly as they saw cows, sheep, lambs and, 'Rabwits!' 'Look! Rabwits!' said Silé.

So they talked and talked until the gig turned sharp right into the semi-circular gravel drive, and crunchingly arrived at the front door of the Wolsey Home for Needy Children. It was a large, long two-storeyed building made of grey stone, red brick coursing, and a slate roof, all in need of repair. The Home was situated off the country road that runs between the village of Appledore and Nok cum Ebony. The distance from London according to an old milestone was 'London Town 73 miles'. There were twenty children in the Home, a large soulless building, originally built to house troops who were to defend England from the promised threat of Napoleon. There were no carpets or curtains, one small stove per dormitory was the only heating. Roofs leaked, floorboards squeaked, windows rattled, panes were missing. Discipline was severe, caning for the smallest offence; all day without food; being made to stand and watch supper being eaten, then being sent to bed hungry. At play-time they were forbidden to run. Not a very nice place for children.

'It's very big,' said Laura.

'Yes, it's bigger dan, dan, dan,' said Silé who couldn't find what it was bigger 'dan', 'dan, dan . . . anythinged,' she concluded.

Clutching their few belongings, Dan led the children down a series of dingy corridors with green, peeling paint, hung with pictures and mottoes that were unreadable because of the gloom. Finally, they arrived at a large, brown-painted door with a polished brass knob. Dan knocked timidly.

'Come in,' snapped an angry voice. Dan ushered the children in.

Inside the room was a large oak desk, behind it sat the headmaster and, standing by him, the headmistress; they were Mr and Mrs Ivan Hewitt. 'These are thur Sparrow children, zur,' said Dan doffing his hat, then backing nervously from the room.

Mr Hewitt eyed the children. He was a large, sweaty, fat man with traces of snuff on his nose. His face was very like a reddish pig wearing spectacles; he had no hair save a few wisps which ran round his head like a lifeless fringe; he had no neck to speak of, so no one spoke of it, his head seeming to be balanced on his collar. He wore a crumpled black suit that appeared to be dead, the shoulders being white with occasional falls of dandruff. His fat, stubby hands, like pigs' trotters, lay clenched on the table next to an engraved silver snuff box that he had just closed.

His wife too wore black. She was taller and thin; her white stringy neck rose from her dress like a plucked turkey; her skin was a pallid grey-green, a long banana-like nose came from her face, on which sat a pair of gold-rimmed pince-nez attached to her neck by a black silk ribbon. Her greying hair was drawn back and packed in a severe bun on the crown of her head and fastened with numerous hair pins. Attached to her waist was a dark, wine-coloured velvet dilly bag in which she kept her handkerchief, a pencil, a notebook, a small mirror, a pair of scissors, the Bible and a little bottle of smelling salts. She stood with her veiny hands clasped on her stomach, which was the curse of her life, for, at the most inconvenient moments, it would emit strange rumbling sounds which had been known to make their dog leap up and start barking. She had tried to make a sort of soundproofing by placing a layer of old vests and bloomers on top. It did take the sound down a bit but her stomach then looked so enormous people tittered at the sight of her, and the dog, Rover, through sharp hearing, still barked when he heard the rumblings.

'So you are the Sparrow children,' said Mr Hewitt in a dark brown voice, with bushy eyebrows.

'Yes, sir,' said Laura, as spokeswoman.

'Well let me tell you, this is a highly disciplined establishment, where you only have one thing to remember, and that is to *do-as-you-are-told*! If not, you will be punished.'

'*Severely* punished,' added Mrs Hewitt with a cruel smile. The Sparrow children drew together as though they were being assaulted. Mr

Mr and Mrs Hewitt

Hewitt looked at his watch. 'You have missed lunch, so the next meal is supper at five-thirty, then prayers, then bed. Mrs Hewitt will show you to the dormitory. At all times you will call her "Mam" and me "Sir"!'

'Come on now,' said Mrs Hewitt, talking as her squeaking boots took her speedily out of the room, taking long steps like a crane. The children had to run to keep up with her. She took them through the long, dark, gloomy corridors with worn, stone-slab floors that echoed to the children's running footsteps. They paused at a large dark green door on which was written 'Dormitory'. Mrs Hewitt felt in her skirt pocket; there was a jangling sound as she withdrew a ring of large iron keys, unlocked the door and let the children in. The dormitory was a long, grim, grey room. At the far end was a picture of Queen Victoria; above her in a cloud was the stylized 'ghost' of Prince Albert holding hands with gloomy angels.

'Your beds are thirteen, fourteen and fifteen. Each of you has a locker in which you will keep everything out of sight. Absolutely *everything*, you understand?'

'I 'aven't got anything,' said Silé and giggled.

'Silence!' said Mrs Hewitt. 'Don't you *dare* raise your voice to me.'

'I don't like her,' said Silé, starting to cry.

'Oh, shut up!' she said.

Laura put her arm around Silé.

'You'll soon get used to it, my girl! You will find your uniforms in your lockers, put them on, then you can have the rest of the day to yourselves, but you must not leave this dormitory! Supper is at five-thirty. When you hear the bell, make for the dining hall. Tomorrow we get up at five-thirty; you will make your bed, wash, put on your uniform and then we start work!' She then left the room at great speed, with squeaky boots. For a moment, the little trio stood mutely amid the empty, iron-framed beds. There were no sheets, only blankets; mattresses were filled with straw. Laura broke the silence.

'It's not too hard,' she said, bumping up and down on her bed. Silé and Séan started jumping on their beds; it went on for five minutes.

'That's made them softer,' said Séan triumphantly.

'Come on,' said Laura. 'We've got to put on our uniforms.'

They delved in their lockers and struggled into the new clothes. They were a dark, battleship-grey colour with white collars. Little Silé's was too big; the skirt came well down over her knees and the sleeves of the jacket nearly hid her hands. Séan's and Laura's fitted fairly well.

'It's too big-ed for my legs,' said Silé, looking down, 'and my arms have gorned in.'

'If you eat lots of dinner it will soon fit you,' said Laura, rolling up the surplus on the sleeves.

'Yes, I'll have to eat-ed a lot of dinner in my legs and arms, den dey will grow long-ed,' said Silé.

Drab as their uniforms were they were still in better condition than their own clothes.

'Coo, I found a piece of string in my pocket,' said Séan, holding it up. This set little Silé searching in her pockets.

'It's not fair, he found a piece of stringed and I didn't,' she said, pulling the linings out.

At half past five the bell for supper went. The three children, who were now quite hungry, made for the dining hall, which they found by following notices 'This way to the dining hall'. It was another cold, cheerless room, a high ceiling and high windows, plain wooden tables and forms, and a stone floor. Children were queueing by a big table, behind which was Dan, the driver of the gig, and an old lady, Mrs Mountain; they were doling out supper. The children went to the end of the line. In turn they picked up a tin tray, a spoon, two bowls, a mug; into one was dolloped a brown stew, into the second rice pudding. Before the children were seated they said grace. 'Sit,' said Mrs Hewitt, then an old woman came around with a big brown jug and poured watery, lukewarm tea into the mugs. The whole meal was eaten in silence, as the Hewitts walked among them swishing their canes. The three children were aware that, as they were newcomers, the other children were watching them. On the stroke of six o'clock Mrs Hewitt rapped the table.

'All stand! Now off to dormitory.'

Even though some children had not finished eating, they all had to troop out. Next they were all made to stand by their beds, change into their night-clothes, which were the same drab grey colour as their uniforms; then, clutching towels, they were marched to the washroom – a long line of brass taps over a zinc metal trough, a small piece of Sunlight soap by every tap. 'All wash!' came the command from Mrs Hewitt. The water was cold. The wash finished, they marched back into the dormitory where towels had to be folded and placed in the locker.

'All kneel!' came the order. In this position they chanted 'Our Father'.

'Now into bed!'

The children clambered in. Mrs Hewitt switched off the gaslight –

the door slammed, the keys rattled and Mrs Hewitt was gone. Immediately, every child was out of bed; one girl stood guard listening at the keyhole, as the children ran around the room, jumping on beds, and pillow-fighting. Several children collected around Laura, Séan and Silé, asking them unending questions: 'Wot's your name?', 'Where are you fromed?', 'Have you got a dad and mum?', 'Got any toffees?', 'Is he your brother?', 'How old are you?'

After excited child conversations, Laura, Séan and Silé – tired after their journey – went to bed. It was at that moment that they all missed their mother. Laura put her head under the clothes and quietly cried herself to sleep. The other children romped and played until it got dark and one by one went to bed. The sun had sunk away in the West, and little by little the small voices went silent. All was quiet. So ended the Sparrows' first day at the Wolsey Home for Needy Children.

4

Hitting Back

Silly Verse for Kids: 1959

Look at all those monkeys; The ABC

Look at all those monkeys

Look at all those monkeys
Jumping in their cage.
Why don't they all go out to work
And earn a decent wage?

How can you say such silly things,
Are you a son of mine?
Imagine monkeys travelling on
The Morden–Edgware line!

But what about the Pekinese!
They have an allocation.
'Don't travel during Peke hour,'
It says on every station.

My Gosh, you're right, my clever boy,
I never thought of that!
And so they left the monkey house,
While an elephant raised his hat.

The ABC

'Twas midnight in the schoolroom
And every desk was shut,
When suddenly from the alphabet
Was heard a loud 'Tut-tut!'

Said A to B, 'I don't like C;
His manners are a lack.
For all I ever see of C
Is a semi-circular back!'

'I disagree,' said D to B,
'I've never found C so.
From where I stand, he seems to be
An uncompleted O.'

C was vexed, 'I'm much perplexed,
You criticize my shape.
I'm made like that, to help spell Cat
and Cow and Cool and Cape.'

'He's right,' said E; said F,
'Whoopee!'
Said G, ''Ip, 'ip, 'ooray!'
'You're dropping me,' roared H to G.
'Don't do it please I pray!'

'Out of my way,' LL said to K.
'I'll make poor I look ILL.'
To stop this stunt, J stood in front,
And presto! ILL was JILL.

'U know,' said V, 'that W
Is twice the age of me,
For as a Roman V is five
I'm half as young as he.'

X and Y yawned sleepily,
'Look at the time!' they said.
'Let's all get off to beddy byes.'
They did, then 'Z-z-z.'

or

alternative last verse

X and Y yawned sleepily,
'Look at the time!' they said.
They all jumped in to beddy byes
And the last one in was Z!

A Dustbin of Milligan: 1961
_____

Come On In, The Fall-out is Lovely; The White Flag

Come On In, The Fall-out is Lovely

or – they're walking backwards to Aldermaston

Aldermaston Marchers hear this and tremble in the foundations of your sodden Left-Wing shoes. At this very moment, if not sooner, the Milligan inter-party, espionage, phone-tapping, radio-hitting counter-espionage movement has gleaned certain information which should be imparted to you who will shortly march forth (or is it April tenth?) for the cause.

Last night I gained access to Downing Street by merely not causing a disturbance, appearing to have no desire to live, looking utterly indifferent to South Africa's death roll, and executing several Non-U turns in a U-turn street. Discreetly I crawled on to the pavement outside Number Ten.

'Looking for something?' said a policeman.

'Yes,' I said, 'a new Government.'

'You won't find it here, sir, this is the old.'

I stood up.

'Who did you vote for?' I said. 'Oh, I don't vote,' he said. 'I'm one of the don't knows.'

'I thought I recognized the uniform,' I said.

'What are you hinferring, madam?' (He had bad eyesight as well.)

'I am suggesting that there are far too many don't knows. One day the don't knows will get in and then what will happen?'

'I don't know,' he said. 'Now move along,' and he pointed further down.

This, dear reader, was all only a cover-up while I made my way to the International Russian-controlled phone-tapping post at Number Seven. I was welcomed at this door by a Russian girl athlete who put me into a cubicle.

'Just listen in on that,' she said pointing to a pair of headphones. 'It's ten roubles for three minutes. If Mac's on form you should get some pretty good copy.'

At last I'd found it, the Gossip Writer's Nirvana where Tanfield and Hickey exchange notes, here in this simple gutter in Downing Street.

The following is the text of a telephone conversation between the P.M. and Selwyn Lloyd:

MAC: Selwyn?

S. LLOYD: Speaking. What are you doing up so early?

MAC: I'm worried, do you hear me? Worried!

S. LLOYD: Is that Profit Tax hurting the book trade? Say the word and I'll take it –

MAC: No, no, no! Haven't you heard? They're marching again this Easter.

S. LLOYD: Not the Aldermaston lot?

MAC: Yes. The first time – well, we all took it as a joke. Last year there were ten thousand of 'em and to make it even more infuriating they were all orderly. Police were powerless.

S. LLOYD: You think that this year –

MAC: Bigger than ever.

S. LLOYD: Say the word and I'll put a tax on marching –

MAC: No, no, no, Selwyn, no. I've already been planning an alternative march. I've been training 'em for the last three months.

S. LLOYD: How? When? Where? Who? What? Which?

MAC: Steady, Selwyn, don't excite yourself. Remember you're a bachelor. You remember the John O' Groats to Lands End March?

S. LLOYD: Yes, I saw it on the telly.

MAC: What may have appeared a simple publicity stunt by Bill Butlin was in fact a heavily disguised training walk by the Young Conservatives.

S. LLOYD: Floreat Macmillan. . . .

MAC: Ta. At this very moment ten thousand true blue Young Tories are encamped in the Vale of Healthy Hampstead disguised as out of season fairground attendants.

S. LLOYD: Master!

MAC: Ta. I, Harold Macmillan, née Prime Minister, née Son of Eden, hope to turn the tide by marching in the exact opposite direction! I will march all the way by Rolls Royce.

S. LLOYD: That should put their shares up.

MAC: Following me will be the 'Atom Bombs for Peace' group with the banner – *Strontium 90 is Good For You; Get Some Today*. Small miniature flower-clad A-bombs will be exploded *en route* to give festive gaiety to the occasion, and from time to time young Tory back-benchers will jump into the centre of simulated mushroom clouds with cries of – 'Look, it doesn't hurt at all!' and/or 'Come on in, the fall-out is lovely!'

S. LLOYD: Is that safe?

MAC: I'm not sure. Anyhow, we can afford a few Tories, the woods are full of 'em, eh? Ha ha!

S. LLOYD: We must not take the opposition too lightly though, Mac. There's people among them who think above the waist – even higher.

MAC: Yes, blast 'em!

S. LLOYD: Say the word, Mac, and I'll put a tax on all J. B. Priestleys.

MAC: No, no, no. You've done enough for England – to get lung cancer now costs tuppence more – well done Selwyn!

At this point the great British G.P.O. system working true to its ecstatic form collapsed . . . however, we had heard enough, so, friends, don't forget to march in the opposite direction to the you-know-whos!

The White Flag

The two great Generals and the two great Armies faced each other across one great battlefield. The two great Generals marched about their two great Armies as they faced each other across one great battlefield. One great General said to himself, 'We can't hold out against this other great Army much longer,' and the other great General said, 'We can't hold out against this other Army much longer,' so the first great General said to one of his great Sergeants, 'Hoist a white flag,' and the second great General said to his great Sergeant, 'Hoist a white flag.'

Private Fred Lengths was commanded by one great General to haul up the flag. At the same time, Private Norrington Blitt had also been signalled by his General to hoist their white flag, and so the two great Armies stood surrendering to each other across the battlefield. It was very quiet, and the two white flags were the only movement seen.

Three days passed, and one great General said, 'What's happened?', as did the other great General. Both great Generals were informed that each side had surrendered to the other. 'Impossible,' said the first General.

'It can't be true,' said the second General.

'My arms are aching,' said Private Blitt, as did Private Lengths.

'How long have they had their flag up?' said the first great General.

'Three days,' at which time the second great General had asked the same question, and received the same answer.

'Tell them *we* surrendered – *first*!'

The message was shouted across the great battlefield.

'No, no,' was the reply. '*We* surrendered first.' Neither side wanted to lose the initiative. Stalemate.

The two great Generals met in a tent in the middle of a field. 'According to my notes,' said the first, 'our flag went up at one minute to eleven on the 1st April.'

'So did ours,' was the reply.

'But,' said the first General, 'I gave the order to put the white flag up at a quarter to eleven . . .' and was met with the same reply. Stalemate II.

The first General screwed his eyes up, screwed his knees up, his nose, teeth and ears. 'Tell you what – my peace flag is whiter than yours.'

'Nonsense,' was the furious reply. 'Hold ours up to the light – not a stain in sight. We use the new Bluinite.'

'Bluinite!' guffawed the facing General. 'My dear fellow, Rinso, the new white Rinso, is my answer to you. That's why I say my flag is whiter.'

'The window test!' they said simultaneously.

In due course, a window was brought, against which the two flags were held. Alas, both were of the same degree of white intensity. Stalemate III.

Meantime, the makers of Bluinite and Rinso had heard of the conflict.

'You aren't going to let that lot get away with it,' said the Managing Director of Bluinite to the first General, at which time, as you can guess, Sir Jim Rinso was inciting the second General.

'I will prove who surrendered first,' he said, as the first great atomic blast exterminated them.

(Traditional)

Puckoon: 1963

Chapter Two

The Dan Milligan cycled tremendously towards the Church of St Theresa of the Little Flowers. Since leaving the area known as his wife he had brightened up a little. 'Man alive! The *size* of her though, she's a danger to shipping, I mean, every time I put me key in the front door I'll wonder what I'm lettin' meself in for.' Away down a lumpy road he pedalled, his right trouser leg being substantially chewed to pulp in the chain. His voice was raised in that high nasal Irish tenor, known and hated the world over.

'Ohhhhhhhhhhhhhhh IIIIIIIIIIIIII
> *Once* knew a judy in Dubleen Town
> Her eyes were blue and her hair was brown,
> One night on the grass I got her down
> And I . . .'

The rest of the words were lost to view as he turned a bend in the road. Farther along, from an overhanging branch, a pure-blooded Irish crow watched the Milligan approach. It also watched him hit the pothole, leave the bike, strike the ground, clutch the shin, scream the agony, swear the word. 'Caw!' said the crow. 'Balls!' said the Milligan. Peering intently from behind a wall was something that Milligan could only hope was a face. The fact that it was hanging from a hat gave credulity to his belief.

'Are you all right, Milligan?' said the face in the hat.

'Oh ho!' Milligan's voice showed recognition. 'It's Murphy. Tell me, why are you wearing dat terrible lookin' trilby?'

'We sold der hat stand, an' dere's no place ter hang it.' Murphy's face was a replica of the King Edwards he grew. He did in fact look like King Edward the Seventh. He also resembled King Edward the Third, Fifth and Second, making a grand total of King Edward the Seventeenth. He had a mobile face, that is, he always took it with him. His nose was what the French call retroussé, or as we say, like a pig; his nostrils were so acutely angled, in stormy weather the rain got in and forced him indoors. His eyebrows grew from his head like Giant Coypu rats, but dear friends, when you and I talk of eyebrows, we know not what eyebrows be until we come face to face with the *Murphy's* eyebrows! The man's head was a veritable plague of eyebrows, black, grey, brown and red they grew, thick as thieves. They covered two-thirds of his skull, both his temples and the entire bridge of his nose. In dry weather they bristled from his head like the spears of an avenging army and careless flies were impaled by the score. In winter they glistened with hoar-frost and steamed by the fire. When wet they hung down over his eyes and he was put to shaking himself like a Cocker Spaniel before he could proceed. For all their size dose eyebrows were as mobile as piglets, and in moments of acute agitation had been seen as far south as his chin. At the first sight of Milligan they had wagged up and down, agitati ma non troppo. As he spoke they both began to revolve round his head at speed.

'I heeerd a crash,' said Murphy. 'I examined meself, and I knew it wasn't me.'

'It was me,' said Milligan. 'I felled off me bi-cycle. Tank heaven the ground broke me fall.'

'Oh yes, it's very handy like dat,' said Murphy, settling his arms along the wall.

'Oh dear, dear!' said Milligan, getting to his feet. 'I've scratched all the paint off the toe of me boot.'

'Is dat right den, you paint yer boots?'

'True, it's the most economical way. Sometimes I paints 'em brown, when I had enough o' dat I paints 'em black again. Dat way people tink you got more than one pair, see? Once when I played the cricket I painted 'em white, you should try dat.'

'Oh no,' said Murphy solemnly. 'Oh no, I don't like inteferring wid nature. Der natural colour of boots is black as God ordained, any udder colour and a man is askin' fer trouble.'

'Oh, and what I may ask is wrong wid brown boots?'

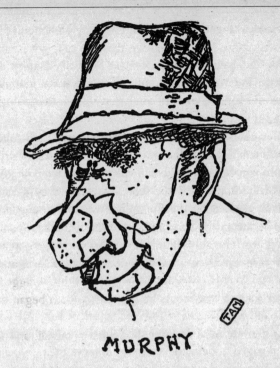

MURPHY

'How do I know? I never had a pair.'

'Take my tip, Murphy, you got to move wid der times man. The rich people in Dublin are all wearin' the brown boots; when scientists spend a lifetime inventin' a thing like the brown boots, we should take advantage of the fact.'

'No, thank you,' said Murphy's eyebrows, 'I'll stick along wid the inventor of the black boots. After all they don't show the dirt.'

'Dat's my argument, black don't show the dirt, brown ones don't show the mud and a good pair of green boots won't show the grass.'

'By Gor', you got something dere,' said the Murphy. 'But wait, when you was wearing dem white boots, what didn't dey show?'

'They didn't show me feet,' said Milligan, throwing himself on to the bike and crashing down on the other side.

'Caw!' said the crow.

'BALLS!' said Milligan. 'I'll be on me way.' He remounted and ped-alled off.

'No, stay and have a little more chat,' called Murphy across the widening gap. 'Parts round here are lonely and sparse populated.'

'Well it's not for the want of you tryin',' came the fading reply.

The day brewed hotter now, it was coming noon. The hedgerows hummed with small things that buzzed and bumbled in the near heat. From the cool woods came a babel of chirruping birds. The greenacious daisy-spattled fields spread out before Milligan, the bayonets of grass shining bravely in the sun, above him the sky was an exaltation of larks. Slowfully Milligan pedalled on his way. Great billy bollers of perspiration were running down his shins into his boots where they escaped through the lace holes as steam. 'Now,' thought the Milligan, 'why are me legs goin' round and round? eh? I don't tink it's me doin' it, in fact, if I had me way dey wouldn't be doin' it at all. But dere dey are goin' round and round; what den was der drivin' force behind dose legs? Me wife! *That's* what's drivin' 'em round and round, dat's the truth, dese legs are terrified of me wife, terrified of bein' kicked in the soles of the feet again.' It was a disgrace how a fine mind like his should be taken along by a pair of terrified legs. If only his mind had a pair of legs of its own they'd be back at the cottage being bronzed in the Celtic sun.

The Milligan had suffered from his legs terribly. During the war in Italy. While his mind was full of great heroisms under shell fire, his legs were carrying the idea, at speed, in the opposite direction. The Battery Major had not understood.

'Gunner Milligan? You have been acting like a coward.'

'No sir, not true. I'm a hero wid coward's legs, I'm a hero from the waist up.'

'Silence! Why did you leave your post?'

'It had woodworm in it, sir, the roof of the trench was falling in.'

'Silence! You acted like a coward!'

'I wasn't acting sir!'

'I could have you shot!'

'Shot? Why didn't they shoot me in peacetime? I was still the same coward.'

'Men like you are a waste of time in war. Understand?'

'Oh? Well den! Men like *you* are a waste of time in peace.'

'Silence when you speak to an officer,' shouted the Sgt. Major at Milligan's neck.

All his arguments were of no avail in the face of military authority. He was court martialled, surrounded by clanking top brass who were not cowards and therefore biased.

'I may be a coward, I'm not denying dat sir,' Milligan told the prosecution. 'But you can't really *blame* me for being a coward. If I am, then you might as well hold me responsible for the shape of me nose, the colour of me hair and the size of me feet.'

'Gunner Milligan,' Captain Martin stroked a cavalry moustache on an infantry face. 'Gunner Milligan,' he said. 'Your personal evaluations of cowardice do not concern the court. To refresh your memory I will read the precise military definition of the word.'

He took a book of King's Regulations, opened a marked page and read 'Cowardice'. Here he paused and gave Milligan a look.

He continued: 'Defection in the face of the enemy. Running away.'

'I was not running away sir, I was retreating.'

'The whole of your Regiment were advancing, and you decided to retreat?'

'Isn't dat what you calls personal initiative?'

'Your action might have caused your comrades to panic and retreat.'

'Oh, I see! One man retreating is called running away, but a whole Regiment running away is called a retreat? I demand to be tried by cowards!'

A light, commissioned-ranks-only laugh passed around the court. But this was no laughing matter. These lunatics could have him shot.

'Have you anything further to add?' asked Captain Martin.

'Yes,' said Milligan. 'Plenty. For one ting I had no desire to partake in dis war. I was dragged in. I warned the Medical Officer, I told him

I was a coward, and he marked me A.1. for Active Service. I gave everyone fair warning! I told me Battery Major before it started, I even wrote to Field Marshal Montgomery. Yes, I warned everybody, and now you're all acting surprised?'

Even as Milligan spoke his mind, three non-cowardly judges made a mental note of Guilty.

'Is that all?' queried Martin with all the assurance of a conviction. Milligan nodded. What was the use? After all, if Albert Einstein stood for a thousand years in front of fifty monkeys explaining the theory of relativity, at the end, they'd still be just monkeys.

Anyhow it was all over now, but he still had these cowardly legs which, he observed, were still going round and round. 'Oh dear, dis weather, I niver knowed it so hot.' It felt as though he could have grabbed a handful of air and squeezed the sweat out of it. 'I wonder,' he mused, 'how long can I go on losin' me body fluids at dis rate before I'm struck down with the dehydration? Ha ha! The answer to me problems,' he said, gleefully drawing level with the front door of the 'Holy Drunkard' pub.

'Hello! Hi-lee, Ho-la, Hup-la!' he shouted through the letter box.

Upstairs, a window flew up like a gun port, and a pig-of-a-face stuck itself out.

'What do you want, Milligan?' said the pig-of-a-face. Milligan doffed his cap.

'Ah, Missis O'Toole, you're looking more lovely dan ever. Is there any chance of a cool libation for a tirsty traveller?'

'Piss off!' said the lovely Mrs O'Toole.

'Oh what a witty tongue you have today,' said Milligan, gallant in defeat. Well, he thought, you can fool some of the people all the time and all the people some of the time, which is just long enough to be President of the United States, and on that useless profundity, Milligan pedalled on, himself, himself.

'Caw!' said a crow.

'Balls!' said Milligan.

Father Patrick Rudden paused as he trod the gravel path of the church drive. He ran his 'kerchief round the inside of his holy clerical collar. Then he walked slowly to the grave of the late Miss Griselda Strains and pontifically lowered his ecclesiastical rump on to the worn slab, muttering a silent apology to the departed lady, but reflecting, it wouldn't be the first time she'd had a man on top of her, least of all one who apologized as he did. He was a tall handsome man touching fifty, but didn't appear to be speeding. His stiff white hair was yellowed with frequent applications of anointment oil. The width of neck and shoulder suggested a rugby player, the broken nose confirmed it. Which shows how wrong you can be as he never played the game in his life. The clock in the church tower said 4.32, as it had done for three hundred years. It was right once a day and that was better than no clock at all. How old the church was no-one knew. It was, like Mary Brannigan's black baby, a mystery. Written records went back to 1530. The only *real* clue was the discovery of a dead skeleton under the ante-chapel. Archaeologists from Dublin had got wind of it and come racing up in a lorry filled with little digging men, instruments and sandwiches.

'It's the bones of an Ionian monk,' said one grey professor. For weeks they took photos of the dear monk. They measured his skull, his shins, his dear elbows; they took scrapings from his pelvis, they took a plaster cast of the dear fellow's teeth, they dusted him with resin and preserving powders and finally the professors had all agreed, the Monk was one thousand five hundred years old. 'Which accounts for him being dead,' said the priest, and that was that.

Money! That was the trouble. Money! The parish was spiritually solvent but financially bankrupt. Money! The Lord will provide, but to date he was behind with his payments. Money! Father Rudden had tried everything to raise funds, he even went to the bank. 'Don't be a fool, Father!' said the manager. 'Put that gun down.' Money! There was the occasion he'd promised to make fire to fall from heaven. The church had been packed. At the psychological moment the priest had mounted the pulpit and called loudly 'I command fire to fall from heaven!' A painful silence followed. The priest seemed uneasy. He repeated his invocation much louder, 'I COMMAND FIRE TO FALL FROM HEAVEN!' The sibilant voice of the verger came wafting hysterically from the loft. 'Just a minute, Father, the cat's pissed on the matches!'

It had been a black day for the church. Money! That was the trouble. His own shoes were so worn he knew every pebble in the church drive by touch. He poked a little gold nut of cheap tobacco into his pipe. As he drew smoke he looked at the honeyed stone of St Theresa, the church he had pastored for thirty years. A pair of nesting doves flew from the ivy on the tower. It was pretty quiet around here. There had been a little excitement during the insurgence; the Sinn Fein had held all their meetings in the bell tower and in consequence were all stone deaf. The priest didn't like bloodshed, after all we only have a limited amount, but what was he to do?

Freedom! The word had been burning through the land for nearly four hundred years. The Irish had won battles for everyone but themselves; now the fever of liberty was at the high peak of delirium, common men were incensed by injustice; now the talk was over and the guns were speaking. Father Rudden had thrown in his lot with 'the lads' and had harboured gunmen on the run. They had won but alas, even then, Ulster had come out against the union. For months since the armistice, dozens of little semi-important men with theodolites and creased trousers, were running in all directions in a frenzy of mensuration, threats and rock-throwing, all trying to agree the new border.

The sound of a male bicycle frame drew the priest's attention. There coming up the drive was the worst Catholic since Genghis Khan.

'Ah, top of the morning to yez, Father,' Milligan said dismounting.

'Well, well, Dan Milligan.' There was surprise and pleasure in the priest's voice. 'Tell me, Dan, what are you doing so far from your dear bed?'

'I'm feeling much better, Father.'

'Oh? You been ill then?'

'No, but I'm feeling much better now dan I felt before.'

There was a short pause, then a longer one, but so close were they together, you couldn't tell the difference.

'It's unexpectedly hot fer dis time of the year, Father.'

'Very hot, Milligan. Almost hot enough to burn a man's conscience, eh?'

'Ha ha, yes, Father,' he laughed weakly, his eyes two revelations of guilt.

'When did you last come to church, Milligan?'

'Oh, er, I forget – but I got it on me Baptismal certificate.'

The priest gave Milligan a long meaning stare which Milligan did not know the meaning of. Then the Milligan, still holding his bike, sat down next to the priest. 'By Gor Father, wot you tink of dis weather?'

'Oh, it's hot all right,' said Father Rudden relighting his pipe. Producing a small clay decoy pipe, Milligan started to pat his empty pockets. 'Here,' said the priest, throwing him his tobacco pouch.

'Oh tank you Father, an unexpected little treat.'

Together the two men sat in silence; sometimes they stood in silence which after all is sitting in silence only higher up. An occasional signal of smoke escaped from the bowl and scurried towards heaven. 'Now Milligan,' the priest eventually said, 'what is the purpose of this visit?' Milligan knew that this was, as the Spaniards say, '*El Momento de la Verdad*', mind you, he didn't think it in Spanish, but if he had, that's what it would have looked like.

'Well Father,' he began, puffing to a match, 'well, I – "puff-puff-puff" – I come to see – "puff-puff" – if dis grass cuttin' – job – "puff-puff" – is still goin'.'

The inquiry shook the priest into stunned silence. In that brief moment the Milligan leaped on to his bike with a 'Ah well, so the job's gone, good-bye.' The priest recovered quickly, restraining Milligan by the seat of the trousers.

'Oh, steady Father,' gasped Milligan, 'dem's more then me trousers yer clutchin'.'

'Sorry, Milligan,' said the priest, releasing his grip. 'We celibates are inclined to forget them parts.' 'Well you can forget mine fer a start,' thought Milligan. Why in God's name did men have to have such tender genitals? He had asked his grandfather that question. 'Don't worry 'bout yer old genitals lad,' said the old man, 'they'll stand up fer themselves.'

What about that terrible, terrible evening so long ago? Dan Milligan was seventeen, he had arrived for his first date with Mary Nolan. Her father had ushered him into the parlour with a forked vermin stick. Alone in the room with him was Mary's youngest brother, a little toddler of four. The little fellow carried in his hand such an innocent thing as a clay lion, but this, plus momentum, and brought unexpectedly into violent contact with Milligan's testicles, caused him to writhe and scream with pain; at which moment the radiant Mary chose to enter the room. To be caught clutching himself so was too much for the sensitive Dan. With only the whites of his eyes showing, he disguised his convulsions as a macabre Highland fling. Cross-eyed, bent double and screaming 'Och aye!' he danced from the room and she never saw him again. For many years after, young Dan Milligan wore an outsized cricketer's protective cup; during the mixed bathing season, many ladies made his acquaintance, only to be disappointed later.

'Yes, there's plenty of work to be done, Dan,' the priest was saying. He led Milligan to the gardener's hut. A small wood plank shed tucked in a cluster of cool elms. 'Michael Collins himself hid in here from the Tans,' said the priest proudly as he opened the door.

'Did he ever cut the grass?'

'No, but once, when the English was after him he set fire to it. What a blaze! Twenty courtin' couples nearly burnt to death! Them's the tools.' The priest pointed to four sentinel scythes standing in the corner like steel flamingoes.

'Ooh!' Milligan backed away. 'They look awful heavy, Father. Would you like ter lift one to see if me fears are well founded?'

'Saints alive, Milligan, there's no weight in 'em at all, man,' said the priest, lifting one and making long sweeping strokes. 'See? No weight in 'em at all,' he repeated, holding his groin for suspected rupture. He stood at the door and pointed out. 'You can start against that wall there and work inwards. If only I was younger.'

So saying the priest made off up the path. As he did, Milligan thought he heard suppressed laughter coming from the holy man. Carefully Milligan folded his jacket and cap and placed them on the roots of a flowering oak. He turned and faced the ocean of tall waving grass. His unshaven face took on that worried look of responsibility. Spitting in his hands he took hold of the instrument. Placing his feet apart he threw the scythe behind him, then, with a cry of 'Hi ayeee! Hoo! Hup-la!' he let go with a mighteous low curling chop; it started way behind him but, never a man of foresight, so great was the initial momentum, by the time the scythe had travelled ninety degrees it was beyond his control. All he could do was hang on; the great blade flashed past his white terrified face disappearing behind his back, taking both of his arms out of sight and sockets, at the same time corkscrewing his legs which gave off an agonized crackling sound from his knees. For a brief poetic moment he stayed twisted and poised, then fell sideways like a felled ox. 'Must be nearly lunch time,' he thought as he hit the ground. The Lord said: 'Six days shalt thou labour and on the seventh thou shalt rest.' He hadn't reckoned wid the unions. Forty-eight hours a week shalt thou labour and on the seventh thou shalt get double time. Ha. It was more profitable to be in the unions.

As Milligan laboured unevenly through the afternoon, long over-grown tombstones came to light,

R.I.P.

Tom Conlon O'Rourke.
Not Dead, just Sleeping.

'He's not kiddin' anyone but himself,' Milligan chuckled irreverently. What was all dis dyin' about, anyhow? It was a strange and mysterious thing, no matter how you looked at it. 'I wonder what heaven is really like? Must be pretty crowded by now, it's been goin' a long time.' Did they have good lunches? Pity dere was so little information. Now, if there was more brochures on the place, more people might be interested in going dere. *Dat's* what the church needed, a good Public Relations man. 'Come to heaven where it's real cool.' 'Come to heaven and enjoy the rest.' 'Come to heaven where old friends meet, book now to avoid disappointment!' Little catch phrases like dat would do the place a power of good. Mind you, derè were other questions, like did people come back to earth after they die, like them Buddhists say.

In dat religion you got to come back as an animal. Mmm, a cat! Dat's the best animal to come back as, sleep all day, independent, ha! that was the life, stretched out in front of a fire, but no, Oh hell, they might give me that terrible cat operation, no no I forgot about that. Come to think of it, who the hell wants to come back again anyhow? Now, honest, how many people in life have had a good enough time to come back? Of course if you could come back as a woman you could see the other side of life? By gor, dat would be an experience, suppose you wakes up one morning and finds you're a woman? What would he do? Go for a walk and see what happens. Oh yes, all this dyin' was a funny business, still, it was better to believe in God than not. You certainly couldn't believe in men. Bernard Shaw said 'Every man over forty is a scoundrel,' ha ha ha, Milligan laughed aloud. 'Every one round dese parts is a scoundrel at sixteen!' Bernard Shaw, dere was a great man, the Irish Noel Coward. A tiny insect with wings hovered stock still in front of Milligan's face. 'I wonder if he's tryin' to hypnotize me,' he thought, waving the creature away.

The sun bled its scarlet way to the horizon and the skies nodded into evening. The birds flew to their secret somewheres, and bats grew restless at the coming of night. Milligan puzzled at the church clock. 4.32? Good heavens, it gets dark early round here.

'How are you getting on then, Dan?'

At the sound of the priest's voice, Milligan put on a brief energetic display of hoeing. The priest blew his nose. 'Farnnnn – farnnnnnnnn,' it went, in a deep melodious E♭. 'I think you've done enough for today, it's nearly seven.'

'Seven?' Milligan cursed in his head. 'Trust me to work to a bloody stopped clock!'

'You mustn't kill yerself, Milligan.'

'I'm in the right place if I do.'

They both laughed.

A cool breeze blew in from the Atlantic, fetching the smell of airborne waves. The first ectoplasms of evening mist were forming over the river. Here and there fishes mouthed an O at the still surface. The Angelus rang out its iron prayer. Murphy, out in his fields, dropped his hoe and joined hands in prayer. 'The Angel of the Lord declared unto Mary.'

The near Godless Milligan trundled his bike towards the Holy Drunkard,

'IIIIIII

> Once knew a Judy in Dubleen town
> Her eyes were blue and her hair was brown
> One night on the grass I got her downnnn
> and the . . .'

The rest of the words were lost to view as the song turned a bend* in the road.

'I wonder if I'll see him again,' pondered Father Rudden. For that reason he had refrained from paying Milligan by the day.

* This was a different bend to the previous one. S.M.

The Little Pot Boiler: 1965

Telephones

The discovery of the telephone came about by accident. In 1873 a young, spotty research chemist, called Dr MacTomjim, had left a plate of virus mould culture on the window-sill to cool before serving and, absent-mindedly, forgot it. Next morning as he was counting the dead children around it, eureka! Whereas the mould had originally been white, there, looming in the middle was an ominous black shape. At first the Doctor thought it was an illegal Jamaican immigrant with a wondrous new way of entering the U.K. But no, closer inspection showed it to be the first telephone. Unaware of his great discovery, the Doctor placed it up on a shelf and forgot it. How then, you say, did he discover it by accident? I'll tell you. It fell on his head.

His devoted Brontë-like wife, who up till then was happily vivisecting away removing the eyes from live rabbits etc., etc., rushed to her beloved's side. Seeing the bruise on his head, she swooned to the floor. There, seeing the telephone, she swooned upright and *instinctively* dialled POLICE – FIRE – AMBULANCE. In a trice the police arrived, set fire to the Doctor and drove away in an ambulance. Friends, the telephone had arrived!

The first telephone proved to be useless until the arrival of the second. It rapidly became the status symbol of the Industrial Nouveau Riche. Daguerreotypes show important men posing alongside their new telephones; families grouped lovingly *around* their telephones; generals

pointing to their military telephones. Tunesmiths wrote 'Will Willy Tinkle Tilly on the Telephone Tonight'. No play was complete without a telephone in the first act. It was a boon to the atrocious plays and playwrights that fouled the English stage from 1926 to '38. Soon millionaires were ordering ornate Victorian-rococo telephones of satin brass and glazed steel. The Czar of all the Russias commanded the famed Romanov court jeweller, Fabergé, to fashion a telephonic master-piece. Made of pure Irish gold, inlaid with lapis lazuli taken from the tomb of Tutankhamen, and blazing with rare Australian fire opals, it caused the fiend Rasputin to say of it, 'This is a great day for Russia!' It turned out he was right; they shot him. (He died defiantly singing 'Anything you can do I kon do better'.)

In British West Pongoland, warring Zulu chiefs were placated with great crates of Victorian telephones. It was common fare to see two chieftains sitting two feet apart talking to each other on the new 'White Magic'; while outside, a snide British Lieutenant was hurriedly running up a Union Jack, and claiming the flagpole for the Queen (back home Prince Albert had gone one better, he was claiming the Queen).

Henry Irving boosted the sale of telephones with his play *The Bells*: the morning after the first night the G.P.O. was beseiged with applications for second night tickets. One man resented the intrusion

of the instrument; William McGonagall, self-appointed Poet Laureate, and idiot, wrote:

> What a sinful thing is the electrified telephone,
> Such a disgrace hitherto before has never been known,
> I would rather see those to whom I speak,
> Otherwise, for all I know I may be speaking to a freak.

The tintinnabulation of the Bells, drove Poe insane; he stabbed himself to death with a state-controlled raven. With good reason; the G.P.O. phone bell could be heard three miles away as the crow flies, and is the direct cause of deafness among crows today. This nerve-shattering bell is the same one installed at the bedsides of wax-frail old ladies in private nursing homes. Now, by shorting the circuit in the early hours, mercenary doctors in need of bed space can set off a carillon that reaps a fine crop of Coronary Occulisions.

My first phone was a 'party' line, that is, when your T.V., radio, wife and mistress break down, you can pick up the phone and listen to the neighbours. It soon became a burden. One of my writers would

phone me at midnight, and indulge in seeing how far he could walk
away from the phone and still be heard; last time he got as far as King's
Road, Chelsea, where he was knocked down by a bus.

My friend Mr Sellers had it bad. He installed a phone in his car.
Rather than let it lie idle all night, he would drive into the Kentish
Weald and phone back to tell his mother he was 'Out'. It was becoming
evident to me that the phone was a drug, and vying with cigarettes
for cancer of the inner ear.

VICTIM: Doctor, I've *got* to have more phone calls.
DR: But Mrs Leigh, you're up to seventy a day!
VICTIM: I know. I've tried to cut them down but I can't.
DR: Very well Mrs Leigh. Do you want them on the G.P.O. or do you
   want to be phoned privately?
VICTIM: My husband is rich.
DR: Very well, I want you to ring this number ten times a day after
   meals.

I invited a fellow sufferer to dine with me. To music by Debussy,
and candlelight, we sat down. As we commenced soup, the phone in
the next room rang. My guest stiffened, half rose and dropped his
spoon. For a moment he listened. 'Aren't you going to answer it?' he
said, his voice strangely castrati. 'We never answer the telephone on
Fridays, we are Catholics, and the Jews next door are watching us.' My

guest was now quite pale, trembling, and his wig had slipped. 'Would you like me to answer it for you?' he whined from his foetus position on the floor. I pointed a threatening obstetrical finger at him but, half-crazed by the bells, he ran screaming to the phone. Lifting the handset he received the following message, 'Your soup's getting cold you silly B——-r.' It had all been prearranged twixt me and a certain Mr Secombe.

Which brings us to the promoters of this malaise, those faceless sons of fun, the G.P.O.! Who from time to time issue little pain-killing brochures telling of fresh G.P.O. triumphs in a world of absolutely no competition. 'VALUE FOR MONEY' says their latest bit of bumph, 'When you pick up your telephone, you have a thousand million pounds' worth of equipment at your fingertips.' That's O.K. with me man, what I complain about are those five-pound-a-week brains that answer them.

A Book of Bits: 1965

Pull Down St. Paul's!

Headline in the Peking Bulletin: 'English Minister of Transport Buys 600 Disused Old Chinese Trams'. As the Minister of Transport so wisely said at the time: 'You never know, we might need them.' It is in this fine tradition that we find that splendid autocrat, Sir Keith Joseph, who will for ever be remembered as the Englishman who did as much for British architecture in London as Attila did for Roman cities. Which brings us to Juxon House.

To date, all we have heard are the asinine criticisms of those who are concerned only with the west face of St. Paul's. St. Paul's indeed! Are they blind to the beauties of Juxon House? Thank heaven there are those who are not, in particular the architect, the builders, the shareholders and the owners, who are all very aware of the new jewel that is raising its clean head in Ludgate Hill.

I am glad to report that the Minister of Housing is being approached with a complaint that St. Paul's is in fact obscuring the new office block's south-west front! He will be requested to pull down part of St. Paul's to afford the public a better view of the building.

For reasons beyond logic, Sir Keith, after considering the idea, said: 'While sympathising with them, the idea was financially not practicable, and it appeared that the public might be strongly averse to such a move.'

In a moment of *laissez-faire*, I phoned the Ministry and asked to speak to the Press representative. After several to eight minutes I was passed to a man called 'Spokesman Said'. I asked him was the Minister likely to stop the building of Juxon House?

Spokesman Said: No.

Me: Why was the plan passed in the first place?

Spokesman Said: It's very simple.

Me: I know that.

Spokesman Said: It's very simple. The building was placed in its present position for historical and commemorative reasons. Juxon House has been built on its present site because it is the identical spot on which

Bishop Juxon stood to admire St. Paul's west face. That is also why the building is called Juxon House.

Me: Splendid. But did not the Minister know that public opinion was in favour of building being suspended prior to an inquiry?

Spokesman Said: Yes, but what the public did not know was that but for Sir Keith's timely intervention, St. Paul's might be no more.

Me: Exploon that: (Yes, exploon!)

Spokesman Said: The original company had plans to pull the cathedral down and build a block of self-contained St. Paul's Cathedrals.

Me: Gloria in Excelsis.

Spokesman Said: I'm sorry, that's for the Foreign Office to answer. What did you say your name was?

Me: Spokesman Listening.

Thus ended the conversation. Mulling it over in my mind, stomach, and knees, I realised if this present spate of objections continued we could get headlines like this:

L.T.E. to sue Balham Gasworks, South Face of Trolleybus Depot in Pratts Road in danger of being Obscured by new Gasometer. L.T.E. appeal to public: 'Save your Balham Bus Depot from visual Vandalism.'

The whole problem of obscuring will certainly divide the country in two, i.e., People versus the Government. To back up the falling prestige of the Ministry of Housing, the Government might encourage Art to abandon chiaroscuro and settle for oscuro alone.

But let us move forward in time and think of St. Paul's 500 years hence, that is, in another ten Sir Keith Josephs from now. Allowing that further uncontrolled building will continue in and around St. Paul's, the official tourist brochure will read like this:

Those wishing to obtain the best view of the west face should apply to the chairman of the Imprudential (whose offices stretch right across the forecourt of St. Paul's – see plan above) enclosing a five shilling postal order. You will be sent a ticket overstamped 'Visitor.

West Front.' This entitles the holder to enter the Imprudential office block, take the lift to the seventeenth floor, where, through the window in a janitor's cupboard, a reasonable view can be had. A complete view can be obtained by photographing those areas visible from office numbers 5, 6, 7, 10, 13, 18 and 20, and piecing them together.

Owing to the heavy shadow cast by the Impru offices, it is advisable to carry a hand torch. Those who cannot afford the postal order can do it all free by following these instructions: walk to the back of the eighty-storey office block directly in front of St. Paul's: there you will find a narrow alley two feet wide; on your left will be the back of the Impru, and on your right the steps of the west face of St. Paul's; lie on your left side facing the step. Turn the head three inches to the right, at the same time craning the neck slightly to the left; cast your eyes to the extreme right and then look slightly up; now hold a small hand-mirror approximately six inches from the face, moving the mirror slowly from 45 to 60 degrees, where it will reflect a fine view of the west face. For those with money to spare the L.T.E. has laid on a special helicopter which takes up to eight passengers. Each passenger in turn is lowered between the Impru and the cathedral in a wicker basket and flown backwards and forwards along the narrow alley, allowing a panoramic view.

I think what Sir Keith Joseph had in mind was to enclose St. Paul's on all sides, thus creating a modern Petra and giving it an air of Eastern mystery.

Sir Keith sees a future in which special guides, chosen for their likeness to Sir Christopher Wren, and dressed in the costume of the period, will carry flaming brands and conduct tourists on horseback down the narrow, ink-black alleys, showing the mysterious and permanently hidden north, south, east and west fronts.

So think twice, irate citizens, ere you condemn Juxon House. As the Queen once said: 'God bless Sir Keith and all who fail with him.'

Exit Milligan pursued by a bear.

Milliganimals: 1968

What the Wiggle-Woggle Said

The Wiggle-Woggle said,
'I wish that I were dead:
I've a pain in my tummy and
It's travelling up the bed.
I wish that I were something
That never got a pain;
A little bit of fluffy stuff
That vanished down the drain.
I could be a tiger's whisker,
A tuba made of bread,
The purple eye
Of a custard pie
With a trouser made of lead.
There *must* be other somethings –
A tiny leather bead?
Or a bit of crumpled paper
Where the water-melons feed?
A yellow thing with lumps on!
A yellow thing without!!
Some hairy stuff
On a powder puff
That snuffs the candles out.
Wish I were a lamp post
(Lamp posts don't get pains),
A leaky rusty gutter
Flooding other people's drains!
All *those* are what I'd like to be,'
The Wiggle-Woggle said.

But he stayed a Wiggle-Woggle
And, what's more, he stayed in bed!

Small Dreams of a Scorpion: 1972

The Dog Lovers

So they bought you
And kept you in a
Very good home
Central heating
TV
A deep freeze
A *very* good home –
No one to take you
For that lovely long run –
But otherwise
'A *very* good home'.
They fed you Pal and Chum
But not that lovely long run,
Until, mad with energy and boredom
You escaped – and ran and ran and ran
Under a car.
Today they will cry for you –
Tomorrow they will buy another dog.

1970

Rommel: Gunner Who? 1973

February 26–28

The second volume of Milligan's war memoirs covered the period from January 1943 in Algeria to the fall of Tunis in May of that year.

My Diary: Feb. 26

'Waggon lines evacuated south of El Aroussa.' *Telephone contact with Waggon Lines was down, so I was sent to open up wireless contact. I threw my gear into Doug Kidgell's lorry (who was up with the rations).*

'Mind if I drive Doug?' Of course he didn't, I took the wheel, put my foot down.

'What's the bleedin' 'urry?' says Kidgell hanging on grimly.

'I want to live,' I said raising one eyebrow like John Barrymore and crossing my eyes. 'I'm young! Lovely! I want to feel the wind of this giant continent blowing through my hair,' I laughed. 'Happy darling?' I said as Kidgell shot two feet up, hitting his nut on the roof.

'Slow down! Fer Christ sake!!!'

'*He's* not in the back is he?'

'Milligan, stop! Or the child will be born premature.'

'If you saw Jerry's artillery back there, you'd realise I'm not doing this for fun!'

'I didn't say it was fun,' he raged.

We hit a large pothole, Kidgell goes up, while he's up we hit another pothole, so while he's on his way down the seat is on its way up to meet him, this time he does a semi-somersault, I have to brake suddenly and there on the floor in the shape of a granny-knot is Kidgell.

We raced past El Aroussa station – now we were safe from Jerry's artillery, I slowed.

'Who taught you to drive?' said Kidgell.

'Eileen Joyce.'

'She's a pianist.'

'That was the trouble.'

We arrived at Waggon Lines at five o'clock, too late to bivvy, so I kipped down in the back of Kidgell's lorry.

27th Feb.: First day at Waggon Lines.

0700. After breakfast, Bombardier/Artificer Donaldson detailed five men to accompany him to the old Waggon Lines to collect equipment left behind in yesterday's panic.

We drove in silence, except for me whistling, which I often did. It was an innocent pastime, free of malice, honest fun, it just drove people mad that's all. In the Carrier with me was Shit-house Orderly Forrest, he was illiterate, but didn't know that because he couldn't read or write. He had a girl in Bradford called Enid — and in reply to her simple letters we would reply on behalf of Forrest, 'Oh dearest Radiant Light of Love, here, where I am serving my monarch and country, a great Symphony-like yearning burgeons within me whenever I think of you. Enid! The name is magic — and your face — whenever I sprinkle the quick lime over the crap, it's your dear face I see.' She never wrote again.

Whistling merrily we arrived at the deserted Waggon Lines. Laying around were the bric-a-brac of hasty evacuation. 'Throw it on the lorry then let's piss off,' said Donaldson, walking up hill. 'I'm going up on ridge to keep KV.'

'Where's the piano?' I said to Forrest.

'What piano?' said the blank face of Forrest.

'The Regimental one.'

'The Regimental piano?'

'Yes, where is it?'

'I don't know. You're not jokin' are you?'

'Joke? About the Regimental piano? You've never seen us playing without a piano!'

'No.'

'Well, until it's found there's no more dances, if the Germans have captured that piano we're finished.'

We threw the last of the salvage on the lorry. 'OK Bom,' I called up to Donaldson, 'you can come down, all the work's done.' The return drive was uneventful except the look the boys gave Forrest when he said 'I wonder what happened to the piano then.'

At Waggon Lines, I shared a tent with BSM McArthur, a regular but only five foot six and a half which made him lack authority to anybody five foot seven and a half. He had a face the shape of a pear held upside down. Smoke blue eyes, a straight fleshy nose, under this hung a brown handlebar moustache. Head on he looked like a motorbike. He had advanced piles and slept face downwards. He greeted me with 'Good news you've been promoted to Lance Bombardier.' I wasn't expecting this, but was quick to capitalise, 'We non-commissioned officers must stick together. Wait till tomorrow, I'll put this bloody lot through their paces.' He was new to the Regiment, having joined a week before sailing. Apparently he had gained the disfavour of someone, and been banished to Waggon Lines as a Khaki Limbo. That night he talked; I thought *I* was a Walter Mitty, but this man was a congenital liar. He started, 'I am born of noble birth, my forebears were Scottish Barons, I have Royal Blood, one of my forebears slept with Prince Charlie, from that a child was born, I am in direct line from that union.'

'Jolly good,' I said, I mean what else can you say to a short sallow Herbert, lying face downwards under three grotty blankets, total value three pounds ten. He didn't stop there. There were the yachts, 'I have one tied up at the Pool of London.'

'Oh yes, if I had one *I'd* tie it up,' I said.

'You see I married a millionairess,' he said lighting a dog-end.

'Why didn't she buy you out?'

'Oh no! I couldn't let the old country down.'

'Why not,' I said. 'Everyone else has.' He was still rambling on when I fell asleep.

Next day I dug a slit trench, roofed it with a small tent and installed the wireless. The Gun Position was nearly fourteen miles away. 'If we move any further, we'll have to get in touch by medium.'

Through the daylight hours I would contact the G.P. every hour.

We had a sudden outbreak of the squitters, and Gunner Forrest had to dig a second latrine to take the overflow. We all had it very bad, and no one dared go more than twenty seconds away from the Karzi without jeopardizing underwear.

The M.O. gave us all some foul tasting pills that left you feeling like you'd slept with an Arab's toe in your mouth. After a few days it all cleared up, but during the attack Bombardier Marsden ran a sweepstake; BSM McArthur swept the pool with twenty-four visits in eight hours, he got two hundred francs and a sore arse.

My Diary: Feb. 28

Torrential rain. Wireless trench flooded.

Contacted Gun Position.

MILLIGAN: Hello! Tell Sergeant Dawson I need a relief.

GUN POSITION: Who do you want?

MILLIGAN: Paulette Goddard.

GUN POSITION: What will be her duties?

MILLIGAN: Me.

The rain! Not only did it come down, it went up 6 feet, and then came down a second time.

'It's good for the crops,' said McArthur.

'I haven't got any,' I said.

'I have. I've got a hundred acres in Somerset and three hundred in Canada.'

'It's not raining there.'

'I know,' he said, pacing up and down, 'and it's very very worrying.'

Goblins: 1978

Obolin Foxtip – A Goblin Juggler

I'm a Goblin Tommy Cooper,
I can do tricks with a hat,
I can walk upside down with a barrow
So they've made me a Water Rat.

I can juggle with seventy skittles
Dive through a rubber tyre
I can sleep on the bottom of the Channel,
Did somebody call me a liar?

I'm a Goblin Tommy Cooper,
I fly round the room on a mat,
You ask me how do I do it,
I'll tell you, 'Just like that'.

There's a Lot of It About: 1983

Life on Earth with David Attenborough

SPIKE IS WEARING AN APPALLING DAVID ATTENBOROUGH WIG,
VOLUMINOUS KHAKI SHORTS, THICK WOOLLY KNEE LENGTH HOSE
AND HEAVY BOOTS. HE IS SITTING INSIDE THE RIB CAGE OF A GIANT
DINOSAUR.

CAPTION: <u>DAVID ATTENBOROUGH AS SPIKE MILLIGAN</u>

SPIKE Good evening and money. Life on Earth. Is there any?
Later on we will be looking at some early expense accounts.
But first let us go back into the mists of time (<u>listens on ear
piece</u>). I'm sorry. Unfortunately it seems that the mists are
too thick so let's go back to a place without the mists of time.
Stonehenge.

WE CUT TO A TROPICAL HAWAIIAN BEACH, SPIKE NOW SITTING IN
A DECK CHAIR NEXT TO A BEAUTIFUL WOMAN WITH CHAMPAGNE
IN A BUCKET.

CAPTION: <u>STONEHENGE</u>

SPIKE Now to the untrained eye this has nothing to do with
Stonehenge but (<u>pours champagne</u>) the light in England is
very bad for filming and (<u>drinks champagne</u>) not very good
for expenses. But here in Hawaii the light and expenses are
perfect, so, here we ask the question: 'Where did the Ancient
Britons get the bricks for it?'

CUT TO BONDI BEACH, AUSTRALIA. WE NOW SEE ATTENBOROUGH
WITH A DIFFERENT BIRD, AND HE ALSO HAS TWO ROLEX OYSTER
WRIST WATCHES ON HIS WRIST. HE WEARS A HAT WITH CORKS
ROUND RIM. IN THE BACKGROUND THERE ARE A LOT OF VERY
GLAMOROUS, TOPLESS GIRLS, ETC.

SPIKE Our search took us – that is not the Jewish tookus, which
are entirely different – took us to this parched arid desert
where the temperatures and my expenses are very high. And

again we asked the question: 'Where did the Ancient Britons get the stone for Stonehenge?'

CUT TO THE INTERIOR OF A LUXURIOUS AIRLINER. SPIKE IS STRETCHED OUT ON A FIRST CLASS SLUMBERETTE. HE IS COVERED WITH A MINK BLANKET. ALONGSIDE THE SEAT IS A CHAMPAGNE BUCKET, ALSO ALONGSIDE IN EQUIVALENT LUXURY IS A BUSTY GIRL, WHO IS TOPLESS, BUT WEARS DARK HORN RIMMED GLASSES AND A STRING OF PEARLS. THEY BOTH HAVE GOOD LOOKING WRIST WATCHES ALL THE WAY UP THEIR LEFT ARMS.

SPIKE Could the answer lie in the luxury first class slumberette of my very good friends at Singapore Airlines? Let us find out.

CUT TO SMILING ORIENTAL, GROVELLING STEWARD AT ENTRÉE TROLLEY.

STEWARD Ah so . . .

SPIKE Professor Ahso, where did the Ancient Britons get the bricks for Stonehenge?

STEWARD Ogaa . . . (stream of Japanese)

SPIKE IS NOW AT A TABLE IN MAXIM'S RESTAURANT WEARING SAFARI GEAR. ALL ELSE IS SUMPTUOUS. THE GIRL WHO WAS ON THE PLANE IS NOW SITTING ALONGSIDE HIM IN A FABULOUS EVENING GOWN. THEY NOW HAVE MORE WRIST WATCHES ON THEIR ARMS.

SPIKE So we came to France and we asked the waiter. Manure.

WAITER Oui, oui . . . (pronounced oo-ee, oo-ee)

SPIKE Où est le Ancient Britons trouvez le bricks pour le Stonehenge?

WAITER PAUSES . . . LOOKS AT THE BIRD AND THEN GIVES A TRADITIONAL GALLIC GESTURE.

SPIKE The mystery deepens (picks up bill and puts it in his pocket). Could the answer lie in the Paul Getty Suite of the Paradise Hilton, Bermuda?

WE CUT TO THE PARADISE HILTON, BERMUDA, WHERE SPIKE IS IN BED IN A SUMPTUOUS SETTING. HE IS WITH THE SAME GIRL, MORE

WRIST WATCHES FOR BOTH, SHE IS NAKED, HE IS STILL WEARING
SAFARI GEAR.

SPIKE No. So we phoned London (girl hands him phone). Hello
England, this is a reverse charge call from David Atten-
borough and Co. Limited, registered in Liberia as an oil
tanker, on expenses in Bermuda. I have a question for you.
Where did the Ancient Britons get the bricks to build
Stonehenge?

HE HOLDS THE PHONE TO HIS EAR AND WE HEAR A TERRIFYING SERIES
OF RASPBERRIES, AS REALISATION DAWNS ON SPIKE'S FACE . . .

SPIKE Our three-year search was over. The Ancient Britons had
shrewdly got the bricks to build Stonehenge from England.
But what was the climate like when the Ancient Britons were
looking for their bricks in England?

WE NOW SEE SPIKE ON THE DECK OF A YACHT IN THE
MEDITERRANEAN. THE WEATHER IS STUNNING, BEAUTIFUL GIRLS
DRAPED AROUND HIM, SPIKE IS STILL ACCOMPANIED BY THE SAME
FEMALE, EVERYBODY IS IN SWIM SUITS, HE IS IN A SAFARI SUIT
. . . MORE WATCHES . . . NOW GOING UP THE OTHER ARM.

SPIKE We found the answer here on the deck of this simple two
thousand pounds a day yacht. So much for the weather. But
what of soil conditions of the Ancient Britons who were finding the bricks in England to build the Stonehenge.

CUT TO SUMPTUOUS ROOM IN THE SAVOY HOTEL. SAME GIRL IN A
NEGLIGÉE AND MORE WATCHES. SPIKE IS IN SAFARI GEAR AND
MORE WATCHES. WAITERS BRING CHAMPAGNE AND FOOD ON
TROLLEYS.

SPIKE Believe it or not Room 29 at the Savoy Hotel, London.
Under the floor of this £680 suite (takes back carpet), lies the
original glacial soil, now covered by this post glacial marquetry floor. This room is living proof that here or within
three hundred miles of here, somewhere, the Ancient Britons

found bricks from which they built Stonehenge. But how did life start on this planet . . .

CUT TO SPIKE ON A HAMMOCK IN THE SEYCHELLES. NOW COVERED IN WRIST WATCHES, ACCOMPANIED BY THE GIRL, WHO WEARS A GRASS SKIRT AND MORE WATCHES.

. . . It started here – well at least it did for me – in this hammock in the Seychelles. Next week our search will lead us to how the first luxury hotels came to this planet, and expense accounts, did they come from outer space?

THE END.

Startling Verse for All the Family: 1987

Soldier, soldier

There was a little soldier
Who went off to the war
To serve the King,
Which is the thing
That soldiers are made for.

But then that little soldier
Was blown to bits, was he.
All for his King
He did this thing:
How silly can you be?

A Mad Medley of Milligan: 1999

More Jam

I hate Jam
I don't want it to know where I am
I want a Jam-free life
Never letting Jam on my knife
Beware of Jam my friend
It can spread from end to end
Eating Jam is a sin
Letting all that Jam go in
Let your life be pure like me
Totally, totally, Jam-free
Be careful my friend
Or Jam will get you in the end

5

Beaming Down

The Goons: 1956

I'm Walking Backwards for Christmas

'I'm Walking Backwards for Christmas'/'Bluebottle Blues' entered the charts on 29 June 1956,
stayed for ten weeks and peaked at number 4.
[Adapted from the website www.shutupeccles.com]

MILLIGAN:
I'm walking backwards for Christmas, across the Irish Sea,
I'm walking backwards for Christmas, it's the only thing for me.
I've tried walking sideways, and walking to the front,
But people just look at me and say it's a publicity stunt.
I'm walking backwards for Christmas,
To prove that I love you.
[Band link]
An immigrant lad loved an Irish colleen from Dublin's Galway
    Bay . . .
He longed for her arms, but she spurned his charms,
And he sailed o'er the foam away.
She left the lad by himself, on his own all alone, a-sorrowing.
And sadly he dreamed, or at least that's the way it seemed,
    buddy,
That an angel choir to him . . . An angel choir did sing.
[eerily] I'm walking backwards for Christmas, across the Irish
    Sea
I'm walking backwards for Christmas, it's the finest thing for me.
    [normal]
And so I've tried walking sideways, and walking to the front.
But people just laughed, and said, 'It's a publicity stunt'.
So I'm walking backwards for Christmas
To prove that I love you. [play out]

Adolf Hitler: My Part in His Downfall: 1971

Dunkirk/Summer 1940

Milligan originally conceived his war memoirs as a trilogy but, like war itself, events soon spun out of his control. Always at pains to point out that the salient facts were true, he relied heavily not just on his own diaries — which he kept painstakingly at all but the most nerve-wracked moments — but also on those of his army colleagues. *Adolf Hitler* was the first volume.

Dunkirk

The first eventful date in my army career was the eve of the final evacuation from Dunkirk, when I was sent to the O.P. at Galley Hill to help the cook. I had only been in the Army twenty-four hours when it happened. Each news bulletin from the BBC told an increasingly depressing story. Things were indeed very grave. For days previously we could hear the distant sound of explosions and heavy gunfire from across the Channel. Sitting in a crude wood O.P. heaped with earth at two in the morning with a Ross Rifle with only five rounds made you feel so bloody useless in relation to what was going on the other side. Five rounds of ammo, and that was between the *whole* O.P. The day of the actual Dunkirk evacuation the Channel was like a piece of polished steel. I'd never seen a sea so calm. One would say it was miraculous. I presume that something like this had happened to create the 'Angels of Mons' legend. That afternoon Bombardier Andrews and I went down for a swim. It would appear we were the only two people on the south coast having one. With the distant booms, the still sea, and just two figures on the landscape, it all seemed very very strange. We swam in silence. Occasionally, a squadron of Spitfires or Hurricanes headed out towards France. I remember so clearly, Bombardier Andrews standing up in the water, putting his hands on his hips, and gazing towards where the B.E.F. was fighting for its life. It was the first time I'd seen genuine concern on a British soldier's face; 'I can't see how they're going to get 'em out,' he said. We sat in the warm water for a while. We felt so helpless. Next day the news of the 'small armada' came through on the afternoon news. As the immensity of the defeat became apparent, somehow the evacuation turned it into a strange victory. I don't think the nation ever reached such a feeling of solidarity as in that week at any other time during the war. Three weeks afterwards, a Bombardier Kean, who had survived the evacuation, was posted to us. 'What was it like?' I asked him.

'Like, son? It was a fuck up, a highly successful fuck up.'

Summer 1940

> Apples be ripe
> Nuts be brown
> Petticoats up
> Trousers down (*Old Sussex Folk Song*)

Apart from light military training in Bexhill there didn't seem to be a war on at all, it was a wonderful 'shirts off' summer. Around us swept the countryside of Sussex. There were the August cornfields that gave off a golden halitus, each trembling ear straining up for the sun. The Land Girls looked brown and inviting and promised an even better harvest. On moonlight nights haystacks bore lovers through their primitive course, by day there was shade a-plenty, oaks, horse chestnuts, willows, all hung out hot wooden arms decked with the green flags of summer.

The W.V.S. Forces Corner on the corner of Sea and Cantalupe Road was open for tea, buns, billiards, ping-pong and deserters. The Women's Voluntary Service girls were 'jolly nice', that is, they were undatable. We tried to bait them with Woodbines disguised in a Players packet and trying to walk like John Wayne. The other excitement was watching German planes trying to knock off the radar installations at Pevensey. Bombardier Rossi used to run a book on it. It was ten to one on against the towers being toppled. Weekends saw most officers off home in mufti. Apparently the same went for the Germans. The phoney war was on. I was now a trainee Signaller, highly inefficient in morse, flags and helio lamps. My duties were simple, a week in every month at an Observation Post overlooking the Channel. We had three: Galley Hill, Bexhill; a Martello Tower, Pevensey; and Constables Farm on the Bexhill–Eastbourne Road. Most of us tried for the Martello on Pevensey Beach as the local birds were easier to lay, but you had to be quick because of the tides. My first confrontation with the enemy was an early autumn evening at Galley Hill O.P. The light was going and a mist was conjuring itself up from the Channel. I'd just finished duty and was strolling along the cliff, enjoying a cigarette; in the absence of a piano I was whistling that bloody awful Warsaw Concerto when suddenly! Nothing happened! But it had happened suddenly, mark you. A moment later I heard the unmistakable sound of a Dornier Bomber, 103 feet long, wing span 80 feet, speed 108 m.p.h., piloted by Fritz Gruber aged twenty-three with a gold filling in his right lower molar. Suddenly, below me, coming out of the mist was the Dornier, flying low to avoid radar and customs duty. I could actually see the pilot and co-pilot's faces lit by a blue light on the instrument panel. What should I do? A pile of bricks! I grabbed one and as the plane roared over me, I threw it. Blast! Missed! But in that moment I envisaged glorious headlines. LONE GUNNER BRINGS DOWN NAZI PLANE WITH LONE BRICK ... INVESTITURE AT PALACE. MILLIGAN M.M. And the Germans! 'Mein Gott, if dis iss vot dey can do vid bricks, vot vill dey get vid guns?' They didn't all get away. That week a Hurricane downed a Dornier on Pevensey marsh. We ran to the crash. It was going to be a bad year for the rear gunner, he was dead. The young blond pilot was being treated by the Battery Cook, Gunner Sherry, who had been discharged from the Army on grounds of Insanity, then invited to join up again on the same grounds. He held the pilot with a carving-knife. We were very short of meat. Before the RAF recovery unit arrived we knocked off anything moveable, including the dead German's boots. The rear gunner's Spandau was handed to Leather Suitcase who tried to raffle it: however, after discussions he decided to use it as an A.A. gun. He really was getting the hang of things. A pit was dug outside 'Trevissick' (the officers' billets). One morning, on the last stag (04:00 to 06:00) I heard a Dornier circling in low cloud. What a chance! I uncovered the Spandau. I could see the headlines again, MILLIGAN DOWNS ANOTHER! KING TAKES BACK M.M. IN PART EXCHANGE FOR V.C. A window opened. The lathered face of Leather Suitcase appeared.

'Milligan? What are you standing there for?'

'Everybody's got to be somewhere sir.'

'What are you doing?'

'Going to have a crack at the Hun sir.'

'Don't be a bloody fool, you'll give our position away. Now cover up that gun before it gets spoilt.' As he spoke there was a lone explosion. The Dornier had dropped a bomb in Devonshire Square.

'You see what you've done,' he said, slamming the window. He must have been worth two divisions to the Germans. It was going to be a long war. Churchill had a tough job on. It was thanks to him that we had any guns at all.

When the '14–'18 War ended, Churchill said the 9.2s were to be dismantled, put in grease and stored in case of 'future eventualities'. There was one drawback. No Ammunition. This didn't deter Leather Suitcase, he soon had all the gun crews shouting 'BANG' in unison. 'Helps keep morale up,' he told visiting Alanbrooke. By luck a 9.2 shell was discovered in Woolwich Rotunda. An official application was made: in due course the shell arrived. A guard was mounted over it. The Mayor was invited to inspect it, the Mayoress was photographed alongside with a V for Victory sign; I don't think she had the vaguest idea what it meant. A month later, application was made to H.Q. Southern Command to fire the shell. The date was set for July 2nd, 1940. The day prior, we went round Bexhill carrying placards.

> THE NOISE YOU WILL HEAR
> TOMORROW AT MIDDAY WILL BE
> THAT OF BEXHILL'S OWN CANNON.
> DO NOT BE AFRAID.

Other men went round telling people to open their windows, otherwise the shock waves might break them. Even better, they were told,

'Break the windows yourself and save the hanging-about.' Dawn! the great day! We were marched to a secret destination on the coast known only to us, and the enemy. Freezing, with a gathering fog, we all sat in the corner of a windy beach that was forever England. They told us, 'Listen for the bang and look for the splash.' Before the visiting brass arrived the fog had obscured the view. The order now became *Listen* for the splash. Zero hour. Tension mounting. A Lance Bombardier was arrested for sneezing. A Jewish gunner fainted on religious grounds. Lieutenant Budden was stung by a bee; lashing out with his hand, he struck Captain Martin's pipe, driving the stem down his throat, leaving just the bowl protruding from his lips and fumigating his nose. Disaster! Sergeant Dawson, A.I.* of Signals, reported the line to the gun position had got a break. Signallers Devine and White, who would do anything for a break, set off. In the haste to defend the Sceptered Isle, the South Coast was a mass of hurriedly-laid, unlabelled telephone lines, along walls, down drains, up men's trouser legs, everywhere!

After thirty military minutes, the O.P. telephone buzzed.

'Ah!' said Dawson hopefully, 'O.P. here.'

'We haven't found the break yet.'

'Right. Keep trying.'

The fog was now settling inland. Top brass had finished the contents of their thermos flasks and withdrawn to the shelter of a deserted fisherman's cottage. All was silent save the sound of frozen gunners singing the International. Every ten minutes for two hours, Signaller Devine phoned and gleefully reported, 'line still broken, Sarge'. The fog was very dense, as were Signallers Devine and White, who were now groping their way through Sussex in Braille. C.O.'s patience being exhausted, a runner was sent to the gun position. Off went Gunner Balfour, the Battery champion athletes foot. Another hour. He was lost. In despair Sergeant Dawson bicycled to the police station, telephoned the Gun Position and told them 'Fire the Bloody Thing!' A distant 'BOOM'. At the O.P. we heard the whistle as the rare projectile passed

---

* Assistant Instructor.

overhead into the Channel, a pause, a splash, then silence . . . it was a dud. How could the Third Reich stand up to this punishment! Next day at low tide we were sent out to look for traces of the lost projectile; we didn't, but it was a nice day for that sort of thing.

Open Heart University: 1978

India! India!

As a boy
I watched India through fresh Empirical eyes.
Inside my young khaki head
I grew not knowing any other world.
My father was a great warrior
My mother was beautiful
                    and never washed dishes,
                    other people did that,
I was only 4, I remember
                    they cleaned my shoes,
                    made my bed.
'Ither ow'
'Kom Kurrow'
Yet, in time I found them gentler
                                than the khaki people
They smiled in their poverty
After dark, when the khaki people
                            were drunk in the mess
I could hear Minnima and
                    her family praying in their godown.
In the bazaar the khaki men
                            are brawling
No wonder they asked us to leave.

Sir Nobonk: 1982

an extract

The full title of this tale was *Sir Nobonk, and the Terrible, Awful, Dreadful, Nasty Dragon*. It was lavishly illustrated by Carole Barker.

THE RETURN

News of the dragon's capture had reached the King's City, and crowds gathered in the Royal Square. The King had declared a holiday and everyone had to wear clean knickers and blow their noses. Nose and knicker wardens went round to check on everyone's noses and knickers.

A cry went up: 'Here they come!' then through the City Gates strained soppy Big Bill, pulling the huge trap with the six-ton dragon, with everyone else on top. In front on his white horse rode Sir Nobonk.

'Make way for the hyena,' said Big Bill, who still hadn't got it right.

The King said, 'Three cheers for the Dragon Catchers. Hip, hip hooray! Hip, hip, hooray!'

'That's only two,' said Sir Nobonk.

'I know,' said the King, 'it's an economy cut. Now step forward, Sir Nobonk. For the capture of this deadly dragon I'm giving you the time. It's exactly half-past three.'

Sir Nobonk bowed low, and hit his nose on the Wizard's head. 'Your Majesty, what a magnificent present, half-past three, just what I've always wanted.'

But by the time he stood up it was three thirty-two!

'Help!' said Sir Nobonk. 'Stop thief! Half-past three is gone, which way did it go?'

'It went towards four o'clock,' said Big Bill.

The King held up his hand for silence. 'Don't worry, it will come back at the same time tomorrow,' he said. 'Now – all stand back while I kill the Dragon.'

The crowd cheered. 'Kill the Dragon!' they shouted, because crowds love violence.

The King took his great bow and arrow and put poison on the tip. He took aim.

'Stop!' said Sir Nobonk. 'Don't kill him, sire.'

'Why not?' said the King. 'He's alive.'

'Because if you kill him he'll die,' said Sir Nobonk.

'Oh,' said the King. 'Do they die when you kill them?'

'Yes,' said the Knight, 'death kills them.'

Sir Nobonk explained that dragons were becoming extinct. 'There are only six left in the world,' he said.

'Only six?' said the King. 'I thought there were 1,000,000,000!'

He sucked his thumb, which he kept on dipping in treacle. He didn't know what to do. In his Kingdom they had *always* killed dragons. 'What good is a live dragon?' he asked.

'What good is a dead one?' asked Sir Nobonk. 'Sire, I shall get the Wizard of Nothing to draw up plans on how to use a live dragon for the benefit of the people,' he said.

That night the townsfolk built a huge bonfire and had a jelly and custard party to celebrate the capture of the Dragon. All the children did ring-a-roses around the Dragon's trap. Next morning the Wizard of Nothing gave the King the plans.

'Good Heavens!' said the King. 'They want us to build a Dragon Zoo.'

The Wizard smiled. 'Yes, we can breed dragons. It will attract tourists from all over the World!'

Suddenly, Sir Nobonk said, 'Look at my present, it's three thirty and that dragon hasn't had any dinner since yesterday, and in my book *Dragons and Their Food* it says that every fifty-six hours they have to be fed or they die of death.'

Sir Nobonk asked what a dragon ate. The Wizard scratched his head, then his leg, then his belly, then his bottom. That's because his fleas were running about very fast.

'I know what dragons eat,' said Little Willy. 'My mother told me. They eat a hundred cows once a week.'

This worried Sir Nobonk, but it worried the cows more.

'We can't afford that,' he said, 'so he'll have to go on a vegetarian diet of trees.'

Now the big surprise for the King was opened on Christmas Day. It was a Dragon Wildlife Park! Soon many people heard of it, and instead of killing dragons they took them to Nobonk's Dragon Sanctuary to be saved. There was also a Dragon Drying Service, where people took all their wet laundry into a field and a dragon would breathe hot air to dry them.

In the winter the dragon would breathe on the lake, and people could swim in warm water. You could hire a dragon for a barbecue, and he would cook food by breathing on it.

In fact, dragons saved the country lots of money in lighting, heating and drying.

Then the dragons had three babies, Plink, Plank and Plonk. They became very tame and let children ride on their backs – it was smashing fun. The children used to take them for walks, and when the children's hands got cold they just put them on the dragon to get warm.

BUT

But! ha! ha! There were people in another country called Dangle who were jealous of Sir Nobonk and his dragons. The leader was called Blackmangle. They liked to eat dragon meat, and because they had killed all their dragons they were all getting hungry.

'We must invade Cornwall and capture their dragons,' said Blackmangle to his witch named Witch-Way.

'Yes,' she shrieked, 'I will put a spell on King Big-Twytt.'

Blackmangle wrote a message:

Dear King Big-Twytt,
I, or one of my Black Knights,
challenge you, or one of your
Knights, to a Joust. If we win,

you must surrender your dragons.
If we lose, we will give you
fifty pence and a smelly sock.

He attached the message to Witch-Way's ankle and sent her off on her broomstick. She screamed as she flew over the sea to Cornwall:

SCREAMMMM!

she went. She kept screaming, because a splinter from her broomstick had stuck in her bottom! As she flew over Cornwall she screamed curses: 'May all your women's teeth go green – heh-heh-heh. May all their dresses catch fire. Heh-heh-heh. May all their heads go bald and grow mushrooms. Heh-heh-heh.'

King Big-Twytt knew something was going wrong when his Queen came in with green teeth, a bald head with mushrooms growing on it and her dress on fire.

'Who are you?' he said.

'Who? I am the Queen.'

'I want a divorce,' said the King.

Soon all the women in Cornwall looked like the Queen. It was terrible, all the daddies ran and locked them away.

'Don't worry,' said the Wizard of Nothing.

'Why? What are you going to do?' said the Queen.

'I'm not going to do anything, all I said was don't worry.'

By now the witch had delivered the challenge to the King.

'They want to fight us for the dragons,' he said.

'What do you intend to do?' asked Sir Nobonk.

'I'm not frightened,' said the King. 'Blackmangle doesn't frighten me. To prove it, I want *you* to fight him.'

BLACKMANGLE ARRIVES: HELP!

What no one knew was that Blackmangle was a *giant* – he was so huge he blacked out the sun. One day a great shadow fell over King Big-Twytt's castle, and everyone thought it was night time. Then they realised that it was the shadow of Blackmangle.

'You didn't tell me he was a giant,' said Sir Nobonk.

Blackmangle let out a great roar: 'Come out and fight!'

Sir Nobonk went out and looked up. 'You'll have to wait, we haven't had breakfast yet.'

'Well, hurry up,' said Blackmangle, 'I'm waiting to kill you.'

'If you kill me,' said Sir Nobonk, 'I'll never speak to you again.'

Blackmangle sat on the grass and waited. It was a hot day. Little Willy rushed in and said to King Big-Twytt, 'Blackmangle has fallen asleep, we must wake him up.'

'Why?' said King Big-Twytt.

'Because', said Little Willy, 'Big Bill is underneath him.'

'No,' said the Wizard, 'while he is asleep he is not dangerous – we must try and keep him asleep.'

'How?' said Sir Nobonk.

'Follow me, I will show you,' said the Wizard.

The Wizard put a ladder up against Blackmangle and they all climbed up on to his belly. As Blackmangle breathed in and out, they all went up and down. The Wizard said: 'Head for his nose.'

Ahead were the giant's nostrils, which looked like two great caves, and the Wizard started to walk in.

'Where are you going?' asked Sir Nobonk.

'I've got to get to his brain,' said the Wizard. 'Once I reach it I can find the piece that makes him bad and switch it off.'

So they all followed the Wizard up the giant's nose, and soon they were in the giant's brain! Different parts were marked 'Good bit', 'Bad bit', 'Naughty bit', 'Nice bit', 'Don't-want-to-go-to-bed bit', 'Eating-too-much-jelly bit', and 'Smelly-poo bit'.

'Ah,' said the Wizard and pointed to a bit marked 'Killing dragon bit'. He saw a switch on it marked ON-OFF. He reached up and put it to OFF, then he switched all the bad bits off. All the giant's body shook like an earthquake!

They all ran down his nose, and on to his belly which was shaking like a jelly! Soon they were safe on the ground. Then the giant woke up.

'Hello, everybody,' he said. 'What a lovely day, let's go and pick blackberries.' He was ever so kind and polite.

'You've done it,' said Sir Nobonk to the Wizard and gave him a chocolate medal.

They all thought now that the Dragon was safe, but no! They'd forgotten Witch-Way. She came roaring through the sky on her great broomstick, screaming and dropping poisoned sweets.

'You can't stop me – I'll kill the Dragon.'

'I challenge you to a duel,' said Sir Nobonk.

'Very well,' screamed the witch. 'Tomorrow at dawn.'

THE DUEL

As the sun rose, the people gathered for the great duel at the jousting ground. At one end, Sir Nobonk on Daz – at the other, on her broomstick, was the witch attended by her hobgoblins all screaming with her. The pages blew their trumpets for the fight to start. The witch pointed her poisoned lance at Sir Nobonk. He knew that even if it only touched him, the poison was so strong it would kill him and his horse. The trumpets sounded for the fight to start.

And the witch screamed, 'Death, death!' She crouched over her broomstick and rushed at Sir Nobonk. She was coming at him so fast that he could hardly see her. He started to gallop towards her, nearer and nearer came the screaming witch.

'She's going too fast for him, she'll kill him,' said King Big-Twytt. 'Look out, Nobonk!'

Just as the witch was going to stick her lance into Sir Nobonk's heart, a giant hand came down and snatched up Sir Nobonk and his horse. The witch screamed past, crashed into the castle wall and exploded in a great ball of fire that turned into black, green and purple frogs which croaked and hopped away.

'Oh, thank you for saving me,' said Sir Nobonk to Blackmangle, and gave him twenty chocolate medals and jelly babies.

And so peace came to Cornwall and they all lived happily ever after – especially the dragons!

101 Limericks: 1982

A Doctor...

A doctor who made a prognosis
Said, 'Madam, 'tis my diagnosis
You have a touch
Of flu in the crutch.'
He was wrong – it was myxomatosis!

Where Have All the Bullets Gone?: 1985

Return to Italy

Most of volume five of Milligan's war memoirs covered his convalescence after the incident at Castelforte, but he also relates his first meetings with band-leader Bill Hall, as well as one Gunner H. Secombe.

The morning of November the second dawns. A hurrying RTO Sergeant proceeds down the corridor. 'Maddaloni in fifteen minutes.' Familiar landscape is in view, the hills behind Caserta are light and dark in the morning sun. We wipe the steamed windows to see it. I've had breakfast: two boiled eggs, boiled bread and boiled tea. How come the Continentals can't make tea? If this is tea, bring me coffee. If this is coffee, bring me tea. The Italian waiter says they don't go much on tea. I tell him if they did it would make it stronger. The black giant locomotive groans and hisses to a clanking steaming halt, there's a long shuddering final hiss as the steam leaches out, like a giant carthorse about to die. We all climb down on to the tracks. A few thank the unshaven smoke-blackened driver. There's a clutch of lorries waiting, they are dead on time. Now the war's over the Army's getting it together. Wearily we clamber on board and arrive at Alexander barracks as the town is coming to life. Shagged-out cats are heading for home and the odd early morning dog sits on the cold pavement, freezing his bum and scratching away the night fleas.

'Wake up, Steven.' I shake the sleeping Yew. 'Wake up, God's in his heaven, all's right with the world.'

'Piss off,' he says, without opening his eyes.

'Wake up Steve my old friend, it's me, Sunny Spike Milligan, back from foreign shores with a tale to tell.'

He raises his lovely head, squints, groans, and lets his head fall back with a thud. Go away Milligan, go a long way away, take a known poison and only come back when you're dead.

I take his eating irons and bring him his breakfast. This thaws him out.

'Breakfast in bed,' he says, sitting up, pulling strings that raise the mosquito net, empty the po, release his shirt, loosen his pyjamas, bring his socks, raise his vest, lower his comb, push his boots . . . So what was England like? It's like 1939 with bomb craters and fruit cake, and there's a lot of it about. I should know, I'm just recovering. Back into the office grind. What news? During the absence of the band on leave, entertainment has come to a halt.

REDIVIVUS

'We've got to do a spot on the Variety Bill this Monday.' Stan Britton welcomes me back. 'They want something funny and musical.' How about 'Ave Maria' naked in gumboots filled with custard? No? Then 'Your Tiny Hand is Frozen' sung from inside a fridge through the keyhole. No? Why am I wasting my time on this man when I could be wasting it on a woman in Sandwich?

SHOCK HORROR ETC. AND OTHER HEADLINES!

I was to get the chop! Not the leg of lamb or the kidney but the chop! While I was helping the women of England get back to normal in Sandwich, Brigadier Henry Woods has decided that either I go or he stays.

> BOMBARDIER MILLIGAN S. 954024
> With effect from November the umpteenth,
> the above will be posted to the CPA,
> Welfare Department, Naples.
> Signed H. Woods, Brigadier and midget.

So, he was the coloured gentleman in the wood pile. I swore I would never go to the pictures with him again. (He died a few years ago. I wish him well.) Why was he persecuting me like this? My only crime was my only crime. Still, like Cold Collation I could take it. I had letters to that effect from several serving women. The papers should hear of this.

DAILY MIRROR

Ace Filing Clerk to be Axed Shock Horror etc.

Today, Bombardier Milligan, the world-renowned corporal with three stripes, and known throughout the Italian theatre of war as the most advanced filing clerk in the British Army, heard that he was to be sacked.

Reuter.

The band boys tried to commiserate with me. We had a last jam session in the band room and rounded off with a great piss up. I was carried to my room for the last time . . .

A NEW LIFE AND A NEW DAWN

A truck is waiting to take me away. How many times have I done this? Yet again the kit is piled in the back, and like a sheep to market, I am driven away, all on the whim of one man who thought I played my trumpet too loud. I am puzzling over what CPA means. Captain's Personal Assistant? Cracked People's Area? Clever Privates' Annexe? None of these, says the driver. It's 'Centril Pule of Hartists (Central Pool of Artists), hits a place where orl dhan-graded squaddies who can hentertain are sent.' Was he a down-graded entertainer?

'Yer.'

'What do you do?'

'Hi sing Hopera.'

'Opera?'

'Yer, you know, *La Bhome*, *Traviahta*, and the like.'

'Were you trained?'

'Now, it cum natural like.'

'Have you ever sung in opera natural like?'

'No, I just done the horditions like. The Captain says 'ees waitin' for a suitable vehicle for me.' Like a bus, I thought.

We have driven through Naples, turned left at the bottom of Via

Roma up the Corso San Antonio, which goes on for ever in an Eastern direction. Finally we arrive at a broken-down Army barracks complex. The walls are peeling, they look as if they have mange. I report to a Captain Philip Ridgeway, a sallow saturnine fellow with a Ronald Colman moustache who looks as if he has mange as well. He sits behind the desk with his hat on. He is the son of the famous Ridgeways' Late Joys Revue that led to the Players Theatre. He looks at my papers. 'So, you play the trumpet. Do you play it well?'

'Well, er loudly.'

'Do you read music?'

'Yes, and the *Daily Herald*.'

He smiled. He would find me a place in 'one of our orchestras'. I was taken by a Corporal Gron, who looked like an unflushed lavatory, and shown to a billet on the first floor, a room with forty single beds around the walls. In them were forty single men. This being Sunday, they were of a religious order that kept them in kip until midday. I drop my kit on a vacant bed, and it collapses to the floor. 'That's why it's vacant,' laughed Corporal Gron, who laughed when babies fell under buses. Next bed is Private Graham Barlow. He helps me repair the bed with some string and money. Nice man – he played the accordion. Noel Coward said, 'No gentleman would ever play the accordion.'

I had no job as such, and as such I had no job. Breakfast was at 8.30, no parade, hang around, lunch, hang further around, tea, extended hanging around, dinner and bed. The CPA Complex had the same ground plan as the Palace of Minos at Knossos, consisting of rehearsal rooms, music stores, costume stores, scenery dock and painting area, Wardrobe Mistress, Executive offices. People went in and were never seen again. The company was assembled from soldier artistes who had been down-graded. They would be formed into concert parties and sent on tour to entertain those Tommies who weren't down-graded. The blind leading the blind. The facilities were primitive, the lavatories were a line of holes in the ground. When I saw eighteen soldiers squatting/balancing over black holes with straining sweating faces for the first time, they looked like the start of the hundred yards for paraplegic dwarfs.

My first step to 'fame' came when I borrowed a guitar from the stores. I was playing in the rehearsal room when a tall cadaverous gunner said, 'You play the guitar then?' This was Bill Hall. If you've ever seen a picture of Niccolò Paganini, this was his double. What's more, he played the violin and played it superbly; be it a Max Bruch Concerto or 'I've Got Rhythm', he was a virtuoso. But bloody scruffy. We teamed up just for the fun of it, and in turn we were joined by Johnny Mulgrew, a short Scots lad from the Recce Corps; as he'd left them they were even shorter of Scots. Curriculum Vitae: Pre-war he played for Ambrose and the Inland Revenue. In the 56 Recce in N. Africa. Trapped behind enemy lines at Madjez-el-Bab. Lay doggo for forty-eight hours in freezing weather. Got pneumonia. Down-graded to B2 . . .

Together we sounded like Le Hot Club de France. When we played, other musicians would come and listen to us – a compliment – and it wasn't long before we were lined up for a show.

In the filling-in time, I used to play the trumpet in a scratch combination. It led to my meeting with someone from Mars, Gunner Secombe, H., singer and lunatic, a little myopic blubber of fat from Wales who had been pronounced a loony after a direct hit by an 88-mm gun in North Africa. He was asleep at the time and didn't know about it till he woke up. General Montgomery saw him and nearly surrendered. He spoke like a speeded up record, no one understood him, he didn't even understand himself; in fact, forty years later he was knighted for not being understood.

The Officers' Club, Naples. We were playing for dancing and cabaret, the latter being the lunatic Secombe. His 'music' consisted of some tatty bits of paper, two parts, one for the drums and one for the piano – the rest of us had to guess. We busked him on with 'I'm Just Wild About Harry'. He told us he had chosen it because his name was Harry, and we said how clever he was. He rushed on, chattering, screaming, farting, sweat pouring off him like a monsoon, and officers moved their chairs back. Then the thing started to shave itself, screaming, chattering and farting; he spoke at high speed; the audience thought he was an imported Polish comic, and many wished he was back in Warsaw being bombed. Shaving soap and hairs flew in all directions, then he launched into a screaming duet with himself, Nelson Eddie and Jeanette MacDonald, but you couldn't tell him apart. A few cries of 'hey hup' and a few more soapy farts, and he's gone, leaving the dance floor smothered in shaving soap. His wasn't an act, it was an interruption.

The dance continues, and officers are going arse over tip in dozens. 'No, not him,' they'd say when Secombe's name came up for a cabaret.

Bill Hall. A law unto himself. He ignored all Army discipline, he ignored all civilian discipline. His regiment had despaired of him and posted him to CPA with an apology note.

Take kit parade. We are all at our beds, kit immaculately laid out for inspection. The Orderly Officer reaches Gunner Hall. There, on an ill-made bed, where there should be 19 items of Army apparel, are a pair of socks, three jack-knives, a vest, a mess tin and a fork. The officer looks at the layout. He puts his glasses on.

OFFICER: Where is the rest of your kit?
GUNNER HALL: It's on holiday, sir.

Apart from Gunner Secombe, CPA contained other stars to be, including Norman Vaughan, Ken Platt and Les Henry (who later formed the Three Monarchs).

There were, of course, failures. Private Dick Scratcher, down-graded with flat feet, was billed as the Great Zoll, the Voltage King. He was given a try-out at the now recovering Officers' Club. His act consisted of a 'Death Throne' made out of wood, cardboard and silver paper, with a surround of light bulbs. On a sign above was a warning: DANGER 1,000,000 VOLTS. The Great Zoll entered as a 'Sultan', with a turban that looked more like a badly bandaged head, and struck a 'gong' which was a dustbin lid painted with cheap silver paint: with its edge cut off it gave a flat 'CLANK'. He was assisted by the driver/opera singer clad in a loin cloth, his body stained brown with boot polish.

The 'Sultan' would be strapped into the chair with silver straps, telling us all the while in Chinese with a north-country accent: 'Chop, chop, my assistant, Tong Bing, now strap me in Death t'chair, and throw switch, and send million volts through my t'body.' Tong Bing then chants some mindless tune which has nothing to do with the tune we are playing. Various bulbs go on and off as the great switch is thrown, the voltage meter goes up and down, the Great Zoll speaks: 'By power of t'mind I will resist the power of t'electricity.' He stared into space, then magnesium flashes go off and fill the club with choking smoke. The final magnesium flash has been placed too near the Great Zoll, it sets fire to his trousers. Tong Bing is trying to beat it out and the room is filled with watery-eyed coughing officers trying to escape.

Dick Scratcher's name went down next to Secombe's in the 'never again' list. After the war, Harry was appearing at the Palladium and was visited by the Great Zoll and his wife. Harry noticed that the woman's legs and arms were bandaged. 'I've changed the act,' says the Great Zoll. 'I'm into knife throwing.'

The best pianist in the CPA was Johnny Bornheim. Late nights we would play in the rehearsal room with a bottle of wine as company. Bornheim was a furrier in civvy street, but should have been a concert pianist. Self-taught, he could literally play anything.

He was fascinated with Bill Hall. He once pointed out, 'No one has ever seen Bill Hall's body alive!' True, he only showered after dark and likewise never took his clothes off with the light on. Was he hiding something? We decided to raid Bill Hall's body.

In darkness we wait by his bed. Comes 0200 hours, Bill shuffles in, he is undressing, he is down to his shirt and socks. Before he can enter his pit, we signal the lights on, and six of us seize him, remove his remaining garments, and hold him down, naked, struggling and swearing. I hold a clipboard with an anatomical list. Bornheim goes to work with a stick. He starts at the top.

'Head, one, with stray hairs attached plus dandruff.'

'Check.'

'Ear'oles and wax, two.'

'Check.'

'Neck, scrawny with Adam's apple, one.'

'Check.'

'Chest, sunken with stray hairs, one.'

'Check.'

'You bastards,' he is yelling and struggling.

'Legs, thin with lumps on knees, two.'

'Check.'

Bornheim elevates Hall's scrotum on the stick. 'Cobblers, red with purple tinges, two.'

'Check.'

'Chopper with foreskin attached, one.'

'Check.'

We released him and he chased us, hurling his and other people's boots. A drunken Secombe enters, sees the naked wraith, embraces him. 'My, you're looking lovely in the moonlight, Amanda.' Amanda says Piss Off. Hall has to fight off the insane raspberrying Welshman. If only his Queen could have seen him that night.

As to Trooper Johnny Mulgrew of Glasgow, he had a wicked sense of humour; his idea of a joke was a huge beaming woman in a wheelchair being pushed through Hyde Park by a dying cripple. Always good for a laugh.

'OVER THE PAGE'

This was the show that launched the Bill Hall Trio. It was the brainchild of Captain Hector Ross, whose play *Men in Shadow* I had destroyed at Maddaloni. It was sheer luck: one of the acts for *Over the Page* had withdrawn at the last moment, a sort of theatrical Coitus Interruptus. Could the Trio fill in? Yes. I knew that just playing jazz never was a winner, so I persuaded the wardrobe to give us the worst ragged costumes we could find. I worked out some patter and introductions.

I never dreamed we would be anything more than just 'another act'. The set for *Over the Page* was a huge book.

The artistes were a mixture of Italian professionals and soldier amateurs. Monday December 6th 1945 the show opened at the Bellini Theatre to a packed house.

We were one incredible hit. When we came off, we were stunned. I couldn't believe that of all that talent out there, we had topped the lot. After the show, a Lieutenant Reg O'List of CPA came backstage. He had been a singer at the Windmill in London, which was rather like being a blood donor in a mortuary. He thinks we're great. Can he take us to dinner? God, we were in the big time already. Off the Via Roma is a wonderful pasta restaurant, we'll love it. Great! Lieutenant O'List does it in style, we go in a horse-drawn carriage. Bill Hall plays his violin as we drift down the Via Roma. Wow! Life is good. The restaurant is all one can dream of: the waiters wear white aprons, the tables have red and white check cloths, there's an oil lamp on every table, a mandolin band playing. As soon as we enter the waiters sweep us up in a cushion of hospitality. 'Si, accomodo, accomodo,' a bottle of wine with the manager's compliments, thank you very much with our compliments. Giddy with success and a free dinner, we eat a mountain of spaghetti. Reg O'List can't stop telling us how good we are and we can't stop agreeing with him. He can't believe we are just the result of a chance meeting in a barrack room. Can we play some jazz after dinner? Yes. 'Hey! I know! why don't we put on a show?' etc! The customers stop eating, they cheer and clap, encore, encore. Free wine is slopping out of us. Enough is enough. Reg O'List is now very pissed; he will do *his* Windmill Act; he starts to sing 'Begin the Beguine'; he has a powerful shivery square voice.

'If he's from the Windmill,' says Gunner Hall, 'why doesn't he take his clothes off?' The night ends with Bill Hall splitting away from us – the last sight we had of him was on a tram playing opera to adoring passengers. What a night. It would lead us slowly down the road to oblivion.

The Mirror Running: 1987

Memory of N. Africa 1943

Gone away is the morning,
　　its teasing light,
The lit of the fire,
　　the burn of its bright,
The chill of the dawning,
　　the pass of the night,
The seeing of bombers
　　passing from sight,
The stirring of gun teams
　　standing down, last stag,
The rummaging down
　　in your old kitbag,
The first morning brew
　　in the kerosene tin,
The waft of the tea
　　as the compo goes in.
Gone away is the morning,
　　the volley of guns;
Gone away the Eyeties,
　　gone away the Huns.

Monkenhurst
June 1985

Peace Work: 1991

Germany I

The war is over, and Milligan and his colleagues in the Bill Hall Trio are working hard to launch themselves in the music business. This is one of several return visits they paid to newly liberated Europe as recorded in volume seven of the war memoirs.

Germany I

Sure enough, there is no work, we all have phoned Leslie MacDonnell. All he has for us is an Army Welfare Troop show tour. Oh Christ, back to that. I move back to Linden Gardens, same room. The Trio have to decide, a troop tour of Germany or bugger-all, we all think bugger-all a bad thing – in fact, none of us thinks much of bugger-all – so it's to be a series of one-nighters in the Fatherland.

So here we are on an RAF converted Wellington Bomber being flown to Berlin from Northolt. It's a small company: Benn Futz, a Polish juggler/acrobat; Vico Wilson, a Liverpudlian comic; Eric Prills, a pianist; Dennis Max-Holm, a comic; and Avis Trenchard, a singer. All about thirty and all about broke, but all very nice people and grateful for the work. Our tour manager is an old queen, William Hodges. 'Now,' he said, as he came along the plane bench seats, 'we're all going to get on, or maybe some of you will get off. Mind if I sit here?'

The pilot shouts, 'No smoking please, till I do!'

'Nothing makes you need a fag more,' says Mulgrew. The plane's engines drown out conversation.

Airborne, the navigator comes round with a large coffee flask with plastic cups. 'You can smoke now,' he says.

'Ta,' says Mulgrew, who already is.

'You're a naughty boy,' says the navigator.

'No sir, he's actually a naughty girl but he had the operation,' I said. Navigator laughs, spills coffee on Mulgrew. 'So sorry.'

After a deafening flight we land at Tempelhof – on the tarmac, all awaiting an AWS coach on to which a Sergeant directs us. Berlin looks grey, the centre is war-torn, great chunks out of the Brandenburg Gate – we are driven to the Schoenbraun Hotel – or rather Hostel. Endless traffic of civilians and soldiers, each one seems due for an important critical meeting at which they will be killed.

A jolly officer of forty summers meets us. He is the living image of Neville Chamberlain, an artillery major, Tom Wells. 'Well, you're all very welcome – you'll all have separate rooms, but I'm afraid the bathrooms are communal. This is Corporal Harris, if you'll follow him.'

'Ba – ba – ba,' I go as we climb the stairs.

'I'm sorry the lift's not working – it was damaged in the war – RAF bombing.'

'You mean that lift was put out of order by us and that's why we're forced to use the stairs?'

The Corporal laughed. 'You can put it that way.'

I can and I have – fancy the RAF targeting lifts. All our rooms are nice, clean, stark, but for the bed there is no furniture, a wall cupboard and a sink.

Hall comes in. 'Handy, the sink, I've just done me socks.' He, this Wretch, seemed in a constant battle with his socks and underwear, night after night he'd wash one or the other – there are times when he only washed one sock, yes, *one sock*, and when asked why, he'd say almost with dignity, 'The other one doesn't need doing.'

We are gathered again by a Corporal, Collins by name, and taken to lunch in a private room. We are waited on by ex-POWs in white jackets and very good they are.

'I don't know,' I said to Hall, 'I think I shot his uncle, and by the way he served food, I wish I had.' I discovered my Kraut was at Cassino – so was I! We involuntarily shake hands, he speaks a smattering of Italian so the conversation is:

'*Me combattere in Cassino. Seben maise. Cassino molto nix good – boom – boom.*'

'*Ich Royal Artillery – grossen Kanonen.*'

'*Grossen nix gut.*'

I say, '*Grossen Kanon molto bono per you.*'

'*Me ich beinen paratruppen.*'

So he was one of the bastards that held us up for sixteen months. '*Me*,' he went on, '*combattere in Castelforte*.'

Castleforte –? My God, we must have killed dozens of his uncles. My heavy battery rained shells on that village for two days. '*Mein Kanon, boom, boom, Castelforte zwei tag –!*'

'*Oh, molto morto, mi amico*.'

'*Mi dispiace – ma c'est la guerre!*'

'What you want ter talk ter these bastards for?' said Hall. 'Two years ago the bastard would have killed you.'

Agreed, but now he's serving me at table and I got him running around me, getting me seconds, he never dreamed from his little funk-hole in Cassino, that one day he'd be serving me apple pie mit der kustard! Anyway, despite trying to kill me in Italy, he wants to know if he can take us to the nightspots. Well, for my nightspots I use Germolene, but we'll see. His name is Ernst Bohem, he 'knows' places.

The evening we are driven to do a concert in a drill hall for REME, there's no stage – we perform at floor level, only the front row see, except for the acrobats. It's a full-blooded soldier reaction – with cries of 'get your knickers down, darlin'' for our singer Miss Trenchard. She came off to cheers in tears. 'I've never been so humiliated in my life. I want to go home.'

Now for the nightlife of Berlin, city of sausage, sin and Sally Bowles. So Ernst takes me to the Blaue Himmel, a cellar, but what a cellar, just table, chairs and a stage, the demimonde are here, men done up as women, women done up as men, waitresses in short skirts with no knickers. We were the only normal ones there.

'*Vobisdu*,' says a ravishing waitress, white-faced, kohl eyes, red lips and bare bum.

A pot of tea for two please.

Tea nix!

'Okay. A bottle of Moselle.'

'Ja, darlink, une Moselle –'

'You like,' said Ernst.

'*Molto bono, ja!*'

'*Ja,*' he said, frothing at the mouth. He leered at everything that went past, there's a drag queen on the stage with a ridiculous act, with a whip, some soppy 'aporth from the audience is standing on stage while she sings, '*Ich slagger barnhoff*' and cuts the buttons off the silly bugger till his clothes fall off – the audience are at that drunken animal stage when anything is suggestive – uproarious laughter for things totally unfunny, every joke was below the waist. 'Oh, *wunderbar,*' says the paratrooper from Cassino. Mind you, it's all a wondrous experience – I mean – Hitler didn't need to shoot himself to avoid the Russians. Believe me, if Hitler had seen this mess he would have committed suicide long before.

Now the main act, a busty, frowsy, over-made-up tart prances on and does a dance, she strips off then a man with white make-up and a long black mac does a sort of dance to piano and violin accompaniment, then whoosh – off flies the black mac with a dramatic chord from the piano. I cried with laughter – then to the signature tune of Laurel and Hardy, he screws, complete with cymbal smashes. All through there are cries of encouragement in German. There were cries of encore, even Heil Hitler, so the male participant tried again, also with the ridiculous Laurel and Hardy tune – not before he took a sip of water from a glass set on a table.

'A lot of fucking good that will do him,' said Wretch Hall. 'What he needs is Guinness and oysters.'

I was by now unfit to talk, I thought it all too funny for words, then no, no, no! As the bloke starts to screw her again – there is an introduction on the piano and she starts to sing, 'Wien Rose', her voice shuddering on each thrust.

'No wonder they lost the war,' said Hall. 'They was all fucked.'

Well, we saw the night out – there were more songs by homos and lesbians made up in fantastic make-up – forget Liza Minnelli in *Cabaret*.

We took a taxi back to the digs and an old German porter let us in with enough grovelling to demand a tip. '*Danke schön! Mein Herren – Ich nix Nazi – Ich bin ein Democrat.*'

'Lying bastard,' said Bill, 'they were all fucking Nazis otherwise they couldn't have kept going so long.'

We walk up the stairs – 'Bloody RAF,' said Mulgrew – so a night's sleep. The noticeboard on our door – Breakfast from 7.30–9.00. So at five to nine we'll be there'

Five to nine queue for breakfast, yes Hall slept well and his socks were dry by the morning. Major Wells moves among us, 'Jolly good show last night, well "we" catch a plane to Hanover this afternoon, do a show at the Opera House and fly back.'

'Not much time to see much,' said Hall.

Well, I told him there wasn't much to see, it's like the Russians left it.

'I'd like to see Hitler's Bunker,' said Mulgrew.

'She's dead,' I said. 'Anyway, it's in the Russian zone so forget it.' It was unbelievable that a man would let a city be razed before shooting himself – had he shot himself a month earlier we'd possibly be staying at a hotel. Oh here we go.

'All on the coach, please answer your names,' says a nameless Sergeant.

Next, the Dakota with bucket seats. 'Seatbelts,' shouts the pilot and we are away over the ruined city, somewhere below us is the male water-supping actor, resting.

Miss Avis Trenchard has not left us, she quite properly dried her tears and said, 'I'm not gwoing to be put orf by some wude soldiers.' She is a darling nineteen-year-old girl, opera-trained, 'dwaddy' is in the Foreign Office, the girl is innocence itself and seems to 'twust' me. 'You'll look after me, won't you, Spywke?' Of course, of course, I'll look after her and fuck her, of course. Our Polish juggler, Benn Futz, is air sick. William Hodges has given him a nylon sock as a sick bag. I watch hypnotically as the sock becomes the shape of a foot. Looking out the window, I am almost stunned at the bomb-damaged landscape. How did they hold out so long, where did they go? There wasn't a building standing.

'Where did they make the Tiger Tanks, there's not a factory in sight,' said smoke-shrouded Mulgrew.

'I've got it,' I said, 'they made them in inch squares and posted them to the front.'

'Fuckin' rubbish,' says Hall.

'Shh Bill,' I whisper, 'not in front of Miss Trenchard.'

'I don't understand,' says Wretch Hall. 'You can say kill out loud but not fuck. I mean, she'd rather be fucked than killed wouldn't she?'

Above the drone of the engines I don't think Miss Trenchard can hear us.

'Seatbelts,' shouts the pilot, 'and fags out.'

We come down slowly.

'Oh, we're not going to cwash are we, Spywke?' Miss Trenchard clutches my arm.

'No, we're as safe as houses.' Looking at the bombing below, there wasn't a house in sight. I told her flying wasn't dangerous, *crashing* was dangerous. A very smooth landing, we all applaud.

'Thanks,' says the pilot, 'but I'm taking you back, by which time – ha, ha, ha,' he twirled his whacko moustache, 'I'll have had a few.'

Someone is saying, 'Anyone want to buy one nylon sock.'

Off the plane, no coach but an army three-tonner is waiting. 'It's getting rougher all the time,' I say as Schnozzle Durante, 'if tings get woise – I'm complainin' to Winston K. Churchill, ha, ha, ha.'

'I give up,' says Mulgrew. 'Let me guess . . . W. C. Fields.'

'You don't know a good impressionist when you see one.'

Mulgrew giggles, 'Er – the Ritz Brothers?'

A new Sergeant appears. 'I'm Sergeant Watson. I'll be looking after you, if you just answer your names,' he smiles. 'Sorry about this.'

As we answer our names we clamber on the three-tonner, helping hands pull Miss Trenchard aboard. She lets out a little squeal of delight or was that me pushing her bottom. Sergeant Watson bolts up the tail board, across the tarmac.

'Hanover is the seat of the Hanoverian kings,' I tell Miss Trenchard.

'Oh weally – I believe we're appwearing in the Opwa House.'

And what a magnificent one, pure Baroque, the interior's like a palace.

'Now if you'd all like to leave your props in your dressing rooms, just choose one,' and laughed. 'There's forty to choose from.'

'I'll take five,' I said, slouching off like Groucho Marx.

'You see my dressing room,' says Hall, who's chosen No. 1. 'Come and 'ave a look.'

Well folks, the room was like a miniature ballroom – so on the polished marble surface Hall deposits his carrier bag of props and 'Is that all?' giggles Hodges, our 'queen'.

'There's one still in the laundry,' says Hall.

'Come on, they're waiting to take us to . . .' Hodges paused, struck a gay pose, 'The Hotel,' he mouthed. 'Hotel Grand Holstein.'

Another Baroque but worn-down building equally lavish in rooms, Mulgrew and I share. I avoid billeting with Wretch Hall, as I'm convinced every night after sock washing he becomes a werewolf. Ah! but we don't eat here – we go to the sergeants' mess for lunch. Oh, now a coach mit zer German driver.

'I'll be leaving you here,' says Sergeant Watson and Adolf here will take over. Adolf is a compressed midget all of five feet five inches. He sits on a high cushion to drive and disappears behind the dashboard when he declutches; as he disappears we all shout, '*Auf Wiedersehen*, Adolf'. He keeps grim-faced and pours with sweat. No. 34 REME Workshops – a sentry halts and checks Adolf's documents; we give the sentry a cheer as we go in.

Yet another i/c party, 'Corporal Allan, follow me, folks.'

I ask Mulgrew, 'Did you know you were a folk?'

'Aw, awa boil yer heed,' he grinned.

'Where's the ladies?' Miss Trenchard is nigh to.

Corporal Allen takes her to ATS toilets. She comes out blushing. Soon we are ushered into a dining room where lunch is being served to eight tables of NCOs. 'You have to help yourself here,' said Corporal Allan. So trays, knives, forks, spoon, cup, steak and kidney, apple pie etc.

'You see,' said Hall the Wretch, 'they'll be askin' us to fuckin' sign on again.'

Mulgrew tells him as things are back home it might not be a bad thing. While we're seated another jolly decent officer appears. They're all between forty and sixty; you can't but feel they haven't been in action, haven't heard a gun go bang, and possibly caught it once.

Fleas, Knees & Hidden Elephants: 1995

The Leg

The other day I gave a cough
There and then my leg fell off
A policeman gave it a stamp
And said 'You cannot leave it there'
I took it to a doctor who said
I'm sorry but this leg is dead
I was shocked into grieving
Then I heard the leg still breathing!
When I knew it wasn't dead
I rushed it to a hospital bed
It was stitched back on by Doctor Hay
But facing alas, the other way
Now when I walk I have found
I only go around and around.

6

Acting Up

The Goon Show, 1956

Series 6, programme 25: Fear of Wages. Broadcast 6 March, 1956

'Fear of Wages', which Milligan's agent Norma Farnes says was his favourite *Goon Show*, was written with long-term collaborator Larry Stephens. *The Wages of Fear*, the classic 1953 film starring Yves Montand parodied here, was directed by Henri-Georges Clouzot. Any subsequent connection with the famous Inspector Clouseau was, of course, entirely accidental.

<u>'THE GOON SHOW' No. 150</u>

(6th series)

<u>NO. 25, 'FEAR OF WAGES'</u>

with

PETER SELLERS

HARRY SECOMBE

SPIKE MILLIGAN

THE RAY ELLINGTON QUARTET

MAX GELDRAY

ORCHESTRA CONDUCTED By WALLY STOTT

ANNOUNCER: WALLACE GREENSLADE

SCRIPT BY SPIKE MILLIGAN

<u>PRODUCED BY PAT DIXON</u>

BILL: This is the BBC Home Service. Enter a short idiot.

HARRY: Good evening folks. I commence by walking backwards for Christmas.

BILL: Why?

HARRY: It's all the rage. Next – an excerpt from East Lynne – Dead – Dead – and never called me mother.

ECCLES: Perhaps you were his father.

HARRY: Shut up the famous Eccles.

ECCLES: Shut up the famous Eccles.

HARRY: Shut up.

ECCLES: Shut up.

BILL: Mr. Seagoon – please remove that false bald woman's wig.

HARRY: And leave myself naked in the mating season?
Never.

BILL: Very well. I sentence you to the highly esteemed Goon
Show.

ORCHESTRA: <u>SHORT DULL CHORD</u>.

HARRY: Presenting – Wallace Greenslade in his daring announcement, entitled –

BILL: La Salaire de la Peur.

HARRY: Meaning The Wages of Fear – er, in England.

PETER: (WOLFIT) The Fear of Wages. Oooooohhhhhh.

ORCHESTRA: <u>NIGHT ON BARE MOUNTAIN TYPE LINK</u>.

BILL: (HEROIC) Part one – The Missing Regiment.

GRAMS: <u>JUNGLE WARFARE – SNIPING SPORADIC M.G. FIRE</u>.

PETER: (BARTON) Burma – 6th March, 1956.

HARRY: These Japs can't hold out much longer.

BLOODNOK: Oh, I don't know. This is the fourteenth year we've
been fighting 'em.

HARRY: Don't worry Major – they can't stand much more of
your drunken singing and bottle throwing.

BLOODNOK: (DIGNITY) I'm only doing my duty sir. And they'd
better surrender soon. We've had no food or pay since that
silly telegram.

HARRY: Telegram? You never – give it here. (READS) Er –
British Forces, Burma. Japan has surrendered. End of World
War Two. Book now for World War Three. Signed – Jim Mount-
batten. Dated – August 1945??

BLOODNOK: Yes – I've never shown it to you before because it's
obviously the work of a practical joker.

HARRY: Well – I hope . . .

ABDUL: Sahib – Sahib – there's a Japanese officer attacking us
with a white flag.

HARRY: Gad – and it's the new Mark <u>III</u> Armour Piercing type
white flag.

THROAT: Cor blimey – I'm orf.

BLOODNOK: Don't panic – I'll show that Jap a thing or two. Help me off with my jodhpurs.

HARRY: No Major – please.

BLOODNOK: Out of my way, Plunger. (SHOUTS) There, you Jap devil – look.

HARRY: Dear listeners – from the waist downwards Bloodnok was tattooed with a pair of false legs – facing the other way.

BLOODNOK: Yes – they're all the rage.

YAKKA: Please, do not shoot.

HARRY: (CALLING) Who are you, you yellow swine?

BLOODNOK: (SURPRISE) You remember me – Dennis Bloodnok. I was at . . .

HARRY: Not you. (CALLS) Come forward military Japanese gentleman – but keep your right leg raised.

YAKKA: Please – I am General Yakkamoto – commander of all Imperial Japanese troops in that tree.

HARRY: Well – yellow devil?

YAKKA: Request – have unexpectedly run short of ammunition. Please could we borrow two boxes until end of war?

BLOODNOK: You Japs are always on the tap – you haven't returned our lawnmower yet.

YAKKA: Very sorry. Have not finished mowing jungle.

BLOODNOK: No – no more credit. Clear off.

YAKKA: Then am forced to surrender, have no alternative. To whom do we surrender Japanese military stores?

BLOODNOK: Stooooooores. You've got stores?

YAKKA: Yes – one thousand cans nitro-glycerine.

BLOODNOK: (DEJECTED) Oohh . . .

YAKKA: And two thousand cans of sake. (ASIDE) Sake being potent Japanese rice wine.

BLOODNOK: (MAD) Sake being potent Japanese rice wine? Oooooohhh – I am forced – forced to accept your two-thousand-cans-of-sake-surrender. Stack it under my bed.

YAKKA: Which are your tent, please?

BLOODNOK: That white one with the red cross on it and the three dummy nurses outside. (PAUSE) Well? Go on – don't say you don't trust me.

YAKKA: I don't trust you.

BLOODNOK: Swine – I told you <u>not</u> to say it. Hand me my Royal Engineers saxophone. Now, you Jap devil – quick – march.

PORGY: <u>SAX. PLAYS MARCH TUNE. FADING OFF</u>.

YAKKA: (<u>GOING OFF. GABBLE</u>)

F.X.: <u>MARCHING</u>.

HARRY: Gad – what a day this has been. A triumph for British arms. Now I must inform the War Office that after fourteen years of fighting, the Japanese Army in that tree has finally surrendered.

F.X.: <u>PENNY IN PHONE COIN BOX</u>.

ORCHESTRA: <u>PPP – UNDER – LAND OF HOPE AND GLORY MELODY PLAYED ON CLARINET – LOW REGISTER</u>.

F.X.: <u>TWO MORE PENNIES IN BOX – THEN DIALLING</u>.

HARRY: (TALKS FROM FALL OF FIRST PENNY) Dial on, brave telephone – send those triumphant electric type impulses athwart the sleeping con-ti-nents to the automatic-type exchange in London – and list . . .

F.X.: <u>BURR BURR OF PHONE AT OTHER END</u>.

HARRY: Even now sounds the tintinnabulation of the phone bell that will arouse the Helmsman of England to whom I carry the victorious news.

F.X.: <u>EVERYTHING STOPS DEAD</u>.

WILLIUM: (<u>DISTORT</u>) Battersea Dogs Home, mate.

HARRY: What? You don't sound like a dog. What breed are you?

BILL: The Fear of Wages, part two. The same day, four hours later.

ORCHESTRA: <u>THREE OR FOUR SINISTER DESCENDING CHORDS</u>.

F.X.: <u>HALF CROWNS BEING COUNTED INTO A HEAP</u>.

MORIARTY: (<u>MUTTERING</u>) Ooohohohhh – money money – lovely money. It's all the rage.

THYNNE: Sssh Moriarty – pull that transparent blind down, you fool. Now – have you sewn that ten thousand pounds into the lining of your socks?

MORIARTY: Yes.

THYNNE: Right. Then help me get this hundred pounds in fivers under my wig – (EFFORT)

MORIARTY: Down on your right – back – waah.

THYNNE: Good man. Any more left?

MORIARTY: Only this fifty thousand pounds in loose silver.

THYNNE: Right – say aah.

MORIARTY: Aaaah.

F.X.: LARGE SHOVELFULS OF SILVER BEING SHOVELLED INTO MORIARTY'S MOUTH.

THYNNE: Now Moriarty, keep your mouth shut. I don't . . .

F.X.: SHORT SHARP PHONE RING. INSTANTLY RECEIVER OFF.

THYNNE: Army Pay Corps here. Chief Cashier speaking – what?

F.X.: PHONE SLAMMED DOWN IMMEDIATELY.

THYNNE: Moriarty?

MORIARTY: (MUFFLED) Yees . . .

F.X.: MONEY FALLS AND CRASHES ALL OVER FLOOR.

MORIARTY: Oueeeeeooooh – I'm sorry I . . .

THYNNE: Never mind about that. Moriarty – we're in the grit cart. Remember the Third Armoured Thunderboxes who vanished in Burma ten years ago?

MORIARTY: Yes.

THYNNE: Well – they're still alive. That was their commander – Seagoon.

MORIARTY: Oooooooohhhhh – type oh. But we've spent all their back pay. Forty thousand pounds. Ooohh sapristi court martial. Cashiered. Shot at dawn. Take aim – fire – bang.

THYNNE: Don't panic, malodorous Gallic Charlie – we'll have to think of something. Meanwhile – Max Geldray and his chromatic plinge.

<u>MAX & ORCHESTRA</u>

(APPLAUSE)

ORCHESTRA: <u>THREE DRAMATIC CHORDS.</u>

GRAMS: <u>JUNGLE BACKGROUND AT NIGHT – CRICKETS,</u>
<u>LIZARDS & TUCKTOOS.</u>

BILL: Night in the jungle encampment of the Fourth Armoured
Thunderboxes.

F.X.: <u>SCRATCHING OF PEN ON PAPER.</u>

BLOODNOK: Dear sirs – I am a keen Art Student over the age of
twenty-one. Please forward me your selection of Continental
Art Studies in the plain wrappers – care of CM – Stroke . . .

HARRY: (<u>SHOUTS</u>) Major Bloodnok.

BLOODNOK: Ooohh – don't come in yet. Abdul – quick – put the
screens round my bed. Come in, Seagoon.

HARRY: Thank you. Major – I was just walking backwards for
Christmas and – Oh. Ahem. I beg your pardon, madam.

BLOODNOK: Get back behind that screen, Gladys. Jeldi, tum
maila bibbi – my wife, you know. But it's all lies – we're just
good friends.

HARRY: Major – grave type news. I've spoken to Whitehall – and
the Pay Corps deny that we're alive.

BLOODNOK: What – I've never had a day's death in my life. And
what about our ten years' back pay? Did you tell them we've
been fighting all this time?

HARRY: I did – but they said these Japs we captured must be
forgeries.

BLOODNOK: You mean – they're worthless?

HARRY: They said no bank would cash them.

BLOODNOK: Then there's only one way to get our back pay. We
must return to England with the entire Japanese Army in
that tree there.

HARRY: Gad yes.

SPIKE: Yes, sorr – what is it, sorrh?

HARRY: Uproot that tree and replant it in the back of a lorry.
  And try not to shake any Japs down.

SPIKE: Will ye be takin' all dat Japanese liquor wid yez?

BLOODNOK: The sake – of course. And don't forget the screens
  round my bed. It's all the rage.

HARRY: You know – I think we'd better leave all that nitro-
  glycerine behind Bloodnok.

F.X.: INSTANTLY SHORT SHARP PHONE RING – RECEIVER OFF
  HOOK.

HARRY: Yes?

THYNNE: (DISTORT) You can't leave all that nitro-glycerine
  behind, Seagoon.

HARRY: I wasn't going – (DRY) I was going to leave it behind
  Bloodnok.

THYNNE: No ad libbing, Neddie. Now listen Nurk – (ASIDE)
  and this, dear listeners, is where we sow the seeds of
  Neddie's demise. (ALOUD) Ahem – Neddie – stand at-t-t-t –
  ease.

F.X.: TEN THOUSAND MEN IN HOBNAILED BOOTS STANDING AT
  EASE ON CONCRETE.

THYNNE: Now Neddie – there's no question of you leaving that
  naughty unexploded nitro-glycerine behind. If you want your
  back pay – all Japanese stores must be surrendered to the
  War Office.

HARRY: But it's so dangerous – nitro-glycerine? In a lorry.

THYNNE: Yes. (GLOATING LAUGH)

ORCHESTRA: THREE OR FOUR DRAMATIC ASCENDING CHORDS –
  TERROR TENSION.

GRAMS: LORRIES WARMING UP – REVVING ETC. OCCASIONAL
  SHOUTS OF I/C CONVOY.

BILL: Dawn – and the Fourth Armoured Thunderboxes prepare
  for the long journey home – Before departure – the surrender
  document is signed.

ORCHESTRA: RATAPLAN DRUMS.

BLOODNOK: Now General Yakkamoto – sign here. We'll fill in the amount later.

F.X.: <u>SIGNING</u>.

HARRY: I watched enthralled as slowly we hauled down the Imperial Japanese credit note and ran up the victorious British bouncing cheque.

YAKKA: There – hon. signature on surrender document.

HARRY: Signed with a cross, eh? You illiterate swine. Pass me the ink pad – uggg – There, there's my thumb print. Now we've <u>both</u> signed mate. Now – get back in your tree.

BLOODNOK: Hurry up, Seagoon. We're ready to leave.

HARRY: Are the lorries warmed up?

BLOODNOK: Yes – had 'em in the oven all night. How do you like yours?

HARRY: Medium rare.

BLOODNOK: Splendid, then you'd better drive the medium rare lorry carrying the nitro.

HARRY: (<u>GULP</u>) I'd – er – I'd rather drive the lorry with the sake.

BLOODNOK: But you're a teetotaller. No, I insist on driving the lorry with the sake.

HARRY: Why?

BLOODNOK: It's a long long story. You see, there's a little yellow idol to the North of Kat . . .

HARRY: Yes, yes, I know – but I refuse to drive the nitro lorry.

BLOODNOK: Why not?

HARRY: It's a long story. You see – there's a little yellow idol to the North of Kat . . .

BLOODNOK: Shut up, Seagoon, and there's a record of me saying it.

<u>GRAMS</u>: (<u>PRE-RECORDED</u>)

    BLOODNOK: (<u>SHOUTS</u>) <u>Shut up Seagoon</u>.

    ECCLES: <u>Shut up Seagoon</u>.

    BLOODNOK: <u>Shut up the famous Eccles</u>.

ECCLES: <u>Shut up the famous Eccles</u>.

BLOODNOK: <u>Shut up</u>.

ECCLES: <u>Shut up</u>.

BLOODNOK: <u>Get off this record at once</u>.

F.X.: <u>FOOTSTEPS RUN SIX PACES</u>.

ECCLES: <u>Hupppp</u>. (<u>END OF PRE-RECORDED</u>)

F.X.: <u>THUD OF HITTING GROUND</u>.

ECCLES: Oooooo Hellooooo.

HARRY: Private Eccles. Just the man – see that lorry that everybody's keeping clear of?

ECCLES: Yer yer yer yer yer?

HARRY: Good good good good good. Well, drive it back to London –
gently.

ECCLES: O.K. – goodbye.

GRAMS: <u>LORRY DRIVES RAPIDLY INTO THE DISTANCE. IT
EXPLODES (SERIES OF EXPLOSIONS)</u>.

ECCLES: A good job I wasn't on it.

HARRY: What? Then who was driving it?

B'BOTTLE: (<u>OFF</u>) You rotten swines, you. (<u>COMES ON</u>) I was kip-
ping in the back of that lorry like a happy boy traveller –
when blangeeee. I was blown backwards out of my boots.

HARRY: Little blackened goon – what were you doing in that
lorry?

B'BOTTLE: Well it's a long story – you see, my capatain –
there's a little cardboard idol to the North of East Finchley –
and the smoke . . .

HARRY: Shhh – here's Ray Ellington.

B'BOTTLE: Oh – smashin'.

QUARTET: <u>'PINK CHAMPAGNE'</u>

(APPLAUSE)

BILL: That was Ray Ellington, the demon plasterer – but then
you will have guessed. And now – the Fear of Wages – part the
Scran. Five weeks of travel saw the lorries well on their way.

F.X.: <u>LORRY</u>.

BLOODNOK: (<u>GULPS</u>)

HARRY: Bloodnok – you must stop drinking that sake. Without it – no back pay.

BLOODNOK: Ohhh – just this one. It's thirsty work, this drinking. (<u>GUZZLES</u>)

YAKKA: (<u>ASIDE</u>) Little do English fool know that it is not sake he drink – but nitro-glycerine – that I substitute. (<u>SMALL LAUGH</u>)

BLOODNOK: Keep quiet up that tree.

YAKKA: Sorry – was just giving listeners story of plot.

BILL: Meanwhile in England at No. 10, Frith Street . . .

ECHO: (<u>MURMURS OF 'RHUBARB'</u>)

MORIARTY: (<u>OVER. ASIDE</u>) You say the nitro exploded when they weren't in the lorry?

THYNNE: Yes, Fred – our little plan went for a burton – that's why I've arranged this meeting.

SPRIGGS: Are you positive that this missing regiment has reappeared and is even now on its way back to England?

THYNNE: Yes, Mr. Chancellor of the Exchequer – and according to our records, their combined back pay and accrued interest amounts to thirty-three million pounds.

SPRIGGS: This will ruin my budget.

W.C.: You've already ruined it yourself.

SPRIGGS: That regiment must be stopped before it reaches England.

THYNNE: Yes – we'll declare war on them.

SPRIGGS: What? England can't declare war on English troops.

THYNNE: Why not – everyone else does.

SPRIGGS: No – we must get a foreign power to do it.

THYNNE: Choose one.

SPRIGGS: Well Japan isn't doing anything at the moment.

THYNNE: I'll inform Tokyo at once. (<u>RAISES VOICE SLIGHTLY</u>) Hello, Tokyo?

HARRY: (SLIGHTLY OFF. JAP) Yakkabakka needle nardle noo.

THYNNE: Declare war on the Fourth Armoured Thunderboxes now in Burma.

HARRY: I do at once. Hello, commander of Imperial Japanese Forces in that tree on back of lorry in Burma.

YAKKA: (SLIGHTLY OFF) Yes?

HARRY: Declare war on Fourth Armoured Thunderboxes.

YAKKA: Velly good. Fire.

GRAMS: RIFLE AND M.G. FIRE AS BEFORE.

HARRY: (ON) Bloodnok – stop the lorry. Those Japs are firing at us.

BLOODNOK: The treacherous devils. Help me off with my jodhpurs.

HARRY: No Major – not again. They know that tattooed leg trick now.

GRAMS: FIRING STOPS.

BLOODNOK: But it's done the trick. They've stopped firing.

YAKKA: Yes – have run out of ammunition.

BLOODNOK: Well – no dice here. You've had enough on tick already.

YAKKA: How much we owe?

BLOODNOK: Seagoon – play him this record of his account.

HARRY: Right, sir.

GRAMS: FEW BARS JAPANESE STRINGED INSTRUMENT – SPEEDED UP.

HARRY: . . . . and sixpence ha'penny.

YAKKA: Ah, please – I promise I pay you back at rate of . . .

GRAMS: BRIEF EXCERPT FROM ABOVE.

YAKKA: . . . a week.

BLOODNOK: Seagoon? How much is –

GRAMS: REPEAT BRIEF EXCERPT.

BLOODNOK: . . . in English money?

HARRY: It's about . . .

GRAMS: BARREL ORGAN – 4 BARS 'OVER THE WAVES'.

HARRY: . . . sir.

BLOODNOK: It's not enough. Here – hold my trousers. I'll soon get 'em out of their tree.

F.X.: SAWING WOOD (LARGE SONG SAW).

GRAMS: (OVER) BURST OF MACHINE GUN FIRE.

BLOODNOK: Ohhh, the treacherous devils – they must have had a parcel from home.

HARRY: Quick – into the driving cab. It's bullet-proof.

BLOODNOK: Splendid. We can drive on and continue engaging the enemy in that tree in the back of the lorry all at the same time.

HARRY: A magnificent exposition of the plot Bloodnok – and under enemy fire too. Have a knighthood.

BLOODNOK: Oh, ta mate.

HARRY: Right then. Drive on Sir Dennis.

BLOODNOK: Beep beep.

GRAMS: (PRE-RECORDING) LORRY STARTS UP AND DRIVES AWAY TAKING WITH IT JAP GABBLE, RIFLE AND M.G. FIRE AND SPORADIC SHOUTS FROM SEAGOON, BLOODNOK ETC. SPEED UP RECORD AS SOUND FADES OFF.

ORCHESTRA: FIRST PHRASE OF 'LAND OF HOPE AND GLORY' AS PER TABS MUSIC – VERY FAST ENDING ON SNAP CYMBAL.

ECHO: (MURMUR OF 'CABINET MEETING RHUBARB')

THYNNE: Thank you for your cabinet meeting rhubarbs. (GRAVE) Gentlemen – our plan to stop the Fourth Armoured Thunderboxes has failed.

SPRIGGS: What? Didn't the Japanese declare World War Three on them?

THYNNE: Yes – but Seagoon has managed to get the war on to the back of a lorry – and is driving it back here.

OMNES: (OUTBURST OF RHUBARBS OF HORROR)

THYNNE: (PACE) I must get in touch with him. Moriarty – what's the number of that lorry?

MORIARTY: GXK 639.

F.X.: DIALLING.

THYNNE: (OVER) G – X – K – 6 – 3 . . . (FADE OUT)
   FADE OUT FADE IN

GRAMS: LORRY ENGINE AND OCCASIONAL SNIPING.
   ESTABLISH – THEN.

F.X.: PHONE RINGS.

HARRY: Take the wheel Bloodnok.

F.X.: RECEIVER UP.

HARRY: Hello – World War Three speaking.

THYNNE: Where are you speaking from?

HARRY: Er – we're just drawing up outside No. 10 Frith
   Street.

F.X.: KNOCK ON DOOR.

HARRY: That's us at the door now.

THYNNE: (FAST – DISTORT) Moriarty – answer it.

F.X.: DOOR OPENS.

MORIARTY: Sapristi measurements – it's Sabrina.

HARRY: Wrong – it's me with my arms folded. Seagoon's the name.

MORIARTY: Ooooh – it can't be – you're a lying charlatan.

HARRY: Rubbish – I'm a truthful charlatan. Now – where's our
   back pay?

MORIARTY: Ooooooeeow Sapristi Aldershot Glasshouse.

THYNNE: (APPROACHING) Moriarty – stop shaving your head.
   Ahh, welcome home, Colonel Seagoon. Now before you get
   your back pay – there's the little matter of handing over the
   enemy stores.

HARRY: Of course – there's the lorry – the captured Japanese
   forces are up that tree – but the nitro-glycerine exploded.

THYNNE: And the thousand cans of sake?

HARRY: (GULP) Er – I'm afraid Bloodnok drank it.

THYNNE: Sorry Seagoon. No sake – no back pay.

HARRY: Wait. (ASIDE) Eccles – get an empty bucket. Now – grab
   his ankles –

BILL: (OVER) Listeners will recall that Bloodnok has not been drinking sake – but nitro-glycerine. Therefore . . .

GRAMS: HUGE EXPLOSION (NOT LONG) MASSES OF FALLING DEBRIS CONTINUES UNDER:–

BILL: (OVER) And so ended World War Three. Book now for World War Four.

B'BOTTLE: Mr. Greenslinge – would you mind telling the nice peopules that I have not been deaded this week.

BILL: Certainly.

B'BOTTLE: (ECHOES BILL'S SPEECH FROM HERE ON)

BILL: Ladies and gentlemen – it is both a privilege and a pleasure to announce that the lad Bluebottle was not deaded this week.

B'BOTTLE: Here – that was a good game. (OVER PLAYOUT) I like dis game.

ORCHESTRA: SIGNATURE TUNE UP AND DOWN FOR:– ('LUCKY STRIKE')

BILL: That was The Goon Show – a BBC recorded programme featuring Peter Sellers, Harry Secombe, Spike Milligan with the Ray Ellington Quartet and Max Geldray. The orchestra was conducted by Wally Stott. Script by Spike Milligan and Larry Stephens. Announcer: Wallace Greenslade. The programme was produced by Pat Dixon.

ORCHESTRA: SIGNATURE TUNE UP TO END.

(APPLAUSE)

MAX & ORCHESTRA: 'CRAZY RHYTHM' PLAYOUT.

Silly Verse for Kids: 1959

Contagion

Elephants are contagious!
Be careful how you tread.
An Elephant that's been trodden on
Should be confined to bed!

Leopards are contagious too.
Be careful tiny tots.
They don't give you a temperature
But lots and lots – of spots.

The Herring is a lucky fish,
From all disease inured.
Should he be ill when caught at sea:
Immediately – he's cured!

A Dustbin of Milligan: 1961

The Gingerbread Boy

Once upon a time there was a baker and his wife. They lived in a little mill by a stream full of fish and fat frogs. It was all very lovely, *but* the baker and his wife were very, *very* unhappy – do you know why? Well they didn't have any children.

'Oh, I *wish* I had a little boy all of my own.'

When the baker saw his wife crying, he said, 'Don't cry, wife. I will try and get us a little boy.'

So, that night, he went to the bakery and said to himself, 'If we can't have a real baby, I'll make one.' So – he got a big bag of white flour and he mixed it with water until it was a big ball of dough – it looked like a big snowball – then he took a jar of ginger and mixed it into the dough. All night he worked, and do you know what he was doing? He was making a gingerbread boy. He made the legs, then the arms, the body, and last he made the gingerbread boy's head. Do you know how he made the eyes? How would you make a gingerbread boy's eyes? Well, this is how the baker made them: he got two currants and popped them in, then he made a little heart out of peppermint and put it inside the body.

When it was all ready he put the gingerbread boy into the oven to make him nice and warm. After a little while the miller heard a tiny voice. 'Let me out, let me out. It's hot in here!' Do you know who was saying it? The gingerbread boy! Quickly, the miller took him out of the oven and he saw the gingerbread boy was alive!

'Hello, my boy,' said the miller.

'Who are *you*?' said the gingerbread boy.

'I am your daddy.' And he picked him up and kissed him.

Then little gingerbread boy said, 'What is my name?' The miller said, 'I don't know yet. I will take you home and ask your mother.'

'Oh, let's hurry,' said gingerbread boy, and off they ran to the miller's house. When his wife opened the door and she saw gingerbread boy she was so happy she clapped her hands with joy. 'At last! At last

I have a little boy all of my own. I shall call him "Gingy" because he is a ginger colour.'

Next morning they took Gingy to start school. At first Gingy was very happy in school, but then one day a naughty boy called Tommy bit Gingy on the arm. 'Oh!' said poor Gingy and Tommy said, 'You taste like a bit of gingerbread,' and he bit poor Gingy again.

The poor little gingerbread boy started to run home – oh dear – it started to rain and he started to get all soggy, and when he arrived home he was just a big ball of dough, like he first was.

When his mother saw him she started to cry and cry. 'Boo-hoo-hoo, what has happened to my poor boy.' And her tears came running down all over gingerbread boy.

'Please don't cry all over me, or I'll fall into little pieces,' said Gingy.

'Come here. I'll make you all better again,' said the baker, and he squeezed all the rain out of gingerbread boy and made him back into a proper boy again.

That night, when they tucked him into bed, gingerbread boy said, 'Mummy, why do I crumble away when it rains?' So mummy had to tell him – he was made of gingerbread, and he was not the same as other girls and boys.

That night little gingerbread boy was very sad. He didn't want to be just made of bread – he wanted to be made of skin.

'I'm going to run away.' So he put on his clothes and took three apples and two oranges in a bag and off he tramped into the forest behind the house. It was dark as black, and a big owl said, 'Where are *yoo* going tooo?'

'Please owl, I'm cold and tired and hungry. Can I shelter under your wing?'

'Oh, all right,' said the owl.

Underneath the wing it was nice and warm, and gingerbread boy went fast asleep. When he woke up it was morning and the owl said, 'I must be off now. I'm going to bed.' And away he flew to bed – because owls don't sleep at night, only in the daytime.

Now gingerbread boy was alone again and he walked through the woods till he came to the top of a hill – and there he saw a house. It was a very funny house – it didn't have any windows, only lots and lots of doors. Gingerbread boy knocked at one door, and out came a funny old man wearing a long blue shirt and no trousers.

'What do you want?' he said.

'I'm hungry,' said gingerbread boy, 'and I'm cold.'

The old man took him inside. 'I'll soon have you warm. Just get into this nice bath of hot water.'

Splash. In jumped gingerbread boy. 'Oh, this is lovely,' he said, and then a terrible bad thing happened – gingerbread boy started to come to pieces in the hot water. 'Help! Help!' he cried. 'Get me out!' But it was too late.

The funny old man rolled all the pieces into a big ball of dough and put it on the mantelpiece. Next morning the funny old man went to the market and tried to sell the big piece of gingerbread. No one would buy it, but then along came gingerbread boy's daddy, the baker.

'I need some dough,' he said, so he bought it off the old man for a penny.

Now, the baker didn't *know* it was really the gingerbread boy he had bought but, when he got back to the bakery, he saw the little peppermint heart sticking out of the lump of gingerbread.

'Hooray, I've found my gingerbread boy again!' And quickly, quickly he made the gingerbread boy all over again, just like he used to be.

'Oh, daddy, daddy,' said gingerbread boy. 'I'll never run away from home again.' And he hugged and kissed him. Just then in came mummy and guess what *she* had – *another* little gingerbread boy.

'This is your new brother,' said daddy. 'When you ran away and we couldn't find you I made *another* little gingerbread boy.'

'Oh, how lovely! Now we can play together.'

And so they did, and they all lived happy ever after.

The Little Pot-Boiler: 1965

Sailor John

Johnny was a sailor lad who sailed the salty sea.
He loved to be on board a ship and feel the wind blo' free!

But then one day a storm blew up. The waves were ten feet high!

"All hands on deck!" The cry went up. "Or we are doomed to die!"

But Johnny was a sailor brave. "Don't worry lads," cried he,

"I'll show you how to save a ship from going down at sea."

A Book of Milliganimals: 1968

Silly Old Baboon

There was a Babooon
Who, one afternoon,
Said, 'I think I will fly to the sun.'
So, with two great palms
Strapped to his arms,
He started his take-off run.

Mile after mile
He galloped in style
But never once left the ground.
'You're running too slow,'
Said a passing crow,
'Try reaching the speed of sound.'

So he put on a spurt –
By God how it hurt!
The soles of his feet caught fire.
There were great clouds of steam
As he raced through a stream
But he still didn't get any higher.

Racing on through the night,
Both his knees caught alight
And smoke billowed out from his rear.
Quick to his aid
Came a fire brigade
Who chased him for over a year.

Many moons passed by.
Did Baboon ever fly?
Did he ever get to the sun?
I've just heard today
That he's well on his way!
He'll be passing through Acton at one.

P.S. Well, what do you expect from a Baboon?

Small Dreams of a Scorpion: 1972

Plastic Woman

What are you saying
Supermarket shopping lady
In the scarlet telephone box.
Lady with a shopping bag
Full of labelled pollution with secret codes
What are you saying?
Is this your dream booth?
Are you telling some plastic operator
You are Princess Grace
And can he put you through
to Buckingham Palace?
Two decimal pence
Is very little to pay for a dream in
    Catford.
If only the label on the door didn't say
'Out of Order'.
Shouldn't it be on you?

1972

Pakistani Daleks

CAPTION: THE ORDINARY WORKING CLASS HOME OF A MIXED
PAKISTANI–CHRISTIAN MARRIAGE. IT IS FRIDAY. WIFE IS LAYING
THE TABLE. SHE'S ABOUT 40-ISH. MIXED ALONG THE HOUSE ARE
TOUCHES OF ISLAMIC INFLUENCES. A BRASS GOD ON THE
MANTELPIECE. A PARROT IN CAGE ON STAND. A STUFFED DOG BY
FIREPLACE. A GRANNY IS DOZING BY THE FIRE. THE WIFE HUMS A
TUNE. THE DOOR TO THE ROOM EXPLODES, AND THROUGH IT
COMES A DALEK WITH TURBAN ON AND A FOLDED UMBRELLA
HANGING FROM HIS SIDE. WOMAN DOESN'T TURN ROUND.

DALEK (Pakistani accent) Hel-oh, Dar-ling, I-am-back.

WOMAN You are late tonight.

DALEK The tubes were full of comm-u-ters.

WOMAN How did you get on then?

DALEK I ext-er-min-ated them.

WOMAN Oh, no wonder you're tired.

DALEK Yes, ex-ter-min-ating is hard work.

WOMAN Never mind, I've got a nice cup of curried tea for you.
How's Mr Banerjee?

DALEK Not ver-y well.

WOMAN Why?

DALEK I ex-ter-min-ated him too.

DOG IN THE GRATE BARKS 'WOOF, WOOF, WOOF'. DALEK POINTS
EXTERMINATOR AT HIM. SHOOTS. DOG EXPLODES.

DALEK Put him in the Cur-ry.

SECOND DOOR TO ROOM EXPLODES, A TWO-THIRD SIZE DALEK WITH
SCHOOL CAP ON COMES IN. IT AIMS AT A VASE ON MANTELPIECE.
IT EXPLODES.

WOMAN Johnny, have you finished your homework?
BOY DALEK Yes. I de-str-o-yed it.

HE POINTS EXTERMINATOR AT SLEEPING GRANNY.

WOMAN You've exterminated granny!
DALEK Put her in the Cur-ry.
PARROT Hello, sailor . . . Hello . . .

SHOOTS PARROT IN CAGE.

DALEK Put him in the Cur-ry.
WOMAN (to camera) Now you know what's wrong with this
country.

ANOTHER EXPLOSION AS TV SET OR SOME OBJECT BEHIND HER
EXPLODES. AS WE FADE OUT THE TWO DALEKS DESTROY VARIOUS
OBJECTS: CLOCK ON MANTELPIECE, VASES, LAMPSTAND.

Harry Secombe Liquefied

<u>A MAGISTRATES' COURT</u>

MAGISTRATE Will the prosecution commence?

SPIKE Your Worship, it is our intention to prove that negligence by Steam Dick's Turkish Bath and Holding Company Ltd resulted in our client suffering a severe change. It has been said not even his own mother would recognize him.:

MAG Did she ever recognize him?

SPIKE No, your Worship – a tree fell on her.

MAG And how was this change wrought?

SPIKE He was reduced from a man of considerable substance to a liquid state.

MAG (<u>puzzled</u>) When you say liquid . . . is he, er, er, dead?

SPIKE We don't know, your Worship.

MAG (<u>agitated</u>) What do you mean, you don't know? Either he's dead or he's not dead.

SPIKE Begging your Worship's indulgence . . .

MAG Is he in court?

SPIKE Ah . . . in a manner of speaking.

MAG Then call him.

CLERK Call Harry Secombe.

VOICES Call 'arry Secombe,

CONSTABLE ENTERS CARRYING A BUCKET.

MAG (<u>after a pause</u>) Are you Harry Secombe?

CONSTABLE No, your Honour, I am Constable Z. Cars, gross take-home pay £18.6.0. with repeats £32.16.4. I just carry the bucket.

SPIKE If I could perhaps explain, your Worship. Inside that bucket is the plaintiff Harry Secombe.

MAG All of him?

SPIKE Yes.

MAG What's he doing?

SPIKE Allow me to elucidate . . . On the night of the 1st of April,
which is by the way of being a Jewish holiday in Morecambe,
my client paid a visit to Steam Dick's Turkish Baths. As is
usual in such establishments, he was shown a chamber, dis-
robed, and there left to steam.

MAG Steam?

SPIKE Steam, your Honour. Owing to a faulty valve, the temperature in Mr Secombe's chamber rose to some 800 degrees Fah-
renheit, the melting-point of the human body. An attendant
rushed in – alas, too late. Mr Secombe now lay in a liquid
state on the floor. The attendant, being a sensitive man,
mopped him up with a sponge, and wrung him carefully in a
bucket – that bucket.

HEAVY OVERACTED MURMURS.

MAG Silence! I will not tolerate overacting in this court. (Coughs)
Can we perhaps see Mr Secombe?

SPIKE Constable?

CONSTABLE POURS FROM A BUCKET INTO A TRANSPARENT CON-
TAINER MARKED WITH LIQUID MEASURE.

MAG And you are suing for negligence?

SPIKE No! We are suing them for short measure. A forensic
report states on entering the baths Mr Secombe weighed
seventeen stone nine pounds, and gaining all the time. According to this conversion table, Mr Secombe should have been
eight and a half imperial pints. I draw the court's attention
 . . . barely six pints. I need to say no more.

MAG Very well, say it.

SPIKE No more.

MAG We are saying that Mr Secombe is 2½ pints short!

SPIKE Yes . . .

MAG Can't you top him up with a little tap water?

COUNS No, it's against his religion.

TAKES OFF HIS ROBES, WIG AND FALSE TEETH – HE IS IN
PYJAMAS.

The defence rests!

COUNSEL FALLS FLAT BACK INTO WAITING BED.

101 Limericks: 1982

A Man from Out of Space ...

A man from out of space
Said, 'I'm from a superior race.
You're all inferior
While I am superior.'
Then he tripped and fell flat on his face.

There's a Lot of It About: 1983

Laugh At A Cretin; TheUnemploymethon

Laugh At A Cretin

ROUSING, FUN TYPE MUSIC, AS SIMILAR AS POSSIBLE TO LONDON
WEEKEND'S 'GAME FOR A LAUGH'. PAN ACROSS GLITTERY CAP-
TION: 'LAUGH AT A CRETIN'. WE HEAR A LOUD, JOLLY VOICE OVER:

VOICE OVER Yes, it's 'Laugh at a Cretin'. The show where the old,
the educationally sub-normal, the poor, the disadvantaged, are
laughed at by a load of awful fat women with false teeth.

BRIEF CUT AWAY TO WEMBLEY CROWD CHEERING.

VOICE OVER And on 'Laugh at a Cretin' tonight: What we did to
a block of flats when all the residents were away at work . . .

STOCK FILM OF A BLOCK OF FLATS BLOWING UP.

. . . The couple who volunteered for a very unusual game of
squash . . .

CUT TO A SHOT OF A YOUNG MAN AND A GIRL IN SQUASH KIT WITH
RACQUETS, STANDING IN A SQUASH COURT, SLOWLY, TWO OF THE
WALLS MOVE INWARDS AND TIGHTLY SQUASH THEM.

. . . The woman who thought her husband was an expert rock
climber, but by hypnosis we made him forget everything he'd
ever learnt . . .

SHOT OF CLIFFS. WE HEAR AN AGONISED SCREAM, THEN SEE A
MALE ROCK CLIMBER PLUMMET PAST.

. . . The old age pensioner who accepted a free trip at our
expense to the Colosseum in Rome . . .

STOCK SHOT, FROM AN EPIC FILM OF A BODY BEING MAULED BY
LIONS IN THE AMPHITHEATRE.

. . . and the housewife from Sydenham who we invited to try
her hand at weight lifting . . .

CUT TO ENORMOUS GREAT BLACK WEIGHT WITH '100 TONS' ON IT.
FROM UNDERNEATH PROTRUDE LEGS. CUT TO STUDIO AUDIENCE
SEATING AREA, STEPS DOWN THE CENTRE. THERE ARE ONLY
ABOUT THREE OR FOUR PEOPLE SITTING IN THE SEATS, BUT WE
HEAR HUGE CHEERS AND DUBBED APPLAUSE.

. . . And here they are. Your hosts tonight on 'Laugh at a
Cretin' . . . A man you have never heard of . . .

GIRL IN BLONDE WIG COMES RUNNING DOWN WAVING.

. . . A man you *have* heard of, but wish to God you hadn't . . .

CUT TO A BUSTY WOMAN IN SWEATER, JEANS, BLACK BEARD AND
BLACK HAIR COMING DOWN THE STEPS WAVING.

. . . And the Irishman we ended up with when we couldn't
afford Terry Wogan!

A DUMMY IN A SMART SUIT AND BIG WELLIES IS CALLOUSLY
HURLED DOWN THE STEPS. MUSIC AND APPLAUSE REACH A
CLIMAX. THE GIRL, WOMAN IN BEARD AND RICHARD III ARE NOW
SITTING ON HIGH STOOLS AGAINST GARISHLY-LIT SET. THE IRISH
DUMMY, NOW REPLACED BY AN ACTOR, GETS UP AND SITS DOWN.

ALL Good evening.
RICHARD III Well that's all we've got time for this week, so
from all of us here . . .
ALL Good night.

MUSIC CRASHES IN AGAIN, PLUS RIOTOUS APPLAUSE.

VOICE OVER Next week in 'Laugh at a Cretin', we meet Breslaw
Quills, the amazing shadow-puppeteer from Dagenham . . .

CUT TO SPIKE IN DUSTY DINNER JACKET, CARDBOARD MOUSTACHE AND
PINCE-NEZ. HE STANDS IN FRONT OF AN OLD VICTORIAN LANTERN
WHICH APPEARS TO PROJECT LIGHT ON TO A SMALL WHITE SCREEN.

SPIKE And now 'Life on a Sussex Farm' . . .

FLEXES FINGERS, THEN THRUSTS THEM IN FRONT OF THE LAN-
TERN. ON THE SCREEN, A CLIP OF VARIOUS NAKED LADIES AS IN

1950s SEX FILM. SPIKE DOES VARIOUS SILLY HAND MOVEMENTS
AS WE WATCH THE FILM. THEN HE WITHDRAWS HIS HANDS AND
THE PICTURE SLIDES OFF THE SIDE. HE BOWS, TO APPLAUSE.
RESUME THEME MUSIC.

CUT TO A FILM OF A HOUSE ON FIRE.

VOICE OVER . . . And now you can see what happened when a
young couple returned from their honeymoon to find we had
arranged a surprise housewarming party . . . All this and
more, next week, on 'Laugh at a Cretin'.

The Unemploymethon

APPALLING GOLD GLITTER SETTING FOR A TELETHON. SPIKE
PLAYS THE TELETHON HOST WEARING A TERRIBLE BLONDE CURLY
WIG, PURPLE FRILLY SHIRT, WHITE SPOTTED BOW TIE AND A GOLD
GLITTER LAMÉ JACKET WITH BEAUTIFULLY CREASED BLACK
TROUSERS AND WHITE LEATHER SHOES. A BOARD WITH TEN
MAJOR EMPLOYERS LISTED AND ALONGSIDE EACH NAME IS A
SQUARE FOR SLIDING THE FIGURES IN. WE HEAR THE MUSIC OF
'HAPPY DAYS ARE HERE AGAIN'.

VOICE OVER Yes, it's time to play something or other and
here's Big Dick Milligan. (music – organ)

SPIKE (running on to storms of applause) Good evening, hello,
and ha ha. Welcome to the Thatcherthon. Yes with me to keep
the tally is lovely Rayleen Body!

RAYLEEN BODY COMES ON TO SCREAMING APPLAUSE.

SPIKE Well Rayleen gribble, grabble, gribble, grabble, boobs gag.

RAYLEEN Oh Dick twitty, twitty, twitty, twitty, giggle and anything rather than work poo.

SPIKE (terrible, insincere laughter) Twitty, twitty, giggle poo,
but more of that later. But seriously folks (false face) Mrs
Thatcher is seriously concerned about the unemployment
figures.

SCREAMS OF LAUGHTER FROM THE AUDIENCE.

SPIKE Yes, you can't beat the oldies, but mind you, round my
way, they beat them all the time. Now as you all know this
morning the unemployment figure stood at two million six hundred thousand – many of them standing in dole queues! Ha,
ha, ha! (roars of laughter from the audience) Wonderful,
wonderful. Now let's set off around the country and see where
that figure stands tonight. (he picks up a glitter phone) . . .
Hello Coventry.

COVENTRY (Irish voice) Hello Dick, British Leyland here. It's been a very difficult decision but this week we can lay off 3,600.

SPIKE Three thousand six hundred.

FIGURES PUT UP ALONGSIDE COVENTRY ON THE SCORE BOARD, WE HEAR THE MUSIC OF 'HAPPY DAYS ARE HERE AGAIN', THE AUDIENCE IS SCREAMING, CUT TO STOCK SHOT OF POP CONCERT AUDIENCE IN ECSTACY.

SPIKE We mustn't get too excited we've got a long way to go. And now, hello Hull.

HULL (coloured Jamaican voice) Hello Dick. Dis am Hull. By sinking three trawlers and setting fire to two boot factories and a dung plant, we have a total of 683 unemployed.

SPIKE Six hundred and eighty-three unemployed!

SCREAMS FROM THE AUDIENCE. FIGURES PUT ON THE SCORE BOARD.

SPIKE So Rayleen, what's the total unemployed so far?

RAYLEEN (looking at card) Well Dick, the total unemployed is two million eight hundred and thirty two thousand.

WE SEE MARGARET THATCHER SMILING, WITH 'SIEG HEIL' CHEERING OVER IT.

SPIKE Wonderful, wonderful. Now can we make it that magic three million? We'll find out after the break.

ELECTRICITY COMMERCIAL

THERE ARE A SERIES OF QUICK CUTS OF ELECTRIC LIGHTS GOING ON AND OFF. CUT TO A FAMILY IN A COSY ROOM WITH TV, ELECTRIC FIRE, KID WITH EARPHONES TO A RADIO, STAND LAMPS AND MASSIVE CHANDELIER. THEY ARE ALL WATCHING THE TV.

VOICE OVER Electricity bills can be high. This winter cut down on electricity. It's very simple.

CLOSE-UP OF MASTER FUSE BOX WITH ON/OFF MASTER SWITCH. SWITCH IS PULLED TO OFF. CUT BACK TO COSY ROOM – BLACKOUT.

VOICE OVER Yes darkness and hypothermia. The ideal

economy. Get a darkness pamphlet and a free guide to hypothermia from your local electricity showrooms.

CAPTION: <u>GLC WORKING FOR LONDON</u>

'PART TWO' CAPTION OF UNEMPLOYMETHON. ACCOMPANIED BY THE MUSIC OF 'HAPPY DAYS ARE HERE AGAIN'.

SPIKE Yes, welcome back, gibber gabber, gibber gabber, joke, joke, joke, weak joke. Anybody here from Manchester? Yes? Well, it's still raining, gibber gabber, laugh, laugh, laugh. But now let's get back on the scrapheap trail, can Britain really make it to the knacker's yard under it's own steam. We topped Crippen, but can we top the magic three million. Hello Glasgow, what have you got for us?

GLASGOW (<u>Pakistani voice</u>) We've got a reverse charge call for you.

SPIKE Reverse charge – a pity they didn't think of that at the Battle of Balaclava . . . joke, joke, joke, laugh, laugh, laugh.

GLASGOW We at Upper Clyde shipyards are proud to be laying off two thousand riveters.

SPIKE Riveting stuff.

GLASGOW Half a dozen platers and Mrs Flora Kilt making a grand total of two thousand and twenty.

SPIKE: Two thousand and twenty!

FLASH IN CLOSE-UP OF MARGARET THATCHER WITH 'SIEG HEIL' CHEERING OVER IT.

SPIKE So now let's have a look at the board. At the moment down there at the bottom with 683 is Hull, then a rank outsider – and they don't come any ranker folks – is Glasgow Shipbuilders who came up with a magnificent two thousand and twenty and Mrs Flora Kilt – but still the overall leader with three thousand six hundred laid off is <u>British Leyland</u>.

WE HEAR THE CROWDS CHEERING, LOUD MUSIC, FILM OF CROWDS
GOING CRAZY WITH JOY. LIGHTS FLASH ON THE BOARD AROUND
BRITISH LEYLAND.

SPIKE And now Rayleen, what have we so far?

RAYLEEN (reading from card) Well Big Dick, the grand total is
two million, nine hundred and ninety-nine thousand, nine hundred and ninety-nine.

STORMS OF APPLAUSE AND LIGHTS FLASH ON THE TOTAL FIGURES.

SPIKE Just one more to reach the magic three million. So come
on South East of England – so far the North have had it all
their own way – there must be someone in your firm you can
lay off. Don't be ashamed. Even if it's only an old crippled
char lady, or your favourite loveable old one-armed com-
missionaire, we're not proud. So don't forget . . . (sings) This
is the ageeeee – (spoken) of the unemployed.

WE SEE PEOPLE IN TRUCKS BEING TRANSPORTED. MUSIC: 'HAPPY
DAYS ARE HERE AGAIN'.

The Flasher II

At Kilburn police station Constable Ward was still smarting over the buried dog affair. This was his seventh year in the force without promotion, his wife had nagged him over his failure. 'There's plenty of murders in London,' she said. 'Why can't you catch one? If you can't catch one, *do* one, you'd be better off in the nick.' He tried, he polished the floor outside her bedroom to a high degree of slipperiness, he waxed the bottom of her slippers, he left the cable bare by her bedside lamp, on holiday he took her for a walk along crumbling cliffs, but fate decreed. With the increased activities of the IRA and the PLO in London he thought he'd ask for a transfer to where the action was. And so he arrived in Kilburn in the centre of the Irish community, *this* is where the IRA would be.

The Irish were 'tick', he'd do some investigating on his own account, he listened to Terry Wogan and copied his accent, he hired a black curly wig, he wore a dark blue suit, a white shirt, green tie and brown boots, the uniform the micks wore to recognise each other when drunk. So disguised, he haunted the Irish pubs: 'God bless all in here, long live der Pope,' he'd say, and they would say, 'It's that cunt of an English polis again.'

He kept his eyes open for suspicious parcels. There was that black plastic bag under the pub seat, just in time he had hurled it through the plate-glass window into the street where, on impact, three tins of Kennomeat rolled out. Outside Harrods he had thrust a suspicious brown paper parcel into a bucket of water and thus prevented a pair of expensive brown shoes from exploding. Superintendent Haymes had called him in. 'For God's sake, Ward, will you stop it! Go for something simple, man, like illegal parking, drunks pissing in doorways, flashers and the like.'

Flashing, according to the *Daily Mirror* poll, was one of the ten most popular crimes among elderly women. Which brings us to Frank Chezenko now strolling on the perimeter of the Kilburn and District Nature Club. The club had a unique beginning, it was formed the moment Leon Marks's wife had caught him and the au pair naked on the ironing board, 'Look darling,' the little fat man said, 'I started a nature club for you.' From his savings he'd been forced to buy a derelict garden and solicit new members, who were not long in coming forward. This day a sea of fat white appalling bodies were socialising in the sun: some were playing badminton, male and female appendages flying gaily in all directions; others disported themselves on the sun terrace. There was a huge fat woman with hairs on her fanny like a deserted crow's nest, and a long thin male with a willy that reached to his knee with a curve in it that made it look like a hockey stick with an egg cosy on the end.

Walking along a hedge that hides all this was limping Frank Chezenko. He hadn't had a decent flash since he paid his rent, and now he felt the need. Peering through the hedge, to his delight he saw a group of nude people playing leap frog, ideal! In one bound Chezenko pushed through the hedge and FLASH . . . FLASH . . . FLASH! The recipients were all stunned, women screamed. One whispered, 'Darling!' 'You filthy swine!' said a male with a small one. 'Can I have your business card?' said a lady. Mad with jealousy, the male nudes threw themselves upon the flasher, holding him and his willy down. 'Phone the police!' cried a man. 'Not too quickly,' said a matron.

Constable Ward put down his football coupon to answer the phone. 'Kilburn police station . . . What? A flasher, where? . . . we'll be right over.' He slammed the phone down, smashing it.

The Noddy car bearing Constable Ward drew up at the Nature Club. 'He's in here,' said a naked man.

'Is he still doing it?'

'Yes, there's a big crowd.'

'Leave it to me, sir,' said Ward, pushing past.

'I'm sorry, sir, it's a club rule, no one's allowed in with clothes on.'

Duty first, the policeman stripped and advanced on the luckless Chezenko.

'Let him up,' said the policeman.

Slowly the Hungarian and his crushed willy rose to his feet.

'I'm arresting you for indecency,' said Ward.

'Who are you?' said Chezenko.

'I am a police cons –'

FLASH – FLASH – FLASH.

'Will you stop doing that while I'm talking to you! I'm a police constable and I'm taking you in.'

'Taking me in what?' Chezenko eyed him up and down – not much opposition there. 'How do I know you are a constable, where's your badges of office?' FLASH – FLASH – FLASH – a woman fainted in ecstasy.

Constable Ward ran to his clothing and returned wearing his helmet and blowing a whistle. Thus adorned, he foolishly handcuffed Chezenko's hands in front where he produced further damning evidence of indecent exposure, including the last turkey in the shop. As Ward drove the flasher away he swore he saw women crying.

Startling Verse for All the Family: 1987

The Twit

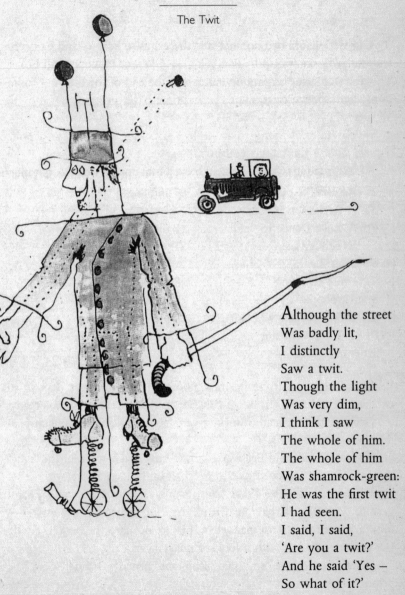

Although the street
Was badly lit,
I distinctly
Saw a twit.
Though the light
Was very dim,
I think I saw
The whole of him.
The whole of him
Was shamrock-green:
He was the first twit
I had seen.
I said, I said,
'Are you a twit?'
And he said 'Yes –
So what of it?'

It Ends with Magic: 1990

The Concert

Yes, indeed; Laura had decreed that there was to be a 'Grand Concert'; and the audience was to be Sam Kidgell, 'Guest of Honour', and Boxer. The day was spent rigging up curtains at the end of the drawing room, using bed sheets as curtains. Séan printed the programme and the 'tickets'.

	CONCERT	
1	A Song by Jeff and Séan	The Grand Old Duke of York
2	Acrobatiks by Silé	Tumbling
3	A Recitation by Séan	'Crusty Bread'
4	A Fairy Dance by Laura	Balleet
5	INTERVAL	Tea and biscuits
6	Séan, Laura, Jeff, Silé	Will do a Ring of Roses
7	Laura will sing	Sea Shells
8	Akrobatiks by Silé	Tumbling
9	Laura and Jeff will skip	Up to a hundred
10	The cast will sing	God Save the King

Laura, now wardrobe mistress, chose all the costumes. It was all excitement and rosy cheeks: finally, at six that evening, all was ready.

'Tickets, please,' said Séan in a very polite official voice. Sam produced his and Boxer's.

'This way, sir,' said Séan with a half bow and a wave of the hand. Sam and Boxer followed to a large chair and a dog basket.

'This is your seat, sir,' said Séan again with a small bow and a hand gesture. 'And this is for your friend,' he said, indicating the basket; it took a while for Sam to manoeuvre his 'friend' into the basket, finally Boxer settled in but with a look of reluctance.

'Your programme, sir,' said Séan and proudly handed Sam the printed sheet.

'Thank you,' said Sam settling.

Sam waited for quite ten minutes; there was no sign of action, only fierce whisperings and bulges from behind the curtains. At last, Jeff appeared through the curtains; he wore a white, billowing-sleeved shirt, black knickerbockers buttoned at the knee, white stockings and black shoes; his face was ghastly-white with Laura's 'special' make-up, but with bright red cheeks, carmine lips and heavy black eyebrows, like miniature umbrellas. He gave a clumsy bow and stumbled.

'Ladies and gentlemen, please take your seats for the grandest concert.'

He turned, fumbled to find the parting in the curtains. A small helping hand and the word 'Here!' was whispered as an opening appeared; gratefully Jeff disappeared, more whispering and running feet from behind the curtain; Boxer leapt up barking at the bulges. Action! The curtains parted, well not exactly; half a curtain parted showing half the opening act – Jeff. A hand appeared on the closed half and manually pulled it back, revealing Séan grinning. Both boys were wearing soldiers' pillbox hats – one a little too big – and sang:

> The Grand Old Duke of York
> [both salute]
> He had ten thousand men
> [both hold up ten fingers]
> He marched them up to the top of the hill
> [vigorously marching right]
> And he marched them down again
> [vigorously marching back again]
> And when they were up they were up
> [pointing upwards]
> And when they were down they were down
> [pointing down]
> And when they were only halfway up
> [halfway up gesture across waist]
> They were neither up nor down.

Warm applause from Sam. The boys bowed and bowed and bowed and bowed – still the curtain wasn't drawn. More bowing, bowing, bowing and looking off. Finally, the curtains wavered to a close; there was a determined tugging to make them overlap and a repeated hissed voice calling, 'Silé! Silé!!!' Through the curtains appeared Séan.

'Ladies and gentlemen, now a display of acrobatics by Miss Silé Sparrow.' Bowing he disappeared.

Laura was heard saying, 'Now!' The curtains parted, each one at different speeds, the stage empty; from the wings, Silé in a black and white clown's costume came head over heels, disappearing on the other side. A pause. Laura's voice hissed, 'Again! Do it again!'

'What?' came the strident voice from the wings.

'Do it again!' came the frantic reply. Again the head-over-heels figure tumbled across the stage, going off-balance, twice wiping her nose on the back of her sleeve before she disappeared again. The curtains closed but not before a brief glimpse was had of the acrobat tumbling across for the third time.

'That's enough!' hissed a frantic voice. A pause. More lumps appeared in the curtain; furious barking from Boxer. Jeff appeared.

'Now ladies and gentlemen, a recitation by Master Séan Sparrow.' He gave an awkward bow, his bottom colliding with someone behind the curtain. 'Ow,' said the someone.

Jeff gone, the curtains parted falteringly, showing Silé still tumbling; a hand appeared and pulled her into the wings. All the while Master S. Sparrow stood waiting, then recited:

A POEM, CRUSTY BREAD
*by E. V. Lucas**

The country is the place for milk
[milking action]
All creamy with a head
[points to head]

---

* With this poem Séan Milligan won first prize for diction in 1961.

And butter fresh as it can be
And bread to spread it on at tea
[spreading motion]
The finest bread you'll ever see
[points to eyes]
The really crusty bread
What? Don't you know the country crust
[points to head]
How crisp it is how sweet it is
Magnificent to eat it is
[furious chewing]
Impossible to beat it is
[beat bottom]
Why sure you must you must
[Bow]

Now what? Sam referred to his programme, ah yes, fairy dance by Laura, a 'Balleet'! From behind the curtains came the sound of a tinkling bell and a sneeze. The curtains parted: there, a vision of loveliness. In a white lacy gown and white satin slippers was the fairy Laura! Her hair all in ringlets, a silver ribbon around her forehead, a silver star centre, a deathly white make-up, raging red cheeks and lips, with heavy-black-arched eyebrows (one slightly longer than the other). Perfection – save the ballet slippers, three sizes too big, the ends turning up. Tinkling her little bell, she tippy-toed around the stage, a terrible fixed smile on her face, eyes blinking at an alarming rate; no one noticed the occasional stumble. All the while she held the little bell by her ear, giving it, when she remembered, a tinkle; round and round went the fairy, the silver slipper only coming off once trailing by ribbons behind her. In mid-dance the curtains suddenly closed, fierce hot whispers of, 'I haven't finished!', curtains opened. The fairy, very angry, stared off-stage; suddenly, the fixed grin again and fluttering eyelids, a wobbly, graceful curtsey. The curtains came nervously together as the fairy fell over. Sam gave appreciative clapping and cries of 'Bravo!'

'Interval.' Sam relit his pipe. From the side of the stage what was recently a fairy, appeared as a waitress, with silver tray and cup of tea.

'Refreshments, sir?' she said.

Sam smilingly took the tea.

'And some for your friend?' she gracefully gave a biscuit to Boxer who nearly took her hand off.

The loud voice of Silé: 'Whenned can I pulled the curtinned Lawa?'

Sam consulted his programme. 'Séan, Laura, Jeff and Silé will do "Ring a Roses".' The curtains quivered apart revealing the quartet, the girls dressed in all red (Laura's idea of 'country costume', as to what country was a mystery), the boys in white shirts and knee-length shorts. All were barefoot; Laura recalled that's how gypsies danced over their bonfires. At the command of 'One' they all held hands; on the command of 'Two' they all raised on tiptoe; on the command 'Three' they all danced in a circle. 'Four,' said Laura jerkily, and they all sang, 'Ring a Ring of Roses, a pocket full of posies, hush ah, hush ah, all fall down'. After several times they all collapsed in a heap; of the heap Laura, Silé and Jeff remained down, while Séan hurried to draw the curtains. Quick-change for Laura. A sea-blue velvet dress, lace collar, the back all undone. 'Never mind, he won't see it,' she hissed, shaking free of Séan's attempts to button her up.

On stage Jeff told a joke about an Englishman, Irishman and Scotsman but couldn't remember the end so, 'Ladies and Gentlemen, Miss Sparrow will now sing.'

> Sea Shells, Sea Shells,
> Sing me a song of the sea;
> Of silver bells and cockle shells . . .

At a critical moment in the song, with Laura's eyes looking heavenwards, a vigorous clown doing head-over-heels crossed behind her. The singer continued like an enraptured diva. 'Hark! Hark!' A hand to her ear. 'I hear the rolling sea.' What she could hear was the rolling Silé, who paused to pull up her socks then – Thud! There came a loud crying;

Silé had fallen off the stage. Ruthlessly the little diva shouted, 'Shut up' through Silé's howls, the song continued in the peace and silence of *Treasure Island*'s distant blue seas.

'Encore, Bravo!' said Sam, clapping enthusiastically. Laura beamed. At last, a star overnight!

The great finale was a 'Britannia' tableau.

'. . . Long to reign over us, God save our Queen,' they sang. It was too late, really; the Queen was dead. Sam clapped, Boxer barked, the players bowed low, Britannia's helmet falling off in the process. The smell of food came wafting into the room and they all trooped off to dinner.

'Sam, this is the best evening of my life,' said Laura, flushed with child happiness.

Condensed Animals: 1991

Salmon; Chimpanzee

Salmon

Salmon salmon
In the River Tweed
You seem to swim
At such a speed
And really salmon
How I wish
You wouldn't end up
On a dish.

Chimpanzee

Chimp-chimp-chimpanzee
Some look like you and some like me
Mr Darwin clearly stated
That some time back we are related.

Fleas, Knees and Hidden Elephants: 1995

Skin Deep

I think that I am lovely
Despite a broken nose
You can detract from it
By wearing fancy clothes
I think I am beautiful
Although I have cross-eyes
You can detract from that as well
By wearing fancy ties
I think I am beautiful
Even though I've got big ears
I cover them with blankets
When anyone appears.
I think I am beautiful
Although my legs are thin
If people want to see them
I say my legs aren't in
If some folk say I'm ugly
As some folk certainly will
I get out my rottweiler
And say kill kill kill.

7

Baring All

Silly Verse for Kids: 1963

Maveric

Maveric Prowles
Had Rumbling Bowels
That thundered in the night.
It shook the bedrooms all around
And gave the folks a fright.

The doctor called;
He was appalled
When through his stethoscope
He heard the sound of a baying hound,
And the acrid smell of smoke.

Was there a cure?
'The higher the fewer,'
The learned doctor said,
Then turned poor Maveric inside out
And stood him on his head.

'Just as I thought
You've been and caught
An Asiatic flu –
You mustn't go near dogs I fear
Unless they come near you.'

Poor Maveric cried.
He went cross-eyed,
His legs went green and blue.
The doctor hit him with a club
And charged him one and two.

And so my friend
This is the end,
A warning to the few:
Stay clear of doctors to the end
Or they'll get rid of you.

A Dustbin of Milligan: 1961

The Violin; My Court Martial

The Violin

It could only happen once in a lifetime. It happened to Joseph Schil-kraut. In the Commercial Road, his pawnshop was the sole survivor in the district of wholesale shut-downs during the 1930 depression.

'There ain't no more money left in the world,' he told his wife at breakfast. 'Nobody *ever* redeems their pledges these days. Look at the stuff I got in the shop! I can't get a penny for any of them, ach! There just *ain't no more money.*'

A host of pawned clocks chimed ten from the shop. In the good old days he would have been open at eight-thirty sharp, but now, there was no point.

He finished his tea, and pulled the shop blinds. It was cold. The windows unseeing with condensation he wiped clear.

Across the road, outside the Labour Exchange groups of grey, cold, unemployed men stood talking. Some wore Army medals – 'Poor fellers,' thought Joe.

Farther down the street some had started a fire with orange boxes. The day passed without a customer.

'I suppose,' thought Joe, 'people ain't got anything to pawn any more!'

It was the shortest day. At four he lit the gas: its light bathed the room in a sea of sepulchral green.

'Ach, might as well close,' Joe muttered. But what was this? Someone coming in! Yes . . . Yes, he was.

The shop door opened, an elderly man made a shuffling entrance. 'You still open, mate?'

Joe shrugged his shoulders. 'Well – mmm, yes. What you got then?'

The old man held up an army sandbag. 'Do you give anything on musical instruments, mate?'

Joe winced. 'Instruments?' He pointed to a host of trumpets that festooned the walls. 'You can see how much I need instruments.'

The old man stood silent – his great shabby overcoat hung from his stooped shoulders like tired wings.

'Oh, all right.' There was a note of pity in Joe's voice. 'What you got?'

The old man laid the sandbag on the counter. 'It's a fiddle, mate,' he said, sliding it from the bag.

At first glance Joe could see it was old, very old. He took it behind the counter under the light and peered into the 'f' holes. The floor of the instrument was thick with dust. All the while the old man stood silent.

'Won't keep you long,' said Joe, removing the dust with a paint brush. *Nicolò Amati. 1604.*

Joe polished his glasses and looked again – *Nicolò Amati. 1604.* That was what the label said.

Steady, Joe, there's a million fakes floating about. This could be another, except, this didn't *feel* like a fake. The label was vellum, and the signature in faded brown ink. Joe had a strange feeling come over him. The old man stood waiting. Joe showed no outward emotion.

'Is it worth *any*thing?' asked the old man.

Joe laid the violin on the sandbag, took off his glasses.

'I don't know, sir. Leave it here a day or two and I'll let you know!'

The old man took a pace forward. 'A *day* or two? – I was hopin' I might get somethin' right away, mate. See I'm skint and hungry – bleedin' hungry. Couldn't you let me have a couple o' bob on account? I mean, it *must* be worth more than that.'

Joe put the violin into the sack.

'All right – two bob.'

The old man took the coin. 'Good luck,' he said spitting on it, and shuffled from the shop.

Heart beating, Joe bolted the shop door. He took the stairs to the loft two at a time. He pulled down his Lexicon of 'Violins – Viols and Cellos'.

For an hour he compared the violin against illustrations. Measurements, wood, scroll – all signs pointed in favour. There was one person who could tell him for sure – Uncle Alfred!

Eight minutes later, the phone rang in Uncle Alf's shop.

'Hello, Alfred Bloom's Antiques here.'

The babbling voice of nephew Joe came racing over the phone. He told all.

'You got to come down now and verify it, or I won't sleep.'

'Me come down now? I'm in Leeds remember?'

'Leeds, Schmeeds, this could mean a fortune – you can have your cut.'

'I'll be down on the night train.'

At six-fifty the following morning Uncle Alfred was in the shop. Without even letting him remove his hat or coat, Joe pushed the violin at him. Screwing an inspection glass in his eye, Uncle Alf roamed the body of the old violin. The glass dropped from his eye, he started to shake.

'Joe – it's real,' he said. 'It's an Amati! Worth forty thousand pounds anywhere in the world.'

The two men stood silent in the room. Then Joe started to speak.

'Forty thousand pounds,' he kept repeating.

'And that's putting it at a minimum,' interjected Uncle Alf.

Joe fell back into his chair. This meant the start of a new life – no more penny pinching, no more bargaining, anti-semitism, bills, arguments, sleepless nights, rent. All over, all over. He started to cry. . . .

Uncle Alf was speaking: 'You ain't told me where you got it.'

'An old feller came in – I gave him two bob deposit.'

'*Two* bob,' Uncle Alf clapped his hands. 'Then he don't know the value. We're home and dry, ha ha!'

Joe held up his hand. 'Just a minute – he's entitled to a slice of the money – it's his violin.'

Uncle's face dropped.

'You mad, Joe? – Who found out it was worth forty thousand? Him? No – it was *you* and *me*. No son, that's the luck of the game –

offer him two quid – and later – send him an anonymous hundred. He'll be happy. Come on, now, wake up! Business is business! – He'd do the same to you –'

A day went by, two, three, a week – the old man never appeared. Joe and his wife were taking sleeping pills. Late one January evening, the old man came.

'Sorry I been so long,' he coughed. 'I been ill wiv the flu. I lives on me own so I di'n' get much attention.'

There was a pause. Joe waited for the man to ask the question. He did.

'Er – did you make up yer mind about the fiddle?'

Joe drew a deep breath. 'Yes,' he exhaled. 'I have.'

'Thank God, I needs a few bob – huh.'

'I'll give you two quid for it.'

At the mention of money the old man swayed.

'Two quid?' he echoed.

'Yes.'

'Oh.' He stood blinking in the middle of the room. 'I fought it might be worth a bit more.'

Joe laughed. 'More? How much you reckon it's worth, then?'

The old man gave Joe a steady gaze. 'Forty thousand pounds,' he said . . .

My Court Martial

The following is just a thought. I recall the incident from my old Army days. In 1917 the British invented the military tank. Under conditions of great secrecy an attack on the German lines was prepared at Cambrai.

The day before the attack, however, to the amazement of all, the Germans attacked the British with tanks. Immediately a member of the House of Commons demanded an inquiry into our security methods.

First day of the inquiry before the Lords Blimley, Grumper, and Chatsshaw-Blurtington.

MR. SMITH, K.C.: Lord Spike, you are a General in the British Army?

LORD SPIKE: Ermm. Yes.

SMITH, K.C.: Your salary is £3,000 a year?

LORD SPIKE: Errrmm. Yes.

SMITH, K.C.: You consider that a living wage?

LORD SPIKE: Errmm. Well, errr –

SMITH: You are living . . . ?

LORD SPIKE: Yes.

SMITH: Then you must be getting a living wage.

(*Laughter*)

SMITH: Lord Spike, you knew of the promised British tank attack three days before it happened?

SPIKE: Yes. I had been told by the Minister for War.

SMITH: You told no one else?

SPIKE: No.

SMITH: Lord Spike, what I am to reveal to the court may displease you, but reveal it I must. I have here before me a receipt addressed to you from the German Army. It says: 'For services rendered, 10,000 Deutschemarks.'

SPIKE: I fail to see why the revelation should displease me.

SMITH: For what reason do you receive these payments from the German Army?

SPIKE: I happen to be a Director: have been for several years.

SMITH: I see; in fact you have shares in the German Army.

SPIKE: Yes.

SMITH: Lord Spike, is not your loyalty divided between the German and British cause?

SPIKE: Of course not; I serve each office faithfully.

SMITH: Let me amplify your position. Supposing, only supposing, the German Army are building up for an attack on the British. What is your immediate reaction.

SPIKE: As a director of the German Army it is my duty to keep secret from the British their intention.

SMITH: But you are General of the British Army. In the light of your knowledge, should you not make defensive preparations?

SPIKE: Of course not. It would ill become my position as a shareholder in the German Army. No sir. When the Germans attacked, and only when, would I react.

SMITH: You actually mean you are almost schizoid in that respect?

SPIKE: Putting it clinically, er – yes.

SMITH: Regarding the tank attack, as the British had only just invented the tank, was it not a great coincidence that the Germans invented it three days before?

SPIKE: It certainly did surprise me – as a British General, that is. Of course, as a shareholder in the German Army I knew all the time.

SMITH: Can you explain why three days prior to the British tank attack a telegram was delivered to the German High Command reading: 'Build tanks'?

SPIKE: It was just coincidence.

SMITH: As the result of the successful German tank attack did not the shares you hold in the German Army increase in value?

SPIKE: Ermmm. Yes.

SMITH: That is all, Lord Spike.

From here on I let the reader take over.

The Little Potboiler: 1965

Once Upon

Once upon an unfortunate time, there was a hairy thing called man. Along with him was a hairier thing called animal. Man had a larger brain which made him think he was superior to animals.

Some men thought they were superior to men. They became leader men. Leader men said 'We have no need to work, we will kill animals to eat.' So they did.

Man increased, animals decreased. Eventually leader men said 'There are not enough animals left to eat. We must grow our own food.' So man grew food.

Now, the only animals man had not destroyed were tiny ones, like rabbits and mices, and these little animals were caught eating some of man's crops. 'These animals are a menace. They must die.'

In China they killed all the sparrows. In Australia they killed all the rabbits. Everywhere man killed all wild life. Soon there was none, and all the birds were poisoned. Leader man said 'At last! We are free of pests.'

Man's numbers increased. The world became crowded with men. They all had to sleep standing up. One day a leader man saw a new creature eating his crops. This creature's name was starving people.

'This creature is a menace!' said leader man . . .

A Book of Bits: 1965

Holy Smoke

I am the Vicar of St Paul's
And I'm ringing the steeple bell,
The floor of the church is on fire,
Or the lid has come off hell.

Shall I ring the fire brigade?
Or should I trust in the Lord?
Oh dear! I've just remembered,
I don't think we're insured!

'What's this then?' said the fire chief.
'Is this church C of E?
It is? Then we can't put it out,
My lads are all R.C.!'

Milliganimals: 1968

The Gofongo

The Gofongo, if you please,
Is a fish with singing knees
And a tail that plays
The Spanish clarionet!

He has toes that whistle tunes
And explode! Like toy balloons.
Hence his many,
Many visits to the vet.

The Gofongo, when he likes,
Swallows jam and rusty bikes,
Orange pips and treacle
Pudding boiled in glue.

He loves chips with rusty nails
And can swallow *iron rails*
That is why they cannot
Keep one in a zoo.

But! Gofongo as a pet
Would cause panic and regret.
People tried it and were
Nearly driven barmy.

For, once inside a house,
He screams, 'I'm a Jewish mouse.'
Then he runs away —
And joins the Arab Army!

Small Dreams of a Scorpion: 1972

England Home and Beauty for Sale

Beautiful Buildings
No longer stand
In Bloomsbury's
Pleasant Land.
The Land (it's said)
Is sold. Who by?
Oh dearie me
Oh dearie my
A place that teaches
Architectural knowledge
London University College!
So when one stands
And sadly stares
At horrid new buildings
In Bloomsbury's Squares
We know the responsibility's
Theirs.

Envoi
A lot of learning can be a little thing.

Open Heart University: 1978

Open Heart University
Dedicated to BBC-TV Open University

We've come a long way
            said the Cigarette Scientist
as he destroyed a live rabbit
            to show the students how it worked.

He took its heart out
            plugged it into an electric pump
            that kept it beating for nearly two hours.

I know rabbits who can keep their hearts
            beating for nearly seven years

And look at the electricity they save.

London
March 1977

Unspun Socks from a Chicken's Laundry: 1981
———————
Standing Room Only;
Bad Report – Good Manners

Standing Room Only

'This population explosion,'
Said Peter to St Paul,
'Is really getting far too much,
Just look at that crowd in the hall.
Even here in heaven
There isn't any room,
I think the world could do with less,
Much less fruit in the womb.'
Thus heaven is overcrowded,
The numbers are starting to tell,
So when the next lot knock at the gates,
Tell 'em to go to hell.

Bad Report – Good Manners

My daddy said, 'My son, my son,
This school report is bad.'
I said, 'I did my best I did,
My dad my dad my dad.'
'Explain, my son, my son,' he said,
'Why *bottom* of the class?'
'I stood aside, my dad my dad,
To let the others pass.'

101 Limericks: 1982

A Young Man from Blighty

There was a young man from Blighty
Who wore a transparent nightie.
The vicar said, 'Son,
It's really not done,
It's not wrong – but it's also not rightie.'

Where Have All the Bullets Gone?: 1985

Landlords Ahoy!

Frightening Folkestone on the Kardboard Kow! The golden seaport hove into view; I would rather have viewed into Hove. It's raining, and doing the gardens good. We are close to the quay.

'It looks so bloody foreboding,' Len says. 'I think I'll go back.'

I remind him that his dear little wife is at this moment panting on her bed with the heating turned up and drinking boiling Horlicks.

The customs are pretty hot. 'Read that, please.' I am handed a foolscap sheet of writing.

'Very good,' I say.

'Have you anything to declare?'

I declare that the war is over. He's not satisfied. What have I got in the case? It's a trumpet. Can he see it? He opens the case. Where did I buy this? In London. Have I got a receipt? Yes. Where is it? It's in an envelope in a drawer in my mother's dressing-table in Reigate.

He hums and haws, he's as stupid as a pissed parrot. 'Empty your kitbag.' I pour out a sea of my second-hand underwear. He turns it over and over. 'Where is it?'

'Where's what?'

'The contents.' He thinks it's the wrapping for something. Why have I got so many underpants? I tell him of my mother's forecast of the coming world shortage that will hit England soon. He is now pretty pissed off. OK. He makes a yellow chalk mark on everything. Next to me he finds a poor squaddie with a bottle of whisky. 'You'll have to pay One Pound Ten Shillings on that,' he says with malice aforethought.

'Oh no I won't,' says the squaddie.

'Then I'll have to confiscate it.'

The squaddie opens the bottle and hands it round to us. With devilish glee we help lower the level to halfway, then the squaddie puts the bottle to his lips and drains it. The customs officer is in a frenzy, says to an MP, 'Arrest that man.'

The MP wants to know why.

'Drunkenness,' he says.

'He's not drunk,' says the MP.

'Wait,' says the customs officer.

From the quay to the station, we are now free of military encumbrances. Just for the hell of it we go into a little teashop in the high road. It's very quiet. Three middle-aged ladies are serving.

'Tea, love?' says one in black with a little white apron.

'Yes, tea love.' That, and a slice of fruit cake that tastes like sawdust. The sugar is rationed to two lumps. The war isn't quite over yet. We pay tenpence. Folkestone station and the 11.40 train to Charing Cross. London is as I left it – black, grimy, rainy but holes in the terraces where bombs have fallen. Len and I split.

'See you in four weeks' time, two stone lighter and skint,' he says.

I buy my first English newspapers for two years. The *Daily Herald*, the *Daily Mail*, the *Express*, the *Mirror*, the *News Chronicle*. I go straight for my beloved Beachcomber and find that Justice Cocklecarrot and the Red Bearded Dwarfs are still in court. He is sentencing a Mrs Grotts for repeatedly pushing the Dwarfs into people's halls.

From Charing Cross I take the tube to Archway. Soon I am knocking on the door of 31 St John's Way. A surprise for Mrs Edgington, she doesn't know I'm coming.

'Oh Spike,' she's drying her hands. 'What are you doing here?'

I tell her I'm doing leave here.

'When are you going back?'

Can I come in first? Tea, would I like some tea? Ah! at last an *English* cup of tea and a dog biscuit. (JOKE) I explain my accommodation difficulty. What is the difficulty? Accommodation. Yes, I can stay here. 'You can sleep in the basement.' Mr Edgington's not in, he's gone out to get a paper. Yes, he's well. Son Doug? He's been called up. The Army. Did I know Harry was getting married on leave? He's been caught at the customs with some material he'd bought for Peg's wedding dress and the bastards have given him detention. Mr Edgington is back.

Ah Spike. 'When are you going back?' He's tall, thin, at one-time handsome. An ex-Guards Sergeant from World War One, he was badly gassed in France. He is in receipt of a small war pension. Alas he smokes, it will do for him one day, as it would his youngest son Doug . . . I dump my gear in the basement. Would I like some lunch? Toad-in-the-hole? Lovely grub. I set myself up in the basement. There's a coal fire, but remember it's rationed! Best not light it until the evening.

Leading question. Can Mrs Edgington see to find room for Sergeant Betty Cranley for a day or so? Yes, there's Doug's bedroom going spare. I tell her, good, because I'm going spare. I phone Betty: Hello Betty, knickers and boobs, can she get up with knickers and boobs this week knickers and boobs? Yes, she can, knickers and boobs.

'Mrs Edgington, can I have egg and chips for tea?' I light the coal fire. Mrs Edgington has lent me Doug's 'wireless', a little Bakelite Echo set. These were the days of quiet broadcasting – Christopher Stone playing gramophone records in steady measured tones, unlike the plastic arse-screaming hyped-up disc jockeys with crappy jokes, who get housewives so hyped up with fast mindless chatter and ghetto-blasting records that they are all on Valium. I spent the afternoon reading the papers and listening to long-forgotten programmes. Sid Dean and his band are broadcasting live from a tea dance in Brighton. How very very nice. The News! Alvar Liddell, ace broadcaster and Master of Wireless is telling us in profound adenoidal tones that Mr Attlee, the Prime Monster, with all the impact of sponge on marble, is meeting with the Soviet Ambassador, where they are promising each other there will never be another war, and babies are found under bushes. Churchill is at home in Chartwell doing the kitchen. Henry Hall has been in a car crash in the key of E flat. Woman's Hour: how to knit socks under water, and hints on how to make the best of rationed food (eat it).

I am staring into the glowing coals, sometimes I stare into the glowing wallpaper or the glowing lino. I decide to take my legs for a walk before supper. Do I want the door key? It's where no burglar can find it, on a string in the letterbox. I'm wearing my red and blue Artillery forage cap. In the London gloom it looks like my head's on fire. I stroll to the Archway and its grumbling grey traffic. The evening is lit with those ghastly green sodium lights that make the English look like a race of seasick Draculas. Down Holloway Road, remembering that it was down here Edward Lear was born. I stop to see what the shops have to offer. Displays of crappy furniture, boasting that you can see the 'natural grain of the cardboard'. I go down to the Seven Sisters Road. None of the sisters show up, so I come back. I pass Hercules Street, with not a person in it weighing more than ten stone. Manor Garden, Alexander Road, Landseer Road; the last two would turn in their graves to see what the names had been used for. Giesbach Road? Who chooses them? What grey, dull, mindless idiots sit and debate these improbable street names, streets that should be called Grotty Road, Dog Shit Street, Crappy Avenue, Terrible Building Road, Who-in-their-right-mind-built-these-Mansions. Mind you, it's got worse since. Ah! this is better. The fish and chip shop. A cheery fat sweating man with six hairs serves me. 'Three pieces of rock salmon and a penn'orth o'chips.' He sees my medal ribbons.

''ello son, you bin in trouble?'

Yes, I said, and her father's after me.

Back at number thirty, I pull the string on the key.

'Is that you Spike?' Mrs Edgington in her nightie, calls from the top of the stairs.

'Yes, would you like some fish and chips?' No, they've had their supper. Remember to bolt the door, but not the food. I say OK.

'If you want a cup of tea it's all there.' Ta. It's 8 o'clock. They go to bed early to save electricity and heating. It's not been an easy war for the working classes. I lie in bed eating fish and chips and sipping tea. The fire glows on to the walls. Geraldo and his band are sparkling on the radio, and Dorothy Carless is thanking her dear for that lovely weekend, reminding me I myself have a very weak end.

Hitler is dead, and I am alive. I cannot understand it. He had so much going for him. Like the Red Army. I fall asleep to the glow of the dying fire, or am I dying to fire by the glow of sleep? It all depends on the size.

The Looney: 1987

The Hindus II

London! Steaming metropolis of grot, grime, grit, gunk and gunge, mugging, Molotov cocktails, rape, football hooligans, bombs and assassinations. Dr Johnson said, 'He who is tired of London is tired of life' – fuck him. Faceless monstrous buildings thrust mindless and screaming up to the sky, a style known as Art Leggo. Buildings that, because of their sterility, denied the artisan work, the woodcarver, the marble and stone mason, the marquetry expert, the brass inlayer, the iron-craft master, the plaster moulder – all now lost in the four million unemployed. Architecture was dead, construction was in, slot square A into slot B continue upwards and voilà! An enclosed space with glass. Classic London squares systematically ruined – vistas of St Paul's blocked out. The cause of conservation is only *just* alive. How can there be any strength in depth when one day Michael Heseltine is Secretary for the Environment, his task to conserve, next he is Minister for War, whose job it is to destroy, next, he's not a minister at all! A big laugh. Even the heir apparent, who can't stand what they are doing and speaks out, he won't stop it. Even as he speaks the Seifert clan are designing a monstrous edifice that will destroy and dwarf the Limehouse area. The conscience of the nation is made up of money and money alone, it seems the whole city exists on a tightrope of finance, a dollar drop in the price of oil and the brokers swallow Valium and shit themselves. Jesus, is this the lot you died for? The young innocent and the confused take to drugs and end up in asylums. This is the city that will welcome the Lalkakas. At this moment they were being awakened from their betel-nutted dreams.

'Vake up, Dutchman.' Von Mugabe was shaking Bapu.

'Oh, vere are ve?'

'Just here hi am droppink you, it is zer Cambridge Circus, zer Frith Street is up zere.'

Wearily the two tired passengers lowered themselves on to even tireder pavements.

*   *   *

Ronnie Scott once said that Frith Street raised the tone of the gutter, 'We're getting a better class of mugger.' Crime existed on an exquisite scale and perverts proliferated. Only the previous night Len Toley the silversmith and his wife were watching the repeat of the repeat of *Dynasty* when they were interrupted by the doorbell. He was greeted at the door by two vicars wearing stocking masks. There was an awkward silence.

''Oo are you?' said Mr Toley. One vicar stepped forward. 'We are Jehovah's Burglars,' he said.

'I don't understand,' said Mr Toley.

'You see,' the man went on, 'we are being persecuted by the Police for our beliefs.'

'Oh,' queried Mr Toley. 'What are you beliefs?'

'We believe,' said the man, pushing Mr Toley back into the hall, 'that you've got a lot of silver in the house.'

Mr Toley remembered the floor coming up to meet him. The vicars tippy-toed into the front room. Mrs Toley sat with her back to the door, which was better than back to the dole. 'That you, Len? You've missed the bit where JR is 'avin' it away with –' She stopped as the blackjack did to her what Toley would love to have done years ago. When they came to, the silver had gone, but worse! *Dynasty* had finished.

Hungry now, the two Hindus vectored in on a promising shop, HAM-BURGERS, ah yes! This was the cheap fast food, wrong! This was *Lew* Hamburgers, betting shop. Down sodden steps into a desperate room anointed with poverty went the hungry pair. Stepping over a drunken punter stretched out on the floor, they approached a counter and addressed Australian Bill Kerr, a policeman dismissed by the Brisbane Police for taking bribes but never sharing them out.

'Excuse me, sir,' said Bapu, 'vot do you recommend?'

The Australian looked up from the betting slips to the race board behind him. 'Well, the popular favourite is Herpes Hal.'

'Very well, we'll have two.'

'Two?' the Aussie queried. 'There's only one Herpes Hal.'

'All right, we'll have one between the two of us.'

'You want it each way?'

'Ve'll have it *anyway*.'

The Australian started to make the betting slip out: 'Herpes Hal, ten to four.'

'Pardon me,' said Bapu, 'we are strangers in this country of yours, vot exactly is a Herpes Hal?'

Bloody Abos! 'It's a horse, mate.'

The Hindus were thunderstruck. 'Horse?' said Bapu.

'Yes, there.' The Australian pointed to the board. 'Two-year-old stakes.'

'Vot?' said Bapu. 'You are selling us two-year-old Herpes Hal steaks made from horsemeat, and you want us to wait till ten to four for them? Ve will be dead from starvation by then. Come, Percy.' So saying, the sons of India took their hunger elsewhere.

Startling Verse for All the Family: 1987

Kids

'Sit up straight,'
Said mum to Mabel.
'Keep your elbows
Off the table.
Do not eat peas
Off a fork.
Your mouth is full –
Don't try and talk.
Keep your mouth shut
When you eat.
Keep still or you'll
Fall off your seat.
If you want more,
You will say "please".
Don't fiddle with
That piece of cheese!'
If then we kids
Cause such a fuss
Why do you go on
Having us?

Dear Robert, Dear Spike: 1991

A selection

Dear Robert, Dear Spike, edited by Milligan's biographer Pauline Scudamore, covers the correspondence of the Goon and the poet Robert Graves, after they had met during the recording of *Muses with Milligan* in 1965.

Orme Court, W.2.
14th January, 1970

My Dear Robert,

It was lovely to get a letter from you at last, especially in the New Year, which it helped to make all the brighter for me.

Sorry that you seem to be having some trouble with your innards. Nervous stomach would appear to be a safe label for a doctor to hang on it. I hope you have taken the precaution to have some X-rays taken.

You're right. Nothing can stop 'progress', especially the destruction of old buildings, that is, nothing except Spike Milligan. I am a pretty old building myself.

I have had some success in the past in Australia. I saved the cottage where Henry Kendall wrote some of his early verse, like 'Bellbirds' and 'Names Upon a Stone'. In England I had success in saving the gas lamps at Constitution Hill. I am giving up two months of my own work to try and organise the various scattered preservation societies into one consolidated unit, which will automatically support one of the members in an attempt to save a building; that is, if the Victorian Society want to save the Town House, they automatically have to support all the societies, like the Georgian Society, and the Holborn Society, etc, etc.

If you would trust me, may I use your name when trying to save something which I think worthwhile?

I was in Dublin last week, to see the Ireland–Springboks match, and was delighted to hear that the canal, which the government wanted to fill in, and build a road over, had been saved. It is now to be a public amenity for barging, sailing, and walks on each side of it. I did my share to save it, so I feel pretty good.

For God's sake, don't stop fighting Robert. Is there anything I can do to help you defend your one unspoilt cove in Majorca, you only have to say. At least seek comfort as a poet. They cannot destroy your skill. Though, most certainly sometimes, they destroy the inspiration.

I have before me, at the moment, the entire tape recording of our evening at the Mermaid Theatre. I have been waiting ever since for the company concerned to get it into a long-playing record, but the fire having gone out of the English personality, the tapes have lain fallow on someone's desk. I have decided to get it together myself, and I will let you know the results.

Love, Light and Peace, to all of you, from all of us,

Spike

Orme Court, W.2.
September 71

My Dear Robert,

I haven't written to you for over a year (it may be 2 or 3), so having found a niche in time, I put this to rights. When one writes a letter, at the conception of it – one imagines one has reams of information for the addressee, then suddenly one becomes aware how repetitive one's life is. Since we last wrote, the only thing of literary note is I wrote the 1st volume of a trilogy entitled *Adolf Hitler, my part in his downfall*, it is a lighthearted account of what befell me in H.M. Army from 1938 to 1947; well, beyond my wildest hopes, it became a BEST SELLER! the first thing I did was to phone my parents in Australia and in doing so I realised in fact I was a little boy of 7, running to his mum and dad to tell them he had got a good conduct star at school. Anyway, it sold 30,000 copies and they had to reprint almost at once, I can't tell you how good that feels, for a person whose education ended at 14 to be top seller. I wrote it in Australia, at Woy Woy, it seems it's the only place where there's peace and no tension, and in that environment I become very productive, not only writing but also music – I played the music to George Martin – and as a result, I'm having an LP made of it by a 25-piece orchestra, and that has really delighted me. On October 7 I fly to Australia to see my mother, write the 2nd volume of the Trilogy. The family are all alive and thriving. Laura, 18, has just passed her 'A' Art exam, Séan (17) has just passed 3 'O' Levels, Silé (13) has passed her piano exams (with honours!). I'm not sure what this all means, but according to 'the System' this is a good thing. I'm not sure that adults should be putting such 'measures' on, as yet, immature young people, we impose adult measures on children, and of course they grow up like us – is that a good thing?

The social and political atmosphere here is depressing – Capitalism and Labour keep meeting head on – and strikes are now commonplace, it would appear that Western civilization is failing due to its preoccupation with money – we have made this the fulcrum of our society and it's become an uncontrollable monster, not for nothing did Jesus drive the money lenders from the Temple. The eve of Autumn has been delightful, sun, a steady 68 degrees . . . I have a portable swim pool in my garden, and I made a point of going in, tho the water temperature was bloody cold the after effect was very invigorating and made you feel ten years younger. I am (and always have been) aware of the myriad world ills – that have their root causes in over-population, and I despair of World leaders (tho I admit Ted Heath can't be accused of proliferating) who seem blandly unaware that over 60% of our troubles could be reduced by stabilising and ultimately reducing it. Straight away we would be easing pressure on housing, hospital beds, schools, jobs, neurosis, crowding – in fact, every social amenity, and yet this insane belief 'Expanding Economy' still prevails. 'Growth' they call it – indeed it is a growth of Cancerous quality.

Wish we could sit and discuss this problem. What are the post-operative qualms of your gall bladder trouble? Are you allowed wine? I hope so. It is a drink that has frequently staved off insanity. I hope you and your Island are resisting the developers, I would guess you are all under pressure from the bastards. You know that Sir Val and Rio Tinto have been given the go-ahead to drill in the Lake District – worse, they are destroying ancient primitive people's way of life on Bougainville – the story of how they did it was almost as odious as Warsaw Ghetto. The World can't hold out much longer against this constant disembowelling. – Robert, the world isn't round – it's bent.

Love, Light and Peace,

Spike

Orme Court, W.2.
April 16 (my birthday)

My Dear Robert,

How delighted I was to see that unexpected film of you on the *This is Your Life* show ... yes, I know you love me – but it's mutual, I wish I had known you were in London recently, I would have loved seeing you again, <u>and</u> to have helped you and Sir John save bridges. If you come again I will take you to where there is food, wine, music, and friendship. Who can refuse such an offer? I go on trying to make a living by my pen, but alas, I finished schooling at 14, and not until I was 35 did I become aware of literature; since then, by assiduous reading, I have tried to teach myself, but it is in the green absorptive years that one should learn. I am instinctively drawn towards Victorianism – War-Nostalgia Comedy – Nonsense – and Poetry – oh, and Children's Stories. I am currently writing the second volume of my war memoirs, and going over war dates (personal and regimental) I find it very nostalgic – almost traumatic – at the end of a day – I find I am immersed in 1939–45, and it takes hours for the aura to wear off – and for a period, even with my family around me, I feel very cut off – at night I can hear the guns going in my mind, the shouts of men under stress, the dramatic incidents that suddenly flash back into mind's eye, are all, well, I feel as if I am 'possessed' and need exorcizing. Here is something very interesting. Four years ago, on the Bayswater Road, I watched a handsome Early Victorian home being 'Developed'; when it was razed to its foundations, the ground floors were exposed to the elements – I was drawn towards the place – why, I don't know – it was like some strange magnetic pull from the past. I stood, in what must have been the front room, littered around amid the ruins were documents, letters, envelopes, news cuttings, snaps – Photographs – Albums Books – a few World War I medals, I don't know why. But I carefully collected all of these under the suspicious gaze of the Navvies. For two years these documents lay in a box in my office, on Nov 11 last (significant date) I started to collate the collection into chronological order. The story and photos go back to about 1848 and terminate in about 1931 – and it was strangely exciting to have a family's story, lasting nearly 150 years on your hands, and it was like being an invisible relative, or am I a ghost? looking at them, and they not being aware of me?

There is a major disaster in the family, two sons killed in World War I, the mother turning to Spiritualism for solace – one son remains – Capt. C. Tate. If you come to London again, do let me know, and I will show you the documents – I must close. London is closing in on me!

Love from

Spike

Fleas, Knees and Hidden Elephants: 1995

Il Papa

The Pope arose at 6pm
And said his morning prayer
When he'd had his breakfast
He said another there
Then just before shaving
He blessed his razor blade
Then a prayer of hope
For his shaving soap
And the place where it was made
Then he prayed to St Theresa
To straighten the Tower of Pisa
While wearing his white fur capel
He blessed the Sistine Chapel
When saying grace before meals
He fell backwards head over heals
He said you see my dearest God
You made me such a clumsy sod.

A Mad Medley of Milligan: 1999

Coronation

Said Prince Charles
When they placed
The Crown on his head
I suppose this means
That Mummy's dead.

8

Trying It On

The Melting Pot: 1983

Episode 2

The Melting Pot was intended as a six-part series for the BBC, and it was recorded with Milligan starring alongside John Bird, John Bluthal (from *Q*) and Bill Kerr (from *Hancock's Half Hour*) but its deeply politically incorrect content fell foul of shifting tastes and it was dropped after the first show was broadcast.

CAST

Mr Van Gogh	Spike Milligan
Mr Rembrandt	John Bird
Paddy O'Brien	Frank Carson
Nefertiti Skupinski	Alexandra Dane
Luigi O'Reilly	Wayne Brown
Eric Lee Fung	Harry Fowler
Richard Armitage	John Bluthal
Sheikh Yamani	Anthony Brothers
Colonel Grope	Robert Dorning
Bluey Notts	Bill Kerr

SCENE 1 THE BATHROOM AT NO. 7, PILES ROAD. THE THREE
SINKS ARE BLOCKED AND FULL OF WATER. NEAR THE SINK
IS A BED WITH TWO BLACK JAMAICANS ASLEEP. BOTH WEAR
WOOLLY HATS WITH BOBBLES ON THE TOP. THE BED HAS
BLANKETS AND TWO OVERCOATS AS WELL; ABOVE IT HANGS A
LINE OF WASHING. DRESSED IN THE SUIT HE ALWAYS WEARS,
VAN GOGH IS STANDING TO WASH HIS PYJAMAS, BUT THE
GEYSER ONLY OCCASIONALLY SQUIRTS WATER. THIS IS ACCOM-
PANIED BY AN EARTHQUAKE-LIKE SHUDDERING, WITH GREAT
RUMBLING AND BUBBLING NOISES. THE STEAM ENVELOPS THE TWO
SLEEPERS. VAN GOGH TRIES TO GATHER THE WATER IN THE
BUCKET. ABOVE HIM IS A HAMMOCK IN WHICH SLEEPS ANOTHER
MAN.

VAN GOGH My God, this is supposed to be a hot water system. (Reads the geyser.) Made by Thomas Crapper, 1889. (Geyser vibrates.) All it does is three squirts an hour. I can do better than that, and they are charging me and my son £18 a week, share bathroom, no women in the room or near offers.

JAMAICAN (In bed.) Please to be keepin' quiet, me an' ma chauffeur am tryin' to get some sleep.

VAN GOGH I wouldn't let my daughter marry one of them.

GEYSER STARTS TO SHUDDER. VAN GOGH RUSHES TO COLLECT THE HOT WATER.

REMBRANDT (Enters with a bucket of water.) Bapu? Are we still blocked up?

VAN GOGH Yes, they are fully blocked, as advertised in the Evening News.

REMBRANDT Then it will have to go down the loo.

VAN GOGH There is no light in here.

REMBRANDT Don't worry, I've done it in the dark before. (He opens WC door and empties bucket.)

BLUEY (Stifled sound from WC, then he appears clutching soaked trousers.) You bloody drongo . . .

REMBRANDT I apologize.

BLUEY Apologize, my arse.

REMBRANDT Very well, I apologize to your arse.

VAN GOGH You should have kept the door shut.

BLUEY Shut? With no window in 'ere? I've 'ad enough. There's too many bloody abos in this country. (Starts to exit.) I'm gonna see about my return passage.

VAN GOGH Is that blocked up too?

JAMAICA (In bed.) For de secon' time, man, we'se tryin' to sleep.

REMBRANDT What is that lot, Bapu?

VAN GOGH They are the British Leyland night shift.

REMBRANDT If I was that colour, that is the shift I'd work on.

VAN GOGH My God, I been here two hours and only got half a
pyjama done. (He holds up bottom half of pyjamas, the
colours have run and the garment is a mess.)

REMBRANDT Are you using Rizzo? With the added Dronkalite
extra blue granules, 2p off? (Sings.) Washes whites whiter.

GEYSER STARTS TO SHUDDER. ENTER A VERY HAIRY, ARROGANT
COCKNEY PLUMBER, CHEWING GUM.

PLUMBER Are these the ones that are blocked up? (Indicates
basin.)

REMBRANDT Ah, yes. (Points to basins.) There.

THE PLUMBER SMASHES THE OUTLET PIPE OF ALL THREE BASINS.
WATER GUSHES TO THE FLOOR.

PLUMBER Twenty-eight pound.

REMBRANDT The landlord is downstairs.

PLUMBER Downstairs? That'll be twenty-eight pound, plus four
pound stairs money. (Exits.) That'll be thirty-two quid . . .

GEYSER GOES MAD, ISSUES FORTH MASSES OF STEAM. VAN GOGH
REACTS. HAMMOCK COLLAPSES AND JAMAICAN OCCUPANT FALLS
INTO BATH AMONG RIZZO SUDS – HE COMES UP WHITE.

SCENE 2 THE ATTIC ROOM. A TRANSISTOR RADIO IS POURING OUT
DISC JOCKEY CRAP MUSIC, COMMERCIAL BREAK GUNGE.
REMBRANDT IS COMPLETING HIS TOILET, LOOKING INTO A MIRROR,
THE SURFACE OF WHICH IS WARPED AND CRACKED. HE HAS
PLASTERED HIS HAIR DOWN, 1935-STYLE.

REMBRANDT May I have the pleasure of the next foxtrot? Oh
yes, my family have been foxtrotting for years. My dear
young lady/gentleman, can I get you a jam sandwich or shall I
play the concertina? My father owns the Bank of Dublin; how
many millions will you inherit? Will you marry me, everything is in working order. (He is in the process of tying his tie,
cutting a piece of white cardboard or paper to the shape of a

breast-pocket handkerchief, when there is a knock on the
door.)

NEFERTITI Can I come in?

REMBRANDT Just a minute. (Picks up aerosol, squirts jacket
armpits.) Come on.

ENTER NEFERTITI. SHE CARRIES A BUNDLE OF NEWSPAPERS.

NEFERTITI I've come to put fresh newspapers in your drawers.
(She sniffs. Picks up aerosol can.) Oh? Fly killer.

REMBRANDT GRABS IT AND LOOKS AT THE LABEL IN SURPRISE.

NEFERTITI Oh. By the way (she reaches inside her bra to
remove a piece of paper.) I've got to show you this . . . (She
can't find it.) Funny, it was there a moment ago.

REMBRANDT It's still there by the look of it.

NEFERTITI (Finds it.) Ah. Mr O'Brien asked me to give it to
you, it's the receipt for last week's rent, and he says, can he
have it?

REMBRANDT Don't worry, we will be drawing our supplemen-
tary benefit this afternoon.

ENTER VAN GOGH. THE TROUSERS OF HIS SUIT ARE NOW A DIRTY
BLEACHED WHITE FROM THE MID THIGHS DOWN. HE IS LITERALLY
STEAMING.

VAN GOGH That bloody Rizzo.

NEFERTITI It's got bleach in it.

REMBRANDT Those cost £1.30 in the Oxfam sale.

NEFERTITI (Looking closely at the trousers.) You could dye
them.

VAN GOGH They are already dead.

NEFERTITI Look, can I speak plainly to you stupid kaffirs?

REMBRANDT Well, you can't speak plainer than that.

HAMMERING ON WALL. VAN GOGH RUNS AND PULLS THE CHAIN ON
CISTERN. IT FLUSHES WC WHICH IS IN THE NEXT ROOM.

NEFERTITI Look, you can take all these crappy clothes to the laundromat and wash the lot for 60p. Or if you like, I'll burn them in the garden for nothing. Oh, my God, the lunch. (<u>She rushes out.</u>)

VAN GOGH (<u>Noticing receipt which Rembrandt is holding.</u>) What is that?

REMBRANDT It is a recipe for the rent.

VAN GOGH Good. At last we'll know how to make it.

SCENE 3 THE FRONT ROOM. SEATED AROUND THE TABLE ARE THE
LODGERS. NEFERTITI IS PUTTING PLATES OF FOOD IN FRONT OF
THEM. REMBRANDT BANGS HIS LAMB CHOP ON HIS PLATE, WHICH
BREAKS.

PADDY God Almighty, Nef, what have you done to these cutlets?

NEFERTITI (<u>Very calmly, continuing to serve burnt food.</u>) I'll tell you what I've done (<u>burst into tears</u>) I've burnt the bloody things. It's that bloody North Sea Gas.

VAN GOGH In India we cook on cow dung.

PADDY Well, we don't have any North Sea cow dung here.

VAN GOGH It is more economical. You just stand behind the cow and wait.

PADDY Look, <u>wogs</u> may cook on cowshit – we don't.

VAN GOGH Wogs – okay, but we are British wogs and we must not be confused with Indian wogs . . . come, my son. We must go to the (<u>reads a card</u>) Laundarama, 239 Terrible Street, Peckham, closed Wednesdays, nearest tube Uxbridge, buy a Red Rover and save one third on a Awayday with Jimmy Savile.

LUIGI O'REILLY (<u>Black Yorkshireman, speaking with mouth full.</u>) You tell 'em, Ram Jam. You bloody Micks, come over t'ere to save 'emselves bein' blown up over there, then start layin' down t' law to people like me – Yorkshire born and bred.

PADDY It must have been brown bread. You wasn't a chip off

the old block, you was a slice off a black pudding. (He bursts out laughing.)

LUIGI Go on, laff, you slit-eyed twit . . . You're one of the Chinese noodles they forgot to take away.

ERIC STANDS UP; HE HAS TABLECLOTH TUCKED INTO HIS SHIRT. IT SPILLS DINNER.

PADDY Stop all this, now. Look, Mr Rembrandt, I'm sorry; I apologize for calling you and yer Dad bloody wogs.

REMBRANDT You didn't say bloody.

PADDY Well, I'm sayin' it now: bloody wogs. I'm sorry. You are British subjects, like Luigi O'Reilly of Yorkshire, Eric Lee Fung of Battersea, and Mrs Nefertiti Skupinski, née O'Brien, late of Johannesburg, who married a Polish RAF pilot who had become British so that she could become English.

VAN GOGH What?

PADDY Of course, the Yid and the Gypo here, now they are bloody foreigners.

YAMANI I'm nay a Gypo . . . the blood of Mohamet runs through my veins.

RICHARD And I bet it runs backwards, like your army.

YAMANI Shut up, Sheenie.

RICHARD Sheenie. If you were any kind of an Arab you'd be on the Golan Heights trying to work out the instructions on yer Chinese rocket-launcher.

REMBRANDT I would . . .

YAMANI Listen, Jew – if Hitler was alive today I'd ask him to make me a gauleiter.

PADDY From what I hear, he couldn't even make a cigarette lighter.

REMBRANDT I'm trying to say, my father and I accept your apology. Now, we go to the laundrette, for a good 60p.

VAN GOGH EMPTIES BURNT DINNER INTO CARRIER BAG.

PADDY You gonna post that to Bangladesh?

SCENE 4 OUTSIDE AN OXFAM SHOP. SOUNDS OF TRAFFIC
CACOPHONY. AEROPLANE GOES OVERHEAD. DRILLS. DISTANT
SOUND OF THE 'HAPPY WANDERERS' ON RADIO. A VERY RAGGED
WORLD WAR TWO HERO, BEDECKED WITH MEDALS, IS SELLING
MATCHES FROM A TRAY WITH A UNION JACK HANGING DOWN. HE
WEARS A BLIND MAN'S GLASSES.

MAN Matches . . . British Toyota matches . . . only 80p a box
plus VAT – £1.20.

VAN GOGH AND REMBRANDT ARRIVE, BOTH CARRYING THEIR
UNION JACK CARRIER BAGS. ONE IS FULL OF LAUNDRY. THEY
READ AN ADVERT IN THE WINDOW OF THE OXFAM SHOP.

REMBRANDT Please help. Fifty million Indians are starving.

WAR HERO (Corner of mouth.) Let the bastards starve. Matches.
British matches . . . as used by the British as central heating.

SCENE 5 INSIDE OXFAM SHOP. BEHIND THE COUNTER IS A LADY OF
GREAT BREEDING. A MASS OF CHARITIES AND GARDEN FETES
WRITTEN ON HER FACE, SHE IS ABOUT FIFTY, GUSHING, TOTALLY
USELESS. SHE WEARS A LAURA ASHLEY GOWN, A LARGE STRAW
GARDEN PARTY HAT, AND A HEARING AID. THE CONTROL IS
ATTACHED TO HER BOSOM, WIRE RUNS TO HER EARPIECE.

WOMAN (She is already talking as Van Gogh and Rembrandt
enter.) Ahhh, how nice, how very nice of you to help like this.
I'm afraid Lady Mitworth-Handleigh isn't here today. She is in
Southall doing wonderful things for the black deaf.

VAN GOGH You hear that? They've got Black Death in Southall.

WOMAN You'll have to speak up, my hearing aid is jammed.

VAN GOGH (To Rembrandt.) What's wrong?

REMBRANDT Someone has put jam on her hearing aid.

THE WOMAN FIDDLES WITH THE CONTROL WHICH OSCILLATES,
THEN WE HEAR A COMMERCIAL FOR CAPITAL RADIO COMING
THROUGH LOUD AND CLEAR.

WOMAN Capital Radio is up the road, dear.

VAN GOGH We don't want Capital Radio . . .

WOMAN What?

VAN GOGH (Shouts.) We don't want Capital Radio.

AS HE IS SPEAKING, TWO JAPANESE TOURISTS COME IN, A MAN
AND WOMAN. THEY STARE AT THE SHOUTING PAKISTANI.

JAPANESE Excuse, is this Buckingham Palace?

VAN GOGH (Shouts.) No, it isn't.

JAPANESE Ahso. (Exits.)

REMBRANDT And Ahso to you.

COLONEL GROPE COMES IN, BUTTONING UP HIS BROWN OVERALL,
ON THE POCKET OF WHICH IS A UNION JACK WITH THE WORDS:
OXFAM VOLUNTARY WORKER.

WOMAN Ah, Colonel Grope, I'm so glad . . .

COLONEL I'm a little late, my dear . . . I lost the bottle opener . . .

WOMAN I must fly, I'm late for my 'Cosi Fan Tutte'.

COLONEL Yes, yes, off you go, Fanny. (Still looking down,
buttoning his coat, unaware of Van Gogh and Rembrandt.)
Now, gentlemen, what can I – (He looks up. His demeanour
changes. Pre-recorded voice of Colonel saying: 'Wogs.' Roll of
drums at execution. Pre-recorded voice of Colonel saying:
'Forty years ago I'd tie them to the mouths of cannons
and . . .' Sound of cannon blasting off. Devilish grin spreads
over his face.) Now, what do you want?

VAN GOGH (Shouts.) We have been told that . . .

REMBRANDT He's not deaf.

COLONEL Who said I was?

VAN GOGH We are told that you feed starving Indians.

COLONEL Yes, but we don't serve the food here. You have to go
to Calcutta, lie on the pavement and hold up one withered arm
with a tin.

PAUSE AS VAN GOGH AND REMBRANDT LAY THE BURNT FOOD OUT
IN FRONT OF THE COLONEL.

COLONEL Very interesting, but what is it?

REMBRANDT Dinner. (Waits.)

PAUSE.

COLONEL I didn't order dinner.

REMBRANDT It is not for you, it is for the people of Calcutta, lying on the pavement, holding up the withered arm.

VAN GOGH Yes, they can put it up their tins.

AS HE TALKS, DEVILISH LOOK APPEARS ON COLONEL'S FACE. PRE-RECORDED ROLL OF DRUMS, DISTANT BUGLE, VOICE OF COLONEL SAYING: 'FORTY YEARS AGO I'D TIE 'EM TO THE MOUTHS OF CANNONS AND . . .' CANNONS ROAR; SCREAMS.

SCENE 6 INTERIOR OF WASHETERIA. SIGN ANNOUNCING IN GOTHIC SCRIPT: 'YE OLD ENGLISH WASHETERIA. PROPRIETOR; DUNCAN SKUPINSKI. REGISTERED AS AN OIL TANKER IN LIBERIA. TRAVELLERS' CHEQUES ENCOURAGED. TREBLE GREEN SHIELD STAMPS'. BENEATH IT ANOTHER GARISH-COLOURED SIGN: 'WITH EVERY 60LB WASH FREE GIVE-AWAY SET, ONE PLASTIC CHAM-PAGNE GLASS, COMPLETE'. THE MANAGERESS STANDS BEHIND A PLASTIC COUNTER, GIVING WASHING POWDER TO AN ARAB WOMAN IN PURDAH.

MANAGERESS Don't eat it, darlin' – puttee in machinee.

PURDAH WOMAN (Gruff cockney soldier's voice.) I know what I'm bleedin' doin . . . it's this or the glass-house.

THE WASHETERIA IS TOTALLY FOUL AND GROTTY. THE MACHINES ARE WORN OUT, SOME SCORCHED AND BLACKENED. ON SEVERAL THERE IS AEROSOL SPRAY GRAFFITI. EMPTY FAG PACKETS, OLD BEER CANS AND NEWSPAPERS ARE SCATTERED ABOUT FLOOR. A DRUNK IS SPRAWLED FACE-DOWN, GROANING AND MUTTERING. THE CUSTOMERS CONSIST OF TWO SIKHS, A GHANAIAN IN TRADITIONAL DRESS, A VERY TWEEDY MIDDLE-AGED ENGLISH LADY IN A TWO-PIECE SUIT, TWO LONDON JAMAICANS (FAT LADIES) IN EUROPEAN DRESS, A HINDU LADY IN A SARI, AND TWO

VERY ITALIAN-LOOKING SOHO-TYPES (MALE). AS THE PURDAH
LADY LEAVES, VAN GOGH AND REMBRANDT APPROACH. THE MAN-
AGERESS HAS A SMALL TV SET ON THE COUNTER FACING HER.
AN AERIAL CABLE SNAKES OVER IT, THROUGH AN ADJACENT DOOR
OR WINDOW.

MALE VOICE (From outside, somewhere high above.) Is that
any better, Rita?

MANAGERESS (Looking at set.) No ... it's shaky ... Reginald
Bosanquet's wig is sliding off his nut.

REMBRANDT Pardon me, sir.

MANAGERESS Sir? Cheeky bugger. I suppose the sexes all look
alike to them. Wot you want, Ram Jam, a curry?

REMBRANDT No, we want to do our laundry.

MANAGERESS Where is it?

REMBRANDT He is wearing it.

MANAGERESS He can't get into my machines wearing it, the
paddles will beat him to death. (Pause.) He doesn't look as if
he's long to go anyway.

VAN GOGH I only want to do the suit.

MANAGERESS He'll have to strip off. 'E's wearing something
underneath, isn't he?

REMBRANDT Oh yes, he's got plenty underneath ...

MALE VOICE (From above.) Wot's on now, Rita?

MANAGERESS 'Crossroads'. (To Rembrandt.) That's me old man,
he's on the roof, fixing the aerial. It won't work down here. It's
these English sets – crap. We can't afford a Japanese one.

MALE VOICE (From above.) Wot's it like now?

MANAGERESS (Pouring powder out for Van Gogh and
Rembrandt.) It's the commercial. There's a tart fast asleep in
a posh bed ... with water crashin' on the rocks. (Pours more
powder – pause.) Now there's a geezer in black, divin' off a
yacht ... Ooh – 'e's killed a shark ...

MALE VOICE (From above.) 'Ow?

MANAGERESS 'E's broken its bleedin' neck. Ooh. Saucy devil,
    'e's climbin' up a rope with 'is teeth . . . (Hands Pakistanis
    powder and drops voice.) That's yours, darlin' . . . and that's
    yours – 60p each.

THEY PUT MONEY DOWN. SHE TAKES THE MONEY, PUTS IT IN THE
TILL, THEN TEARS OFF GREEN SHIELD STAMPS, REACHES UNDER
THE DESK, AND HANDS THEM EACH A VERY NASTY PLASTIC CHAM-
PAGNE GLASS.

MANAGERESS That's yer champagne glass, darlin'.
REMBRANDT Champagne? Oh!
MANAGERESS Now the geezer in the black's come leapin'
    through the tart's window and 'e's putting somethin' on her
    bed.
MALE VOICE (From above.) What is it?
MANAGERESS (She raises her voice.) A roll of kazi paper . . .
    'Pink Magic . . . the perfect gift from a stranger.'
MALE VOICE (From above.) 'As he left 'is card? How!
MANAGERESS Machine number nine . . . that's the one with the
    door still on.

VAN GOGH AND REMBRANDT SIT NEXT TO THE TWEEDY ENGLISH
LADY WHO IS READING THE TIMES. SHE HOLDS THE TIMES UP
BETWEEN HERSELF AND THE INDIANS AS A DEFENCE.

VAN GOGH Ah, number nine – doctor's orders.
REMBRANDT (Takes Van Gogh's glass.) I will hold it until they
    bring it round.
VAN GOGH Fancy, they are serving champagne in laundries.
    That's the benefit of going into the Common European Market.
    (Starts to take his suit off.) Yes, we did a . . . (low gasp of
    horror from tweedy English lady) . . . good thing leaving the
    Calcutta gutters.

VAN GOGH REMOVES SUIT, STARTS TO STUFF IT INTO MACHINE.
THE DOOR FALLS OFF BUT HE MANAGES TO GET IT BACK.
REMBRANDT THROWS THE POWDER IN RATHER DRAMATICALLY.

VAN GOGH PUTS IN ENTIRE BOX OF RIZZO. HE IS NOW IN OUTSIZED LONG UNDERWEAR AND LONG-SLEEVED VEST. HE HAS HIS LONG JOHNS ON BACK TO FRONT. THE TWEEDY ENGLISH LADY WITH THE TIMES IS SLOWLY TEARING A SMALL HOLE IN THE PAGE TO SPY THROUGH. OCCASIONAL GASPS OF HORROR ISSUE FORTH. DISTANT SOUNDS OF 'CROSSROADS' ON THE TELLY. VAN GOGH SWITCHES THE MACHINE ON.

VAN GOGH I think this was made by Thomas Crapper, too.

FROM HIS UNION JACK CARRIER BAG REMBRANDT TAKES OUT A BANANA AND STARTS TO EAT.

REMBRANDT (Looks up.) Isn't it wonderful, in this country, electric light in every room.

VAN GOGH In Bangladesh we had oil lamps in every room.

REMBRANDT We only had one room.

VAN GOGH And we had an oil lamp in it.

REMBRANDT So?

VAN GOGH So we had an oil lamp in every room . . .

A VERY SMART GUARDSMAN ENTERS HOLDING HANDS WITH A DELIGHTFUL GAY BOY. THE GAY BOY WEARS FLARED RED CORDUROYS, SLEEVELESS BODY VEST, A PINK OSTRICH-FEATHER BOA. THEY ARE HOLDING HANDS AND CARRYING LAUNDRY BAGS. THE GAY WEARS AN AFRO WIG WHICH HE REMOVES AND PUTS IN THE WASHING MACHINE. HE SITS BACK WITH THE GUARDSMAN, TO THE AMAZEMENT OF VAN GOGH AND REMBRANDT.

GUARDSMAN Wot you starin' at? It's legal now, isn't it?

THE TWEEDY ENGLISH LADY IS NOW MISSING. SOUND OF POLICE SIREN APPROACHING. SEVERAL CUSTOMERS RUSH TO HIDE BEHIND MACHINES. A COLOURED JAMAICAN CONSTABLE ENTERS WITH SIX-FOOT TRAINEE POLICE CADET. HE HAS AN ALSATIAN ON A LEAD.

MANAGERESS Hello, come in for the dropsy, 'ave yer?

CONSTABLE We had a 'phone call from a lady.

TWEEDY LADY (Comes in.) That was me, Officer.

CONSTABLE You complained about a case of indecent
exposure.

MANAGERESS A flasher, was there? 'Ave I missed it?

TWEEDY LADY That's the man. (<u>Points to Van Gogh.</u>)

MANAGERESS IMMEDIATELY SEARCHES HIM WITH HER EYES. CON-
STABLE AND DOG HANDLER STROLL AROUND THE BACK OF VAN
GOGH, WHO IS NOW STANDING. HE REVOLVES WITH THEM.

CONSTABLE This lady has accused you of gross indecency and
flashing.

VAN GOGH Rubbish. I was born like this.

CONSTABLE Why aren't you wearing any clothes?

VAN GOGH They are in the machine.

CONSTABLE I'm sorry, Madam, there seems to be a mistake.
Are you sure you haven't been seeing things?

VAN GOGH If she was, it wasn't mine.

SOUND OF BREAKING GLASS FROM STREET. SCREAMS. PISTOL
SHOTS. THE POLICEMAN, CADET AND DOG RUSH OFF, FOLLOWED BY
MANAGERESS. THE TWEEDY LADY GROANS AND FAINTS TO THE
FLOOR. REMBRANDT RUNS OUT AFTER THE POLICE. SOUND OF AN
AFFRAY, WITH POLICE WHISTLES. POLICE DOG GROWLING, RIPPING
CLOTH. VAN GOGH IS LEFT WITH THE FAINTED TWEEDY LADY.

VAN GOGH She has fallen face down. I must give her artificial
insemination. (<u>Gets across her back and starts to carry out
vigorous massage.</u>) I shouldn't be doing this. Someone from
the National Health should be pumping.

TWEEDY LADY Oooohhh . . . ooohh . . .

VAN GOGH Alright, missy, you'll soon be home.

THE MANAGERESS COMES BACK IN, SEES A COMPROMISING
SITUATION.

MANAGERESS 'Ere, stop that. No shaggin' in my laundries.
(<u>She picks up a bucket full of starch and water and throws it
over them. Immediately the washing machine starts to</u>

<u>smoke.</u>) My machine. You haven't been putting bloody curry in there, 'ave you? 'Ow long you had it on?

VAN GOGH LOOKS AT HIS WRIST – HIS WATCH IS MISSING.

VAN GOGH My watch. My wrist has been mugged.

MANAGERESS Police. Police. (<u>Exits.</u>)

TWEEDY LADY (<u>Sits up behind Van Gogh.</u>) Oohhh, a black one.

SHE FAINTS AGAIN. VAN GOGH GIVES MORE ARTIFICIAL RESPIRATION. REMBRANDT RUSHES BACK IN. HE HAS BEEN IN A PUNCH-UP. HIS RIGHT TROUSER LEG IS IN SHREDS.

REMBRANDT Bloody police dog . . . trained in Brixton.

WASHING MACHINE EXPLODES. THE MANAGERESS THROWS ANOTHER BUCKET OF STARCH OVER VAN GOGH AS SHE RE-ENTERS. BLACK CONSTABLE ENTERS. HIS TROUSER LEGS ARE SHREDDED. SOUND OF BARKING, OFF. POLICEMAN AND REMBRANDT IMMEDIATELY LEAP UP ON TOP OF THE WASHING MACHINE.

CONSTABLE Look out, he's not properly trained.

REMBRANDT You think I don't know that?

POLICE CADET RE-ENTERS, CRYING, WITH DOG.

CADET (<u>Sobbing.</u>) I can't control him, Sarge.

CONSTABLE (<u>On walkie talkie.</u>) Hello? Can you send in a net and two pounds of raw meat to the laundromat? Hurry.

MANAGERESS Arrest that coon for damaging my property.

DRUNK STANDS UP SINGING 'LIFE IS A CABARET, OLD CHUM'. TO HIS AMAZEMENT, HE IS NOW COVERED FROM HEAD TO FOOT IN WHITE STARCH.

SCENE 7 THE FRONT ROOM OF NO. 7, PILES ROAD, LATE AT NIGHT. RAIN IS SEEPING THROUGH THE CEILING. AROUND THE ROOM IS A MIXTURE OF BUCKETS, JUGS, TIN BATHS. THE FLOOR IS COVERED WITH NEWSPAPERS TO ABSORB THE DAMP. THERE IS A SAUCEPAN ON TOP OF THE PIANO. THE TV IS ON WITH AN UMBRELLA ON IT.

ALL THE OCCUPANTS ARE THERE EXCEPT VAN GOGH AND REM-
BRANDT. PADDY IS JUST WALKING FROM THE TABLE TO THE TV.

NEFERTITI (Mending socks on the couch.) How in God's name
do you get such big holes in your socks?

BLUEY I'll tell you how, he wears 'em as a balaclava.

PADDY Look at this, race riots in Golders Green.

RICHARD (Leaps up from table where he has been using a hand
adding-machine.) Golders Green: my property, my property.
(He rushes to set.)

YAMANI (At the table, writing a letter home.) Property? What
you got there, a crematorium?

RICHARD You fascist. Jews don't burn their dead in Golders
Green.

YAMANI Only because it's a smokeless zone.

RICHARD (Wags finger.) One day, one day you'll run out of oil.
Then back to the camels.

BLUEY Will you two bungs shut up. Y're ruining 'Blankety Blank'.

RICHARD (Staggered.) How could anything ruin 'Blankety
Blank'?

BLUEY You should take this lot and do what we did with the
Abos, bung 'em up North.

PADDY North? That's Scotland, what in God's name would they
do?

LUIGI They'd bloody eat 'em, wouldn't they?

SOUND OF POLICE SIREN APPROACHING. STOPS OUTSIDE. CAR
DOORS SLAM. PADDY LEAPS TO HIS FEET, SWITCHES OFF TV, PULLS
A WHITE CLOTH OVER IT, PLACES A CRUCIFIX ON TOP, KNEELS AND
CHANTS IN LATIN. ALL THE OTHERS KNEEL AS WELL. THE LOUNGE
DOOR OPENS, IN COMES THE BLACK CONSTABLE.

CONSTABLE Good evening. I'm sorry to interrupt the service,
Father.

PADDY What TV set, Officer? I –

CONSTABLE One of your lodgers has had an accident.

PADDY I know nothing about a TV set, Officer.

THE DOOR SLOWLY OPENS AND VAN GOGH AND REMBRANDT WALK
IN. VAN GOGH HAS GONE STIFF WITH STARCH. HE WALKS STIFF-
LEGGED, SUPPORTED BY REMBRANDT.

PADDY Good God, where have you been – the sales?

VAN GOGH The laundry. The woman is fainting and I am trying
to give her artificial insemination.

PADDY Oh dear –

REMBRANDT And they are throwing a bucket of starch over him.

PADDY Get him on the dinner table.

VAN GOGH My God – they're going to eat me.

PADDY Don't be bloody silly. Get a hammer – I'll try and break
him down.

MEANWHILE ALL THE LODGERS ARE CARRYING THE STIFFENED
VAN GOGH AND LAYING HIM ON THE DINING TABLE. THEY AD LIB
UNDER THE DIALOGUE.

REMBRANDT Get his legs.

LUIGI Mind the jam.

PADDY Get his hat off.

ERIC FUNG Don't get the bread knives up his jacksie.

PADDY (Hammering Van Gogh with a wooden mallet.) Don't
worry. You'll be able to claim sick benefit.

THE TABLE COLLAPSES. FROM THE TV WE HEAR THE NEWS.

NEWSCASTER Another bomb has exploded in the House of
Lords toilet. Max Byegroul gets an OBE. More clues have been
uncovered in the Nude Vicar Murders . . .

The Looney: 1987

The Village of Drool

The village of Drool slumbered in its unending tissue of mist-haunted rain, lost in what seemed like a timeless valley encased in nodding green hills. It all rested on the bones of the giant Irish elk buried in tissues of basalt black peat underfoot, where lay million-year-old mutating Irish oaks. Fat, patched cattle mooed in lush shamrock-strewn meadows; cuddling the village like a liquid arm ran the River Murragh; sliding in its watery music, wary of fly-decked hooks, were the glittering homing salmon, the river princes.

Many a moon-mad night Rory Mullins and Father Dan Costello dipped their illegal nets and scooped up plump supper-promised trout while Garda O'Brien kept an eye out for the law. There had been that fatal star-kissed night, all three were caught by Sergeant Kelly. He had let them off with a caution and a bribe, confiscated the salmon and sold it to his superintendent.

As the Looney entourage passed through the main street, little pink pinched faces peered through little windows, eyes following them, lips made for gossip spoke, ''Tis shamus Looney with a small s and dat rich brudder from the London.' The same Shamus Looney who had sired ten kids in ten years, whose poor wife had pleaded with Father Costello, 'Father we can't afford another child.'

The Pope-orientated priest spoke sternly: this woman wanted to take the accursed Protestant Pill. 'No, Mrs Looney, 'tis mortal sin to take that sinful terrible pill.'

'But I don't want any more kids,' she said.

'Then,' said the priest, 'you must *stop* the sexual intercourse!'

'Listen, father,' she said, 'I don't have intercourse with him, he has it with *me*, he does it while I'm asleep!'

'Don't you ever wake up?'

'God, no father, I'm too tired.'

'Then how do you know he does it?'

'Nine months later!'

Costello sent for Shamus. 'Listen, man, you must stop havin' the sexual intercourses with yer wife when she's asleep.'

'Oh, it seems a pity ter wake her up father, I do it as quiet as possible.'

'You *must* stop it, man! You must use the rhythm method.'

Shamus's brows ruffled. 'Rhythm method? Wot's dat?'

'It means you only do it at certain times.'

'I always do it at certain times, twenty past twelve.'

'Look, read this book, it's by the Pope, it explains all the method.'

How could *he* know about it? No one in the Vatican screwed! Shamus took time learning how to open the book, he read it and re-read it. Good God, here was the church telling people when and how to screw, intercourse was *only* meant to beget children! That's what the sex act was for, Tommy Cooper had a better act than that! While Shamus Looney's family slept four in a bed the Pope slept luxuriously alone.

Just outside Drool, Shamus reined up the horse. 'Dis is it,' he said, pointing to a blot on the landscape. 'Dis is der cottage. Four walls, a fireplace, a few sticks of furniture, no more. Still, it's free,' said Shamus.

'I should tink so,' said Mrs Looney. 'No one in dere right bloody mind would pay for dis.' She dumped down her rain-soaked bags on the floor.

'It'll look better when youse has yer bits and pieces in,' said Shamus.

'It's *all* bits and bloody pieces,' she said.

'I'll get der fire goin',' said Looney, breaking up a chair.

'Oh, we got der electric,' boasted Shamus, switching on the light.

'God, it looked better in the dark,' said Mrs Looney.

'Will youse stop complaining!' said Looney. 'Dis is only temporary.'

'Dat's fer sure,' she said. 'It won't last the bloody night.'

Above the door was a holy picture of the Sacred Heart – 'I will bless the house wherein this picture is shown' – something had gone wrong.

In the coming weeks, bit by bit, the cottage was put into shape, a coat of whitewash here, a shelf there, a bit of plasterwork, a wall here, a floor and a roof there. It was hard work but Mrs Looney finally finished it. Drool! This was where the seat of the family was and he was sitting on it! Searching for his royal ancestry Looney asked the folks around about his royal father and grandfather, sure they *all* knew them. 'Oh, those two cunts,' they'd say.

The Mirror Running: 1987

Journey

I think I am going out of my mind
The journey shouldn't take long
Once I get outside I'll be fine
I won't have to worry about thinking
I'll sit on a green bank of Sodium Amytal
    and watch my mind float away
Ah! my mind has a visitor!
A white-washed nurse
    a tray of NHS food
If only it would fit my mind
It's my stomach they're treating
    letting my head starve to death.

January 1981

The Bible According to Spike Milligan: 1993

Chapter IV

The Bible was the first of several free-wheeling adaptations which Milligan undertook in his later years. Subsequent titles included *Lady Chatterley's Lover*, *Wuthering Heights*, *Black Beauty*, *Frankenstein*, *The Hound of the Baskervilles*, *Robin Hood* and *Treasure Island*.

CHAPTER IV

And in time all the souls that came out of the loins of Jacob were seventy souls. And Jacob died and his wives gave thanks for the rest. And, lo, the children of Israel went into Egypt where there was a higher rate of pay, better working conditions and BUPA. But Pharaoh saw how fast the children of Israel multiplied – already all the gown shops were Jewish – so he enslaved them, made their lives bitter with hard bondage in mortar, in brick double glazing and pyramid aftersales, but still the children of Israel multiplied finding time to do it in the lunch break and, lo, the lunch breaks grew longer and longer. So Pharaoh sayeth all male babies would be thrown in the river. This would require a mighty throw as the river was a mile away.

2. The wife of Levi, thanks to a good lunch break, bore a son. 'Wrong!' said Levi. 'You know very well boys have got to be drowned.'

'I thought it was bank managers,' she said. That night the wife took the babe to the river and floated him away with some smoked salmon sandwiches.

'What are they for?' said Levi.

'He's a growing boy,' said the wife.

3. So the babe floated away on a compass bearing of Nor Nor East. It so happened that Pharaoh's daughter, there being no mains water at the palace, was having a bath in the river on a compass bearing of Nor Nor East, when floating by came the little basket.

4. 'Oh look,' said the princess, 'smoked salmon sandwiches. But wait! What's that next to them; it's a baby, what's he doing in there?'

And she looked and he had done everything in there. 'This is one of the Hebrews' children; see, he's had a bit snicked off.'

And she called him Moses because that was his name. And he grew up as her son with an inside leg measurement of thirty-seven inches, and an area set aside for things. When the tailor asked which side he dressed, he said near the window.

5. When Moses had grown he went on a day trip to see the Hebrews building a temple and he saw their overseers beateth the shit out of them. He spied an Egyptian smiting a Hebrew, Wallop Thud Kerpow, so he slew the Egyptian and buried him in the sand. And the Lord said, 'Moses, what hast thou done?'

And he said, 'I done him.'

When Pharaoh heard this, he sought to slay Moses, but running like the clappers, Moses fled to a B&B area and a job centre.

6. And it came to pass that while reading *The Oldie* the Pharaoh died of boredom and the children of Israel gave a great sigh. God heard their groaning; it kept Him awake all night and he fitteth double glazing. Moses had a fleximite job looking after sheep.

7A. An angel of the Lord appeared to him in a burning bush.

'You all right in there?' said Moses.

God called unto him from the burning bush.

'How do you do that?' said Moses.

'It's better than Paul Daniels,' God said. 'Draw not nigh: for this land where thou standest is holy ground owned by the Church Commissioners.'

So Moses taketh off his shoes and God said, 'Verily, thou needest OdorEaters.'

7B. God went on a bit, then He said, 'I am come to deliver the children of Israel.'

'It'll take it out of you,' said Moses; 'they have about ten kids a week.'

'Nay, I am come,' said God, 'to take them into the land of milk and honey unto the place of Canaanites, Hittites, Amorites, Perizzites, Hivites and Jebusites, all good Jewish third-division teams.'

Moses went unto the children of Israel and said, 'I will lead you to a land of milk and honey.'

And they said, 'We won't last long on that, we need protein.'

8. And the Lord spake unto Moses and his footbath: 'Go to Pharaoh and say let my people go or I will smite all thy borders with frogs: the frogs shall come upon thee, verily, frogs will be everywhere, even in private parts.'

'It soundeth a bit kinky, but I shall do it,' said Moses. So he sayeth it all to the Pharaoh, who called for a psychiatrist's report. Moses stretched his hand over the waters and, lo, Egypt was covered with frogs and not a French chef in sight.

Then spoke the Pharaoh from under a hundred and sixty frogs, 'Moses, call them off and your people can go.'

So Moses sprinkled Dettol and the frogs goeth. Moses said unto the children of Israel, 'Our people can go.' Some went but some had already been.

9. And so the children of Israel left Egypt – many Egyptian bank managers committed suicide. And Moses said, 'The Lord sayeth for seven days thou shalt eat unleavened bread, thou shalt not eat leaven bread.'

'Are chips all right?' said the children of Israel.

The Lord said unto Moses, 'Every firstborn lamb thou shall redeem; if thou will not redeem it, break its neck.'

'How's that?' said Moses.

'When thy son asketh what is that, thou will say it's a lamb with a broken neck,' said the Lord.

'What about vegetarians?' said Moses.

'The same applies, only with a carrot,' said the Lord.

10. So Moses led the children of Israel into the desert. The Lord went before them by day in a pillar of cloud and by night in a pillar of fire. It was very distracting. Back in Egypt Pharaoh regretted letting the children of Israel go, there wasn't a decent tailor in town. He hardened his heart and arteries and, taking six hundred chariots and three aspirins, he set off in pursuit of them. The children of Israel were

camping by the sea, then they saw the approaching Egyptians and were sore afraid, some were sorer than others and had to use ointment.

11. Many burnt their bank statements. And Moses said unto the people, 'Fear not, for the Egyptians whom ye have seen today, ye shall see them again no more for ever.'

'Pardon???' said the children of Israel.

'Watch this,' said Moses and, using an east wind, he held his hand over the sea and, lo, the seas divided and the children of Israel escaped along the bottom.

'What did I tell you?' said Moses.

'Oh wow,' said the children of Israel.

But the Egyptians pursued them and Pharaoh shouted, 'Charge!'

And the Israelites were sore afraid, they did not like being charged for anything and they cried out to the Lord, 'Can't we settle out of court?'

12. And it came to pass that in the morning the Lord was on a pillar of fire and cloud, and when it cleared, he saw the Egyptians close upon the children of Israel. And the Lord said unto Moses, 'Stretch out thine hand over the sea.'

But Moses was sore afraid. 'Will it work a second time?' And, lo, it did. The waters returned, marked not known here, and drowneth the Egyptian Army and its chariots. Thus the Lord had saved Israel, who saw the Egyptians dead on the seashore. 'Oi vay,' said Moses, 'this will ruin the holiday trade.'

9

Epilogue

There's a Lot of It About: 1993

Milligan Obituary

WE SEE A BLACK AND WHITE PHOTO OF SPIKE AS A VERY OLD
MILLIGAN, GREY WIG, BEARD, VICTORIAN CLOTHING. SPIKE
STARTS ANNOUNCING . . .

ANNOUNCER (grave, reverential tones) Well, as you may have
heard on the news, earlier this evening the comedian and
writer Spike Milligan died at his home in Barnet, aged 104.

AT THIS POINT THE PICTURE ON THE SCREEN UNFREEZES AND
SPIKE SLOWLY BEGINS TO LOOK UNEASY. HE BEGINS TO FEEL HIS
PULSE, CANNOT FIND IT. HE UNBUTTONS HIS SHIRT, SLIPS HIS
HAND INSIDE TO FEEL HIS HEART. HE THEN PRODUCES A SMALL
MIRROR AND LIFTS HIS EYELIDS UP TO INSPECT HIS EYES. HE
GROWS MORE AND MORE WORRIED BY WHAT IS BEING SAID ABOUT
HIM.

ANNOUNCER (continuing over this) Widely regarded as one of
the country's true comic geniuses, the late Mr Milligan had
only just completed recording a new series of his zany, wacky
half hour shows for the BBC. That's BBC 2 of course, and not
BBC 1, who tended to regard him as something of a light entertainment leper. And though millions will mourn the tragic
passing of Mr Milligan's unique and eccentric talent, we have
been asked by the trustee of his estate – a Miss Glenda
Plunge, of Latex Dungeons, Soho, to honour his memory in
the way that he would surely have wished. BBC 2 is now
proud to present – George Formby in 'Spare a Copper'.

CUT TO BEGINNING OF A FORMBY FILM, OR WHAT PASSES FOR IT,
SCRATCHY OLD BLACK AND WHITE FILM WITH MUSIC AND TITLES.
A BEAT, THEN SPIKE CRASHES THROUGH THE PICTURE. HE IS IN
COLOUR NOW.

SPIKE (very old) Stop this! Stop I say! (music stops and film

freezes around him) I may be dead, but I still have my pride.
Cue Telecine! Ah . . . (collapses)

WE SEE SPIKE DRESSED AS A SCOTSMAN WITH SOME BAGPIPES
THAT HE IS FILLING UP WITH WIND.

CAPTION: A DUKE OF EDINBURGH.

HE BLOWS AND BLOWS AND AS THE BAG BECOMES INFLATED HE
FLOATS AWAY. A HUNTER ENTERS WITH A SHOTGUN AND AIMS
AND FIRES AT HIM. A DUMMY OF KENNETH McKELLER FALLS TO
THE FLOOR WITH THE SOUND OF DEFLATING BAGPIPES.